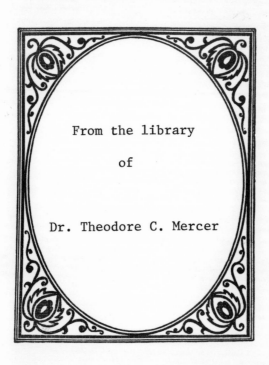

CHRISTIAN FOUNDATIONS

VOLUME ONE

Containing the
Complete Texts of:

CONFESS YOUR SINS

THE WAY OF RECONCILIATION

John R. W. Stott

THE BODY OF CHRIST

A NEW TESTAMENT IMAGE OF THE CHURCH

Alan Cole

CALLED TO SERVE

MINISTRY AND MINISTERS IN THE CHURCH

Michael Green

BUT FOR THE GRACE OF GOD

DIVINE INITIATVE AND HUMAN NEED

Philip E. Hughes

Published by The Westminster Press ®
Philadelphia, Pennsylvania

PRINTED IN THE UNITED STATES OF AMERICA

CONFESS YOUR SINS

THE WAY OF RECONCILIATION

by

JOHN R. W. STOTT

CONTENTS

FOREWORD

CHRISTIAN FOUNDATIONS is a series of books written by evangelical churchmen and designed to reaffirm the doctrine of the New Testament in the light of the past history, the present needs, and the future development of the Church. The series appears under the auspices of the Evangelical Fellowship in the Anglican Communion, and the authors are all members of that Communion. But their concern is for the whole Church, and not for just one portion of it. They have no desire to promote any kind of narrow denominationalism or to avoid involvement in the contemporary ecumenical debate. As the Archbishop of Sydney said in his Foreword to the British edition, 'These books have a truly catholic scope, and accordingly they can speak with clarity and also charity to those on either side of Anglicanism, and indeed, to many who at present are outside the fellowship of Christian believers.' The unity that the authors covet for the Church is unity in the truth – not unity at any price, least of all at the price of dispensing with the foundations of the faith which has been once delivered to the Church. They are convinced that, as evangelicals, they have a full and essential contribution to make, especially in advocating the recovery of the dynamic witness, the apostolic teaching, the fellowship in worship, and the victorious living of the New Testament; for these, they believe, are the vital principles of Christian unity in faith and action.

In view of the fact that some of the books deal with controversial issues, it is not expected that there will always be agreement with each particular position that may be propounded; but it is hoped that the books will be received in the spirit in which they are offered, which is not one of contention but of goodwill and reasonableness. The authors only ask for an unprejudiced hearing. Naturally they seek to persuade; yet where they fail to do that, they will be content if any discussion that arises is conducted before the bar of the scriptural revelation. They wish that all together, however different their viewpoints, might follow the example of the Christians in Beroea who searched the

Scriptures to see whether the things they had been told were true (Acts 17: 10f.). To do just this could in itself hardly fail to have the effect of bringing us all closer together.

Basic to the biblical doctrine of man is the concept of man as God's creature who has fallen into sin and is in need of redemption. The biblical doctrine of grace explains how God took the initiative for the purpose of redeeming our fallen race by the coming of His Son into the world to die the death that was due to man's sin and thereby to open the way for man to return to God as his Father. But man, for his part, must confess that he is a sinner, and this confession means acknowledging not only his sinfulness but also his need for forgiveness and restoration. The Gospel assures every repentant and believing heart of forgiveness through the grace of God in Christ Jesus. Many persons, however, are troubled by uncertainty as to how and to whom they should confess their sins, and as to how and from whom they may receive the assurance of absolution or forgiveness.

Mr. Stott is an experienced pastor of souls, both in his large parish in the heart of London's West End and also in the many different countries to which, by his travels, his ministry has been extended, and particularly on university campuses. In this book he discusses the necessity for the confession of sins and distinguishes between three different types of confession – namely, confession in secret to God, confession in private to a person whom our sin has injured, and confession in public in the presence of the Christian congregation – showing how this threefold distinction, which answers to different types of sin, is biblically founded, as John Jewel, who was Bishop of Salisbury under Queen Elizabeth I, pointed out four hundred years ago. A fourth type of confession, auricular confession to a priest, on the necessity of which the Church of Rome insists and which in these days of ecumenical 'conversation' demands renewed attention, is also helpfully examined by Mr. Stott.

Sin is the dark background to the ray of divine grace. The Church today tends to underemphasize sin and the direness of its consequences, and the inevitable consequence of this squeamishness is that people are not adequately prepared, because they are not shown their need, for the reception of the Gospel. Mr. Stott's book points the way for the Church to recapture its old virility in this important respect.

P. E. H.

Note: In this book and in others of the CHRISTIAN FOUNDATIONS series, mention of the 'Articles' in general, or of certain 'Articles' in particular (for example, 'Article XI' or 'Article XXXVII'), should be understood to refer to the Thirty-Nine Articles of Religion of the Church of England (1563). Parallels to many of the statements in these doctrinal formulae could have been cited, of course, from sixteenth-century Reformation confessions such as the Augsburg Confession (1530), the Second Helvetic Confession (1566), and the Scottish Confession (1560), and from later statements such as the Westminister Confession (1647).

INTRODUCTION

THE title of this book *Confess Your Sins* will no doubt seem to some a clear indication of the unhealthy preoccupation of Christians with their sins. A year or two ago a lay correspondent wrote to *The Times* to complain of this very tendency. He found it disconcerting, whenever he attended a Church of England service, to be reminded of his sins. At Morning and Evening Prayer he was obliged to associate himself with the rest of the congregation as a crowd of 'miserable offenders'. At every baptism he was informed that he was 'conceived and born in sin', at every wedding that marriage was 'a remedy against sin', and at every funeral that death delivered men 'out of the miseries of this sinful world'. He had come to the conclusion that sin was with churchmen a veritable obsession.

There is no need for us to be offended by this criticism. We are not in the least ashamed of the fact that we think and talk a lot about sin. We do so for the simple reason that we are realists. Sin is an ugly fact. It is to be neither ignored nor ridiculed, but honestly faced. Indeed, Christianity is the only religion in the world which takes sin seriously and offers a satisfactory remedy for it. And the way to enjoy this remedy is not to deny the disease, but to confess it.

So far, so good. But to whom should we confess our sins? Some people say that it is necessary to confess them to a priest, and that this is in fact the way which God has appointed for us to be forgiven. Is this so? What is the character of Christian confession and the way of Christian forgiveness?

It may be useful to approach these questions by clearing the ground a bit, and by taking our stand on the common ground which is (or should be) shared by all Christians alike, whatever our particular persuasion. The truths on which we should be able to agree concern the fact and guilt of *sin*, the possibility of *forgiveness* and the need for *confession*. Sin–confession–forgiveness are, in fact, an inseparable trio. Let me elaborate these truths in three straightforward Christian propositions.

1. *Our sins involve us in guilt, so that we need to be forgiven.*

I cannot delay to establish the fact of human sin; I must assume that this is not in dispute between us. We have fallen short of our own ideals, let alone God's standards. We have broken our own rules of conduct, let alone God's holy laws. We are sinners.

But we must go further and add that we are *guilty* sinners. This is because sin, according to the Bible, is primarily an offence against God. Its gravity lies here. However much our misdeeds may bring disgrace to ourselves and sorrow and suffering to others, their greatest evil is that they constitute a rebellion against God, our Creator and our Lord. One of the Bible's simplest definitions of sin is that 'sin is lawlessness' (I Jn. 3: 4). The two words are convertible. Sin is an infringement of God's known will, a revolt against His authority. It therefore makes us 'guilty before God' (Rom. 3: 19), bringing us under His righteous displeasure and judgment. Only divine forgiveness can expunge our guilt and restore us to fellowship with God.

FORGIVENESS

2. *Forgiveness is offered to us by God on the sole ground of the death of His Son.*

All Christians believe that God is a forgiving God. It is part of our basic creed. 'I believe in ... the forgiveness of sins.' Christianity is fundamentally a religion of salvation, and salvation includes forgiveness. Thus, one of the great promises of the New Covenant, foretold through Jeremiah, which Jesus said would be ratified by the shedding of His blood, was: 'I will forgive their iniquity, and I will remember their sin no more' (Jer. 31: 34; Mt. 26: 28). When the apostles began to preach the gospel, they were faithful to their Lord's commission and proclaimed forgiveness of sins to those who repented and believed (Lk. 24: 47; Acts 2: 38; 3: 19; 13: 38f.). What they preached in their sermons, they also wrote in their epistles – for example, as a recognizable echo of Matthew 26: 28, that in Christ 'We have redemption through His blood, the forgiveness of sins, according to the riches of His grace' (Eph. 1: 7).

This last quotation not only makes it plain that redemption and forgiveness are to some extent equivalent terms and that they are a present, conscious possession which in Christ 'we have', but that they are both attributable to 'His blood', that is to say, His death on the cross. The Scripture teaches that when He died, He 'bore our sins', an Old Testament expression meaning that He suffered the consequences of our sins; and that only because He was 'made . . . to be sin for us' can we 'be made the righteousness of God in Him', that is, be forgiven and accepted (I Pet. 2: 24; II Cor. 5: 21).

What the Bible asserts, the Prayer Book faithfully reflects. In the Holy Communion service we are told (in the first exhortation) that 'we obtain remission of our sins' by 'His meritorious Cross and Passion . . . alone'. In confessing our sins we therefore pray that God will have mercy upon us and for His 'Son our Lord Jesus Christ's sake forgive us all that is past', and in the prayer of oblation, after receiving the sacrament, we pray again that 'by the merits and death of Thy Son Jesus Christ, and through faith in His blood, we and all Thy whole Church may obtain remission of our sins . . .' We cannot escape this indissoluble link in Bible and Prayer Book between the death of Christ and the forgiveness of our sins. Each of us needs to pray for our soul: 'wash it, we pray Thee, in the blood of that immaculate Lamb, that was slain to take away the sins of the world' (The Visitation of the Sick).

CONFESSION

3. *The confession of sin is a necessary condition of receiving the forgiveness of God.*

The clearest statement of this third proposition is in one of the Scripture sentences which introduces Morning and Evening Prayer: 'If we say that we have no sin, we deceive ourselves, and the truth is not in us: but, if we confess our sins, He is faithful and just to forgive us our sins, and to cleanse us from all unrighteousness' (I Jn. 1: 8f.). Here are two 'if' sentences placed in contrast to one another, stating the result on the one hand of denying that we are sinners and on the other of confessing our sins. If we deny our sin, we deceive ourselves; if we confess our sins, we are forgiven. So the forgiveness of sins by God is made conditional upon the confession of sins by man. The Prayer Book exhortation goes on to enforce this truth, that we should 'acknowledge and confess our manifold sins and wickedness, and that we should not dissemble, nor cloke them, before the face of Almighty God our heavenly Father, but confess them . . . *to the end that* we may obtain forgiveness of the same . . .' Forgiveness depends on confession.

So much is agreed among us. We are guilty sinners. Our merciful God offers us forgiveness through Jesus Christ. We must confess our sins. But how, and to whom, should our confession be made? This is the question, and a preliminary answer may already be given, because an important principle emerges from the three agreed propositions above. We have seen that they belong together. Sin, forgiveness, and confession cannot be separated. Moreover, confession is the link between sin and its forgiveness, and can for this reason be understood only in relation to the sin that has been committed and the forgiveness that is desired. To be more precise, confession must be made *to* the person *against* whom we have sinned and *from* whom we need and desire to receive forgiveness. Therefore, before we can judge whether it is proper for us to confess our sins to somebody, whether God or man, we must ask two questions. First, have I sinned against him, that I should confess my sin to him? Secondly, has he authority to forgive me, that I should ask him to do so?

If we apply this principle, we can immediately distinguish between three different kinds of confession corresponding to three different kinds of sin. There is 'secret confession' to God because there are 'secret sins' (Ps. 90: 8) committed against God alone. Next, there is 'private confession', because some of our sins are committed against man as well as God, a private individual, or two or three such, and must be confessed to the offended party. Thirdly, there is 'public confession', because some sins are committed against a group of people, a community or the whole local congregation, and must therefore be confessed publicly.

The nature and the necessity of these three kinds of confession will be considered in the first three chapters of this book. We shall then be in a position in the last two chapters to ask: where does 'auricular confession' to a priest fit into this biblical scheme?

CHAPTER ONE

SECRET CONFESSION

THE awful dilemma of 'to confess' or 'not to confess' probably conjures up in our minds some of the most painful recollections of our schooldays. Some damage has been done to school property. The crime has been discovered, but the culprit has not been caught. The school is paraded. 'Who is responsible for this act of vandalism?' The headmaster's voice repeats the question. Tense silence. Somebody is experiencing a bitter inner struggle between duty and fear. The tension is only relieved when at last he owns up.

The adult has the same struggle in his relationship to God. Indeed it has been so ever since man first disobeyed God and fell from his original state of innocence. 'Adam and his wife hid themselves from the presence of the Lord God amongst the trees of the garden.' 'I was afraid,' Adam said, when God called him, '. . . and I hid myself.' Self-consciously aware of their nakedness (the physical counterpart, no doubt, to a sense of moral shame), Adam and Eve even 'sewed fig leaves together, and made themselves aprons' (Gen. 3: 7–10). It is all very well smiling at their naïvety; we too have our aprons of fig leaves, pathetic attempts to cover up, to conceal from God what we know ourselves to be.

The alternative between 'covering' our sins and 'confessing' them is set before us very clearly in Proverbs 28: 13: 'He that covereth his sins shall not prosper: but whoso confesseth and forsaketh them shall have mercy.' As so often in the book of Proverbs, the contrast is not merely between two opposite courses of action, but between the consequences of each. No one who covers his sins will prosper; it is he who confesses them who will find mercy. What is at stake, we are told, is our spiritual prosperity, whether we receive or forfeit the mercy of God. Many of us are not prospering in our Christian lives. We are making little or no progress. We have got stuck and do not appear to be enjoying the mercy of God. Is the reason partly or wholly that we have neglected the plain teaching of this Scripture about the secret confession of our sins to God?

The practice of covering or concealing sin is characteristic of unbelievers. They neither acknowledge their sins nor feel their guilt or peril. Consequently, they do not cry to God to have mercy on them or flee to Jesus Christ for refuge from the judgment their sins deserve. Indeed, this old-fashioned language means nothing to them. If they heard it, they would laugh at it. But their position is far more serious than they realize. 'He that covereth his sins shall not prosper.' They are on the broad road which leads to destruction.

We must not suppose, however, that this verse has no reference to Christian believers. It has. There is a common and dangerous tendency among us to 'cover' our sins. We may go to church and join in the general confession, and in our private prayers say we are sorry for our sins. But our words have a hollow sound. Our confession is largely a formality. The truth is that we do more covering up than uncovering. We know little of the uncomfortable discipline of confessing and forsaking our sins and so finding mercy. It is not difficult to rationalize our distaste for it.

Some people would have us believe that the whole idea of confessing sin is morbid and unhealthy. 'It's such an un-wholesome thing,' they say, 'to concentrate on your sins; it only adds to the number of neurotics who suffer from a guilt complex.' Well, some forms of confession *are* unhealthy, especially if we keep raking over our past which should have been long ago confessed, forsaken, and forgiven. But true confession, the honest, shamefaced uncovering before God of the sins of the past day or week, far from being unhealthy, is an essential condition of spiritual health. It is the person who covers his sins who is unhealthy; he 'shall not prosper'. There can be no mental or spiritual health without honesty.

The Bible gives us a graphic account of the inner turmoil of a man who tried to cover his sins: 'When I declared not my sin, my body wasted away through my groaning all day long. For day and night Thy hand was heavy upon me; my strength was dried up as by the heat of summer. I acknowledged my sin unto Thee, and I did not hide my iniquity; I said, "I will confess my transgressions to the Lord"; then Thou didst forgive the guilt of my sin' (Ps. 32: 3–5, R.S.V.).

I could echo these words from my own experience. There is no misery of mind or spirit to compare with estrangement from God through sin and the refusal to confess it in penitence; and there is no joy like fellowship with God through repentance, confession, and forgiveness.

Other people do not confess their sins for a very different reason. They imagine they have no need to do so. They have an unbalanced view of holiness. They suppose they have attained such a degree of perfection that there is nothing left to confess. All one can say to them is that Jesus was not of their opinion. He taught us to pray, 'forgive us our trespasses'. He evidently did not anticipate a time when His disciples could dispense with this petition. Similarly, the Church of England puts a general confession on our lips every time we come to worship, whether at Morning or Evening Prayer or at Holy Communion. It may indeed be that, by the grace of God, there are days when no actual transgression stains the conscience or memory of the Christian. But still there are sins of omission to confess, for no man has loved God with all his heart, mind, soul, and strength; and there is the infection and corruption of our fallen nature to mourn, as we acknowledge that 'there is no health in us'.

Yet other people, ready to catch at the flimsiest straw in their desperate anxiety to cover their sins and justify themselves, resort to a biblical argument. 'We are *meant* to cover our sins,' they say; 'the Scriptures themselves plainly teach that "love covers a multitude of sins". Didn't you know that this is written several times in the book of Proverbs (10: 12; 11: 13; 17: 9), and twice in the New Testament too (Jas. 5: 20; I Pet. 4: 8)? It is quite wrong to uncover our sins in the way you are suggesting.' I cannot imagine that the reader will be deceived by this. It is easy to misquote Scripture. The devil himself is an expert at it. But these verses have nothing whatever to do with the subject before us. They teach that if we truly love other people, we shall want to cover their sins. We shall not gossip about them, or expose them to criticism or ridicule, but rather seek to lead them to Christ, so that God may forgive them. There is nothing here to dissuade us from uncovering our own sins in secret confession to God.

All these are superficial excuses. They disguise the real

reason why we tend to cover our sins before God, which is that we want to conceal them even from ourselves. We cannot bear the humiliation of seeing and facing ourselves as we really are. Such is our innate pride that we prefer fiction to fact. We are in love with the fantasy image of ourselves which we have created, and refuse to escape from our dreamland. It is sheer vanity. We cannot endure the injury to our self-esteem which an honest uncovering and confession of our sins would bring to us. So we try to cover our sins from ourselves and God, so as to leave our comfortable complacency undisturbed. It is this that is unhealthy, the covering of our sins, not the uncovering of them. Such self-deception is ruinous to all spiritual health, for one of the most elementary rules of mental and spiritual health is to know the truth about ourselves and to admit it.

The folly of trying to cover our sins would be hard to exaggerate. 'He that covereth his sins shall not prosper', either in this world or the next.

For one thing, however successful we may be in concealing our sins from ourselves and from others, we cannot conceal them from God. Adam and Eve tried to hide themselves among the trees of the garden, but the Lord God found them there. He knows us as we are, not as we would like to think we are. He knows our secret thoughts, motives, and deceptions. All things are naked and open before Him. He is called in the Bible the 'heart-knower'. We do not, therefore, confess our sins to Him to inform Him of what He is ignorant, but rather to 'acknowledge and bewail' what He already knows.

Not only does God know us as we are now, but one day we are going to be made known as we are. Let me put the same truth in another way: if we cover our sins in this life, they will be uncovered in the next. The Bible tells us that the Day of Judgment will be an occasion of acute embarrassment for all hypocrites who have covered themselves up. So Jesus said: 'Nothing is covered up that will not be revealed, or hidden that will not be known. Whatever you have said in the dark shall be heard in the light, and what you have whispered in private rooms shall be proclaimed upon the housetops' (Lk. 12: 2f., R.S.V.). We shall not be able to retain any secrets on that dreadful day. We shall be exposed in the poverty-stricken nakedness of our sin, selfishness, and shame. We shall long to escape from this exposure, and the judgment which will follow it, but we shall not be able, even though we cry 'to the mountains and rocks, "Fall on us and hide us from the face of Him who is seated on the throne, and from the wrath of the Lamb; for the great day of their wrath has come, and who can stand before it?" ' (Rev. 6: 16f.; cf. Hos. 10: 8; Lk. 23: 30).

It is in these ways that 'he that covereth his sins shall not prosper'. No lie ever did prosper. To cover our sins is to court spiritual ruin.

THE WISDOM OF CONFESSING SIN

If the way to forfeit prosperity is to cover our sins, the way to find mercy is to uncover them, to bring them out of the darkness of secrecy and deception into the burning light of God's presence. Such uncovering of sin before God leads first to confessing it, then to forsaking it, so that we may find mercy. In these two activities, confessing and forsaking, is revealed the double purpose of uncovering our sins.

First, we need to uncover our sins, in order that God may forgive them. I referred earlier in this chapter to Psalm 32, in which we are given a graphic description of the pain of covering our sins. The same Psalm describes the joy of the man 'in whose spirit there is no guile', who does not deceive himself but confesses his sin, so that God forgives or 'covers' it. There is a deliberate contrast and play on words between these two experiences. The psalmist writes: 'Blessed is he whose transgression is forgiven, whose sin is covered' (v.1), and later: 'I acknowledged my sin to Thee and I did not hide my iniquity' (v.5). The words 'covered' and 'hide' in these verses translate the same Hebrew verb. It means to 'cover', in the sense of to conceal. It is used of clothes covering the body and a veil covering the face, of water covering the earth and the clouds covering the sun; and it occurs metaphorically in Psalm 32 both of *men* covering their sins in a refusal to confess them, and of *God* covering their sins by His merciful forgiveness.[1]

[1] Examples of the 'covering' of sin in an attempt to hide it are Job 31: 33; Ps. 32: 5; Prov. 28: 13, and of God's 'covering' of sin in forgiveness Neh. 4: 5; Ps. 32: 1; 85: 2.

Indeed, the two are alternatives. As soon as David uncovered his sins, God covered them, for God can only cover with His forgiveness the sins which we uncover in our confession. It is God's loving desire to cover our sins, to 'blot out' our transgressions, to put them from us as far as the east is from the west, to cast them behind His back, to bury them in the depths of the sea, to remember them no more. These are the vivid expressions found in the Bible for the forgiveness of sins.[2] Happy indeed is the man who has experienced this forgiveness! The relief and joy are indescribable.

But this covering of sin is for Him to do, not for us. Some people foolishly try to cover their own sins, to forget them, only to find that they continue to haunt them. The means which God has appointed for the putting away of sins is that we should deliberately recall them and bring them out with shame into the open, and let Him cover them through the merit of His Son's death.

The reason why we are to uncover our sins is not only that God may forgive them, but that we may forsake them. There is a closer link than we often realize between the confessing of sins and the forsaking of them. How can we expect to overcome in the future if we do not deal seriously with our failures of the past?

One of the greatest snares to which Christians are exposed in the contemporary world is the tendency to grow accustomed to sin. It is not just that sin is ingrained in our nature, or that the devil refuses to leave us alone, but that the influences of 'the world', the pressures of a godless, secular society, are so insidious. Wherever we look, sin stares us in the face. The standards of press, radio, television, and advertisement hoardings are, to say the least, sub-Christian. We cannot escape this continuous assault upon us. It is frighteningly easy to become morally insensitive, and to find that we are no longer hurt or grieved or shocked by the evil with which we are surrounded.

One of the surest antidotes to this process of moral hardening is the disciplined practice of uncovering our sins of thought and outlook, as well as of word and deed, and the repentant forsaking of them. It is not enough to confess

[2] Is. 44: 22; Ps. 103: 12; Is. 38: 17; Mic. 7: 19; Jer. 31: 34; and Heb. 8: 12.

them, asking for forgiveness and cleansing; we need deliberately, definitely, specifically to forsake them. We would not be so plagued by 'besetting sins' if we did this. It is important, when we bring our sins into the open before God, not to stop there, but to go on to adopt a right attitude towards both God and the sin itself. First, we confess the sin, humbling ourselves with a contrite heart before God. Secondly, we forsake it, rejecting and repudiating it. This is a vital part of what is meant by 'mortification' in the New Testament. It is taking up towards sin an attitude of resolute antagonism. The uncovering of sin is in itself of little value; it must lead us to an attitude both of humility towards God and of hostility towards sin. 'Ye that love the Lord hate evil', or 'the Lord loves those who hate evil' (Ps. 97: 10, A.V. and R.S.V.); and it is this holy hatred of evil which is promoted by the faithful, systematic uncovering and confession of our sins.

IS IT REALLY NECESSARY?

There are two important objections to this practice of secret confession to God which need to be considered at this stage. The first concerns the question why we should confess our sins *to God*. 'Why should I confess all my sins to Him?' someone asks. 'I admit that I am sometimes beastly to other people and that I ought to apologize to *them*; but what has it got to do with God?' This may sound a reasonable objection, but not if we accept the biblical view of sin which has already been outlined in the Introduction. The Bible views sin as being fundamentally 'lawlessness', whether positively or negatively. It is both a 'transgression', the stepping over a forbidden boundary, a 'trespass' into territory where we have no right to be, and also a 'missing the mark', a failure to do what we should do or be what we should be. In either case, an absolute moral standard is implied, whether we are said to break it or to fail to attain it. And this moral standard is God's law. Therefore, even if our sins are an offence to our fellow-men, because we hate them or envy them or are rude or unkind to them, they are also a sin against God, because they are a breach of His great commandment: 'Thou shalt love thy neighbour as thyself.'

The most striking example of this is David's sin with Bathsheba, which probably lies behind the confession of Psalm 51. He saw her bathing and was attracted by her beauty, lusted after her, took her for himself, had a child by her, and arranged for her husband to be killed in battle. One after another he broke four of the last five commandments: he coveted, he stole, he committed adultery, he murdered. And yet, when through the ministry of the prophet Nathan he was brought to repentance, he cried: 'Against Thee, Thee only, have I sinned, and done this evil in Thy sight' (Ps. 51: 4). This is not a denial that he had sinned against Bathsheba, against her lawful husband, and against the whole nation of which he was king; but it is a recognition that all sins are first and foremost a defiance of the holy laws of God.

True confession is, therefore, not merely an admission that I have sinned, but that I have sinned *against God*. The compilers of the Book of Common Prayer were quite clear about this and make us acknowledge it when we confess our sins in church. 'We have ... strayed *from Thy ways* like lost sheep ... We have offended *against Thy holy laws* ... We acknowledge and bewail our manifold sins and wickedness, which we, from time to time most grievously have committed, by thought, word, and deed, *against Thy Divine Majesty*.' It is because we are 'miserable offenders' in this sense, having defied God's authority and broken His laws, that we have 'provoked most justly His wrath and indignation against us'. 'He it is that is offended with us,' wrote Bullinger 'and therefore of Him we must desire forgiveness ...'[3] and, further, to Him we must confess our sins.

'But,' a second objector may now say, 'what is this confession, which you are making a condition of forgiveness? I have always understood that we are "justified by faith alone"; aren't you guilty of destroying the Reformation principle of *sola fides* by adding another condition of salvation?' This is an important argument to consider, although it is not difficult to answer. Justification is indeed through faith alone. It is God's acceptance of the sinner, on the sole ground of Christ's death for his sins, when by faith he lays hold of Christ as his Saviour. But no man ever thus

[3] p. 71.

21

believes in Christ who has not first acknowledged his need. And our need of Christ's salvation is found in our sin and guilt. This is why repentance is so often coupled with faith in Bible and Prayer Book. 'Repent and believe the good news' was the message of Jesus and His apostles;[4] forgiveness is granted to those who 'truly repent and unfeignedly believe His holy gospel' (the absolution). Turning trustfully to Jesus Christ for deliverance presupposes a recognition of our sin and a renunciation of it. And confession is simply a part of repentance. We have already seen in Proverbs 28: 13 how 'confessing and forsaking' belong together. Similarly, in the general confession we pray: 'Spare Thou them, O God, which *confess* their faults. Restore Thou them that are *penitent*.' Bible and Prayer Book know nothing of a formal confession in words, which is not the expression of a 'humble, lowly, penitent, and obedient heart' (the exhortation).

It is in this connection that something needs to be said about the twofold use of the word 'confess' in the New Testament, first the confession of sin, and secondly the confession of faith in God and in Jesus Christ. Often they occur quite separately and independently,[5] but sometimes they are in significant association.[6] As Charles Biber has written, 'These are the two aspects of one and the same revolution: Jesus Christ came, indeed, to bring the forgiveness of sins.'[7] It is inconceivable that the Christian should ever think of sin without also thinking of his Saviour. Humble confession of the one leads to thankful confession of the Other. The confession of sin is not, therefore, an additional condition of salvation; it is itself an integral part of true, saving faith in Christ.

[4] E.g. Mk. 1: 15; Acts 2: 38, 44; Acts 20: 21; Heb. 6: 1.
[5] For the confession of sin see Lev. 5: 5; 16: 21, 26, 40; Num. 5: 7; Josh. 7: 19; Ezra 10: 1; Neh. 1: 6; Ps. 32: 5; Prov. 28: 13; Dan. 9: 4, 20; Mt. 3: 6 = Mk. 1: 5; Acts 19: 18; Jas. 5: 16; I Jn. 1: 9.
For the confession of faith see Mt. 10: 32f. = Lk. 12: 8f.; Jn. 1: 20; 9: 22; 12: 42; Rom. 10: 9; II Cor. 9: 13; Phil. 2: 11; I Tim. 6: 12f.; I Jn. 2: 23; 4: 2; II Jn. 7.
[6] E.g. Neh. 9; Ps. 32, 40, 51; I Jn. 1: 5–2: 2.
[7] Ch. Biber: *Confess* (in *Vocabulary of the Bible* by J.-J. von Allmen).

In view of all this plain biblical teaching regarding the necessity of confessing our sins, let me plead that we should take it more seriously and be more disciplined in it. In particular, the Christian's confession of sin should be both immediate and detailed.

It is a great mistake to imagine that, when we are conscious of having sinned, we must wait, before confessing it, until the following Sunday or Holy Communion service, or even until our time of prayer that night. The apostle Paul affirmed before Felix: 'I always take pains to have a clear conscience toward God and toward men' (Acts 24: 16, R.S.V.). We should have the same ambition. As soon as any sin is on our conscience, whether committed against God or men, we must confess it. This is what it means to 'walk in the light' (I Jn. 1: 7). It has been described as living in a house without ceiling or walls – permitting no barrier to arise between us and either God or our fellows. It is a very serious thing to tamper with our conscience or to let it remain burdened and unrelieved. As soon as we have sinned against our neighbour we should apologize. As soon as we are conscious of God's face having become clouded, so that we are estranged from Him, we need to get away quietly, to uncover our sin, to confess and forsake it. As Thomas Becon, Archbishop Cranmer's chaplain, put it: 'This kind of confession ought every Christian man daily and hourly to make unto God, so oft as he is brought unto the knowledge of his sin.'[8] It is an indispensable condition of abiding continuously in Christ.

Our confession must also be detailed. An omnibus confession is not enough: 'O God, I'm sorry for my sins. Amen.' Such a general confession may be suitable for public worship in church; in private devotion our confession must be particular. The biblical promise of divine forgiveness is made to those who confess their 'sins' in the plural (I Jn. 1: 9). I believe this should always be part of our response to God's Word after we have read the Bible, for the Bible is not only a revelation of God's Name, calling us to worship and faith, but a revelation of man's sin, calling us to

[8] Thomas Becon: *The Potation for Lent* (*Early works of Thomas Becon*, Parker Society, 1843) p. 100.

repentance and confession. What sin has been exposed in the passage we read this morning? Whatever it is, it lurks in our heart. If it has erupted in sinful thoughts, words or deeds, we must confess them. The other time in which to be specific in confession is at night. Do we not look back over the day to recall God's mercies, so that we 'forget not all His benefits', and thank Him for them one by one? We must also look back over the day, asking the Holy Spirit to search us and to remind and convict us of our sins, so that we can uncover them in humility before God one by one. I must insist again that this is not morbid introspection, provided that the discovering and uncovering of our sins are not an end in themselves. We must never look back at our past sins or into our wicked hearts without immediately looking away from them in repentance and up to Jesus Christ in faith. The whole purpose of uncovering our sins is that we go on first to confess them, asking for cleansing through the blood of Christ, and then to forsake them, praying for grace to overcome.

Another time for detailed confession is before and at Holy Communion to which we come seeking in a special way forgiveness through the death of Christ (I Cor. 11: 28, 31). The first and third exhortations urge us before we come to examine ourselves 'by the rule of God's commandments' (cf. Rom. 3: 20). We continue this private self-examination in public when the Ten Commandments are read, first confessing our infringement of each ('Lord, have mercy upon us'), and then praying for grace to obey it in future ('and incline our hearts to keep this law'). It would be a sad day if this recitation of the commandments at Holy Communion were to be generally abandoned.

Such confessing and forsaking, immediate and detailed, are required of every Christian. It is a question of honesty versus hypocrisy. The uncovering of sins is painful and humiliating. It brings us to our knees in lowliness before God. But if we want to receive mercy, both forgiveness for the past and power for the future, there is no other way. Let it never be said of us that we take sin lightly or presume on the mercy of God.

CHAPTER TWO

PRIVATE CONFESSION

WE have considered the necessity of confessing our sins secretly to God. We have sinned against Him and must confess our sins to Him, if we desire Him to forgive us. This is plain. But is there any biblical warrant for confessing our sins also to a fellow-man? Yes, there is. Although all misdeeds are sins against God, some are sins against men as well; and when our sin has offended men as well as God, we must confess to them and seek forgiveness from them too. We have to say to the injured party, in the prodigal's words to his father: 'I have sinned against heaven *and in thy sight*' (Lk. 15: 18, 21). The principle is clear. Let William Tyndale state it for us: 'To whom a man trespasseth, unto him he ought to confess.'[1] We must seek forgiveness from him whom we have offended; we must confess to him from whom we seek forgiveness.

Indeed, the Bible lays great emphasis on the importance of right relations with our fellow-men, teaching that a right relationship with God is impossible without them. The great Hebrew prophets of the seventh and eighth centuries B.C. constantly reiterated this theme. The offering of sacrifices to God was not only useless, but positively nauseating to Him, they said, if the worshippers were living lives of immorality or injustice to men. 'Bring no more vain oblations; incense is an abomination unto me ... Your new moons and your appointed feasts my soul hateth ... And when ye spread forth your hands, I will hide mine eyes from you: yea, when ye make many prayers, I will not hear: your hands are full of blood. Wash you, make you clean; put away the evil of your doings from before mine eyes; cease to do evil; learn to do well; seek judgment (s.c. justice), relieve the oppressed, judge the fatherless, plead for the widow.'[2]

[1] p. 266.
[2] Is. 1: 13–17. Cf. also Is. 59: 1 ff.; Hos. 6: 6; Amos 5: 21–24; Mic. 6: 6–8, etc.

Granted that right relations with their fellow-men are necessary for the people of God, what are they to do when these relationships go wrong? It may be helpful to distinguish between three separate duties – confession, restitution, and rebuke.

CONFESSION

If we have sinned against our neighbour, we must confess our sin to him and ask for his forgiveness. It sounds easy; yet we all know from common experience how costly it is simply to apologize to somebody and to say that we are sorry. It is a rare Christian grace. D. L. Moody, the famous American evangelist of the last century, exhibited it, and I think I was more struck by this than by anything else about him when reading a recent biography. Let me give you two examples which impressed me. In the early days at their home in Northfield, Massachusetts, Moody was anxious to have a lawn like those he had greatly admired in England. But one day his two sons, Paul and Will, let the horses loose from the barn. They galloped over his precious lawn and ruined it. And Moody lost his temper with them. But the boys never forgot how, after they had gone to bed that night, they heard his heavy footsteps as he approached and entered their room, and, laying a heavy hand on their head, said to them: 'I want you to forgive me; that wasn't the way Christ taught.'[3] On another occasion a theological student interrupted him during an address and Moody snapped an irritated retort. Let J. C. Pollock describe what happened at the end of the sermon: 'He reached his close. He paused. Then he said: "Friends, I want to confess before you all that I made a great mistake at the beginning of this meeting. I answered my young brother down there foolishly. I ask God to forgive me. I ask *him* to forgive me." And before anyone realized what was happening the world's most famous evangelist had stepped off the platform, dashed across to the insignificant anonymous youth and taken him by the hand. As another present said, "The man of iron will proved that he had mastered the hardest of all earth's languages, 'I am sorry'."' Someone else called it 'the greatest thing I ever saw D. L. Moody do'.[4]

[3] J. C. Pollock: *Moody without Sankey* (London, 1963) pp. 234f.
[4] Ibid. p. 189.

Perhaps a word of caution may be written here. All sins, whether of thought, word, or deed, must be confessed to God, because He sees them all. 'O Lord, Thou hast searched me, and known me. Thou knowest my downsitting and mine uprising, Thou understandest my *thought* afar off. Thou compassest my path and my lying down, and art acquainted with all my *ways*. For there is not a *word* in my tongue, but, lo, O Lord, Thou knowest it altogether' (Ps. 139: 1–4). But we need to remember that men do not share the omniscience of God. They hear our words and see our works; they cannot read our hidden thoughts. It is, therefore, social sins of word and deed which we must confess to our fellow-men, not the sinful thoughts we may have harboured about them. Some zealous believers, in their anxiety to be open and honest, go too far in this matter. To say 'I'm sorry I was rude to you' or 'I'm sorry I showed off in front of you' is right; but not 'I'm afraid I've had jealous thoughts about you all day'. Such a confession does not help; it only embarrasses. If the sin remains secret in the mind and does not erupt into words or deeds, it must be confessed to God alone. It is true that, according to the teaching of Jesus, 'whosoever looketh on a woman to lust after her hath committed adultery with her already in his heart' (Mt. 5: 28); but this is adultery *in the sight of God* and is to be confessed to Him, not to her. The rule is always that secret sins must be confessed secretly (to God), and private sins must be confessed privately (to the injured party).

The clearest teaching in the New Testament about such private confession came from the lips of our Lord Himself, in the course of the Sermon on the Mount: 'If thou bring thy gift to the altar, and there rememberest that thy brother hath aught against thee; leave there thy gift before the altar, and go thy way; first be reconciled to thy brother, and then come and offer thy gift' (Mt. 5: 23f.). The situation is obvious. We are going to church, and on the way we suddenly remember somebody who has a grievance against us. It is not that he has wronged us, but we him. The teaching of Jesus is clear. It is no use going to church when such a sin comes to our mind and burdens our conscience. We cannot draw near to God while we are estranged from a brother. The command is: 'first go . . .; then come . . .' First 'be reconciled to thy brother' (which means 'ask for his forgiveness'), and then your offering will be acceptable to God.

This need to be 'in love and charity with our neighbours' is much insisted upon in the Prayer Book. It is an indispensable condition of coming to the Lord's Supper: 'And if ye shall perceive your offences to be such as are not only against God, but also against your neighbours; then ye shall reconcile yourselves unto them' (first exhortation). Similarly, in the Visitation of the Sick, the minister is to examine the sick person whether he 'be in charity with all the world, exhorting him to forgive, from the bottom of his heart, all persons that have offended him, and if he hath offended any other, to ask them forgiveness . . .'

It seems appropriate at this point to mention the command of St. James: 'Confess your faults one to another, and pray one for another, that ye may be healed' (5: 16). There is certainly here no reference whatever to the practice of auricular confession to a priest, despite the fact that 'the elders of the church' (v. 14), whom the sick person is to send for, are in the Rhemish New Testament of 1582 inaccurately labelled 'priests'! Commentators have rightly pointed out that if auricular confession is in view, then the priest must confess to the penitent as well as the penitent to the priest, since the confession is to be reciprocal 'one to another'.[5] Nor do I think there is a reference here to the reciprocal, private confession of secret sins, because the biblical principle is consistently that 'confession' is due to the party who has been offended. Thus, sins against man are confessed to God and man, since they are committed against both. But sins against God are *confessed* to God alone and not to man, since they are *committed* against God alone and not man. The great sixteenth-century Swiss theologian, Heinrich Bullinger, was surely right in interpreting this verse as a command to those who have 'mutually offended one another' to confess these sins to one another.[6] It suits the context too, that physical healing may be hindered by a breach of fellowship with our fellowmen.

[5] Cf. *Of Repentance* in the Second Book of Homilies (1562), p. 575.
[6] IV, p. 85.

Real repentance often involves restitution. True, in sins committed against God no restitution of any kind is possible; we can only worship Him that, on the ground of the death of His Son for our sins, He is ready to blot out fully and freely all our transgressions. But in some sins against men we can make restitution, and when we can we must.

This whole issue became very confused in the Middle Ages through the so-called sacrament of penance, and we need to understand the changes which the Reformation brought. In the article on 'Penance' in the *Oxford Dictionary of the Christian Church* it is conceded that of its early history 'very little is known'. It seems to be clear, however, that the first use of penance was public, not private. The Commination Service starts with the statement that 'in the Primitive Church there was a godly discipline, that, at the beginning of Lent, such persons as stood convicted of notorious sin were put to open penance ...' That is, open penance was the penalty for open sin. These 'penitents' were only restored to Communion after a period of submission to strenuous discipline in prayer, fasting, and almsgiving. As Hooker put it, 'The course of discipline in former ages reformed open transgressors by putting them unto offices of open penitence, especially confession, whereby they declared their own crimes in the hearing of the whole church ...'[7] Hooker goes on to explain how, when such 'public confessions became dangerous and prejudicial to the safety of well-minded men and ... advantageous to the enemies of God's Church',[8] they were gradually superseded by a system of private confession, whose purpose was concerned with discipline, not absolution, however. 'Penitential Books' were published from about the fifth century, in which a catalogue of sins was supplied with suitable penances. The Fourth Lateran Council of 1215 made private confession and penance compulsory for every Christian at least once a year.

The medieval schoolmen went further and developed their elaborate sacrament of penance, which consisted of three parts – contrition, confession and satisfaction. It is the last

[7] Book VI, iv, 2.
[8] Book VI, iv, 3.

of these which concerns us now, for 'satisfaction' was regarded as an attempt to make amends for sin, an act of restitution to the injured party. The schoolmen taught that the sinner could and must make some satisfaction to God for his sins. They distinguished between the *culpa* (guilt) of sin and the *poena* (penalty) of sin. They agreed that the satisfaction of Christ on the cross was sufficient to deliver the penitent from the *culpa* of sin, but not from the *poena*. The 'eternal' *poena* had to be removed by the sinner's penance, while the 'temporal' *poena* would only be finally paid off by the pains of a fiery purgatory, unless it was remitted earlier by the purchase of indulgences.

This dreadful doctrine the Reformers vigorously attacked as being derogatory to the death of Christ. They insisted that all the consequences of sin may be put away by His death. 'God forgiveth us both the pain and the guiltiness of sins', cried Latimer in one of his eloquent sermons.[9] Cranmer's prayer of consecration insists that Christ on the cross made '(by His one oblation of Himself once offered) a full, perfect, and sufficient sacrifice, oblation, and satisfaction, for the sins of the whole world'. Article XXXI adds: 'and there is none other satisfaction for sin, but that alone'.[10]

While denying that sinners could make any satisfaction for their sins to God, or needed to since Christ had done it fully and finally in His death, the Reformers qualified their dismissal of the medieval notion of satisfaction in two respects. First, they emphasized the necessity of true 'penitence' as opposed to 'penance' and of good works in the life of the penitent believer. He cannot 'make amends' to God for his sins; but he can and must 'amend his life'. His good works are not 'meritorious'. They 'cannot put away sins' or earn his salvation. 'Yet are they pleasing and acceptable to God in Christ, and do spring out necessarily of a true and lively faith' (Article XII, *Of Good Works*). They may be said to 'satisfy' God only in the sense that they are pleasing to Him, not because they atone for sin or win His favour. Similarly, the Christian believer may be called upon to suffer, but his sufferings have no redeeming merit like the

[9] *Sermons of Hugh Latimer* (Parker Society, 1844), Vol. I, i, 426.
[10] This phrase from Article XXXI (*Of the One Oblation of Christ finished upon the Cross*) already occurred in the Forty-two Articles published in 1552.

sufferings of Christ; their value lies in their power to promote within him holiness, humility, faith, and patience.

Secondly, the Reformers fully agreed that, although no satisfaction could be made for sins against God, the case was very different with sins against men, both corporately and individually. They wanted the restoration of ecclesiastical discipline, with public penance and confession. Jewel urges it in the *Defence of the Apology* as 'necessary for the satisfaction of the Church'.[11] They also stressed the need to 'satisfy', that is, make restitution to an offended brother: 'Thou must make him amends or satisfaction, or, at the leastway, if thou be not able, ask him forgiveness'.[12] The Book of Common Prayer contains the same requirement: 'Ye shall reconcile yourselves unto them (s.c. your offended neighbours), being ready to make restitution and satisfaction, according to the uttermost of your powers, for all injuries and wrongs done by you to any other' (Holy Communion, first exhortation). Similarly, in the Visitation of the Sick, the minister is to exhort the sick person not only to forgive others and ask their forgiveness, as we have seen, but also 'where he hath done injury or wrong to any man, that he make amends to the uttermost of his power'.

This Prayer Book emphasis is thoroughly biblical. Already in the Law of Moses we find restitution demanded: 'When a man or woman commits any of the sins that men commit by breaking faith with the Lord, and that person is guilty, he shall confess his sin which he has committed; and he shall make full restitution for his wrong, adding a fifth to it, and giving it to him to whom he did the wrong' (Num. 5: 5-7, R.S.V.). The chief difference between the sin-offering and the trespass-offering (R.S.V. 'guilt offering') seems to have lain here, that the latter was the divine provision for social sins and had to be accompanied by restitution: 'When one has sinned and become guilty, he shall restore what he took by robbery, or what he got by oppression, or the deposit which was committed to him, or the lost thing which he found, or anything about which he has sworn falsely; he shall restore it in full, and shall add a fifth to it, and give it to him to whom it belongs, on the day of his guilt offering' (Lev. 6: 4f., R.S.V.).

[11] Vol. III, p. 352.
[12] Tyndale, p. 267.

In the New Testament, Zacchaeus, the dishonest tax-collector of Jericho,[13] stands out as one of the most striking examples of restitution. When Jesus brought salvation to his house, he was not content to add to the stolen money which he resolved to return the one-fifth that the law required. He promised the Lord that he would restore *fourfold* the money of which he had defrauded people. He said he would go further even than that. No doubt because there were many of his ill-fated customers whom he could never trace and therefore never repay, he proposed an equivalent: 'Behold, Lord, the half of my goods I give to the poor'. In this way he was willing 'to make satisfaction unto all them that he had done injury and wrong unto'.[14] This man meant business in his dealings with God. He was beginning a new life through Jesus. He knew perfectly well that his lifelong dishonesty could never be forgiven if he continued to live on the proceeds.

This moral issue is as live today as it was in the days of Moses or during the ministry of Jesus. Those sins which we have committed against man as well as God can never be forgiven if we do not make amends to the utmost of our ability to those we have offended. There may be some stolen money or property to return, some damage to repair, an evil and false report to contradict, a lie to repudiate, or a broken relationship to mend. We must be realistic and practical about this. It is plain logic. Our sins have devastating consequences. Their effects upon God and His law only He can remedy; their effects upon men we can sometimes remedy ourselves. Without such restitution, divine forgiveness is impossible.

REBUKE AND RESTORATION

Wrong relationships can be reciprocal. So far we have concentrated on the injuries we have done to others; what about the injuries which others have done to us? The Bible declares that we have a duty in this matter too. We have to confess and make restitution to those we have wronged, that they may forgive us; we have also to seek to bring to repentance those who have wronged us, that we may forgive

[13] Lk. 19: 1-10.
[14] *Of Repentance* in the Second Book of Homilies (1562), p. 580.

them. This is a widely neglected duty. Most of us are as irresponsible as Cain in imagining that we are not our brother's keeper.

The obligation to administer a rebuke to sinners does not rest only upon prophets like John the Baptist[15] or Christian leaders like Timothy and Titus;[16] it rests upon all Christian believers.[17] It is a ministry on which much valuable teaching is given in the book of Proverbs. The contrast which is drawn in this book between the portraits of the wise man and the fool is particularly sharp in this matter. It is characteristic of the 'wise man' that he listens to instruction, admonition, and rebuke, and heeds them (13: 1; 15: 31). He knows that this is the way to 'gain understanding' (15: 32; 19: 25). He realizes that the reprover rebukes him for his good, out of love for him, and that 'open rebuke is better than secret love' (27: 5). He therefore prefers rebuke to flattery (28: 23), and even loves the man who reproves him (9: 8). The 'scoffer', on the other hand, refuses to listen to rebuke, and both hates and insults the one who seeks to correct him (13: 1; 9: 7, 8). He is as stupid to reject reproof as the wise man is prudent to welcome it (12: 1; 15: 15), for in refusing reproof he goes yet further astray (10: 17). Indeed, 'he that being often reproved hardeneth his neck, shall suddenly be destroyed, and that without remedy' (29: 1); and 'he that hateth reproof shall die' (15 :10).

This teaching in the book of Proverbs is concerned largely with how to *receive* reproof; Jesus taught us how to *give* it. One of His instructions which is more commonly disregarded and disobeyed than others, is found in Matthew 18: 5: 'If thy brother shall trespass against thee, go and tell him his fault between thee and him alone; if he shall hear thee, thou hast gained thy brother.' 'If your brother sins against you' is a pretty common experience. We have probably all done it to others, and had others do it to us. What do we do when a fellow-Christian sins against us? Sometimes we harbour resentment or even begin to plot our revenge. These things are always wrong. At other times we do nothing and imagine ourselves to be fine Christians

[15] Lk. 3: 19.
[16] I Tim. 5: 20; II Tim. 4: 2; Tit. 1: 13; 2: 15.
[17] Eph. 5: 11.

33

for overlooking the fault. But Jesus told us there was something for us to do: 'Go and tell him his fault.' There is no need to gossip about him, or to nurse our self-pity by attracting the pity of others. No. 'Go and tell him his fault *between you and him alone*.' Just as, when we have offended somebody, we confess our sin to him privately, so when somebody has offended us, we are to approach him about it privately. It is not necessary at this stage for anybody else to know.

Notice next that our purpose in speaking to him privately is clearly defined. It is to 'gain' him. It is not to humiliate him, but to win him. This is important. There are those who try to avoid the responsibility of this verse by quoting what Jesus said about the 'mote' and the 'beam' (Mt. 7: 1–5). They imagine that our Lord was prohibiting altogether the attempt to remove specks out of other people's eyes! He was doing nothing of the kind. What He was condemning was the spirit of proud, hypocritical superiority, when we busy ourselves with the specks in the eyes of others and are blind or indifferent to the logs in our own. He concluded: 'You hypocrite, first take the log out of your own eye, and then you will see clearly to take the speck out of your brother's eye' (R.S.V.). We must indeed be more critical of ourselves than we are of others, but we cannot shelve our responsibility towards other people in this way. It is our God-given duty to go to a brother who has sinned against us, and to tell him his fault, not out of pride, but out of love, 'in a spirit of meekness' (Gal. 6: 1). We desire to 'gain' him (Mt. 18: 15), to 'restore' him (Gal. 6: 1), to 'save' him (Jas. 5: 19f.). If our purpose is thus constructive, and our spirit meek, an apparently perilous activity will become safe.

A great deal of tension in Christian congregations would be eased if we obeyed this plain command of Jesus: 'Go and tell him his fault between you and him alone.' Instead of having the courage to face a person with his fault, frankly but privately, we whisper behind his back and poison other people's minds against him. The whole atmosphere of the church becomes foul. The best way to open the windows and let in some fresh air is to do what our Lord commanded: to go and tell him his fault privately, and otherwise to keep our lips sealed. If he listens to us, we shall have 'gained' him; a real victory will have been won for Christ and His cause. What we are to do if he does not listen to us belongs to the next chapter.

In Lk. 17: 3f. similar teaching of Jesus is recorded, but with a significant addition: 'If thy brother trespass against thee, rebuke him; and if he repent, forgive him. And if he trespass against thee seven times in a day, and seven times in a day turn to thee, saying, "I repent", thou shalt forgive him.' The passage in St. Matthew's Gospel concentrates on *rebuking* a brother; this passage in St. Luke concentrates rather on *forgiving* him. We are to rebuke a brother if he sins against us; we are to forgive him if he repents – and only if he repents. We must beware of cheapening forgiveness. Although God's forgiveness of us and our forgiveness of one another are quite different (since God is God, and we are merely private individuals, and sinners besides), yet both are conditional upon repentance. If a brother who has sinned against us refuses to repent, we should not forgive him. Does this startle you? It is what Jesus taught. Oh, we must 'forgive' him in the sense that our thoughts towards him are free of all animosity and full of love. But this is not Christian forgiveness. 'Forgiveness' means more than that; it includes restoration to fellowship. If we can restore to full and intimate fellowship with ourselves a sinning and unrepentant brother, we reveal not the depth of our love, but its shallowness, for we are doing what is not for his highest good. A forgiveness which bypasses the need for repentance issues not from love but from sentimentality.

But 'if he repents, forgive him'. Yes, and 'until seventy times seven' (Mt. 18: 22), for, as Jesus goes on to teach in the parable of the unmerciful servant, how can we refuse to forgive the little debts which others owe us when God has freely forgiven us 'all that debt', which we owed Him? The parable turns on the comparative size of the debts. The greater our awareness of the magnitude of our sin and of God's forgiveness, the more the sins of others against us will be eclipsed. God will not forgive us if we do not forgive others; for if we do not forgive others, it is evident that we have never seen our own sins as they are and therefore have never truly repented (Mt. 6: 12–15; Mk. 11: 25).

God's purpose for His people, as revealed in His Word, is that we should live in harmony with Himself and with each other. We are called to peace (Col. 3: 15). We are to seek peace and to pursue it (I Pet. 3: 11). Christianity is in essence a religion of peace and of reconciliation. Therefore we must take seriously every situation in which fellowship is marred or broken. So far as it depends on *us*, we are to live peaceably with all men, and to remember the special blessing which Jesus pronounced upon peacemakers (Rom. 12: 18; Mt. 5: 9). We can 'make peace' both by confessing our faults to those against whom we have sinned, and by reproving, in order to 'restore', those who have sinned against us. But if these activities are truly to promote peace, they must both be kept entirely private.

CHAPTER THREE

PUBLIC CONFESSION

'THREE kinds of confession are expressed unto us in the Scriptures,' wrote the great John Jewel, Bishop of Salisbury from 1559, in his *Defence of the Apology*: 'The first made secretly unto God alone; the second openly before the whole congregation; the third privately unto our brother.'[1] We have already considered secret confession to God and private confession to an offended individual; we must now turn to the subject of public confession to the Church.

There are three forms which this public confession may be said to take, although, as I hope to show, the first two forms are public and open without, strictly speaking, being 'confession to the Church'.

GENERAL AND FORMAL CONFESSION

The Prayer Books of the Anglican Communion all contain a formal General Confession both in the Holy Communion service and in the services of Morning and Evening Prayer. The pattern of the penitential introduction, consisting of Scripture sentences, exhortation, general confession, and absolution, has been universally recognized as fitting, inasmuch as the people of God may not presume to approach God in worship until they have first been cleansed and forgiven. 'It is impossible that a sinner should truly draw near to God in the name of Christ without such a sense of his corruption and guilt being awakened within him as to make him introduce and intersperse his prayer with confession of sin and lamentation on account of it,' says Alexander Whyte in his *Commentary on the Shorter Catechism* of the Church of Scotland. 'Let the student pass his mind over the record of Scripture, and mark how universal and how acceptable this state of mind was in God's people.' [2]

[1] Vol. III, p. 351.
[2] Ibid., p. 191.

The general confession of Anglican worship is so called because it is intended for the use of all, and is an acknowledgment rather of our general sinfulness than of particular sins. It gives a true and comprehensive description of our sinful condition, in six short sentences. We have strayed from God's ways like lost sheep (an echo of Isaiah 53: 6), and offended against His laws. This departure from His ways and infringement of His laws is due to 'the devices and desires of our own hearts', which are prone to lead us astray and which 'we have followed too much'. Our sins are sins of omission as well as commission, concerning not only what we have 'done' but what we have 'left undone'. We are obliged to conclude that 'there is no health in us'. That is, our sin is not to be measured in deeds alone; but in the disease of our fallen nature. So we are 'miserable offenders', which means, offenders in need of the pity of God. We therefore address Him as 'most merciful' as well as 'almighty', and cry to Him to have mercy on us who repent and confess our sins. We deserve only to be condemned, but we pray that He will both 'spare' us and 'restore' us, our only confidence being in His promises given to us through Jesus Christ. Finally, we look beyond our promised forgiveness and pray for grace to live lives of holiness towards God, others, and ourselves ('godly, righteous, and sober'), to the glory of His Name.

In his *Small Catechism* Luther distinguishes two parts of confession: firstly, the actual confession of sins, and, secondly, the reception of absolution. Absolution, however, is not indiscriminate: it applies only where there is genuine repentance and faith. Thus in the Anglican Prayer Book the minister proclaims that God 'pardoneth and absolveth all them that truly repent and unfeignedly believe His holy Gospel'; and the Wurtemberg Confession declares: 'Seeing that God promises unto us His free mercy for Christ His Son's sake, and requires of us that we should obediently believe the Gospel of His Son, He also requires that we should mortify the doubting of the flesh and have an assured trust in His mercy' (Chapter 14, *Concerning Confession*). Public confession which is merely an outward formality, unrelated to inward contrition and trust, has no part in the absolution and forgiveness of God which the minister pronounces.

If the general confession is a formal and public acknowledgment to God of our *general* sinfulness, is there any room for the public confession of *specific* sins?

One or two biblical precedents have been advanced for this practice. The first belongs to the ministry of John the Baptist. Large numbers of people from Judea flocked to him at the River Jordan. They listened to his preaching and were baptized by him, 'confessing their sins' (Mt. 3: 6 = Mk. 1: 5). We are given no information about what form this public confession took. It may have been couched in entirely general terms. On the other hand, since John preached 'a baptism of repentance for the forgiveness of sins' (Mk. 1: 4 = Lk. 3: 3), and since he applied his teaching in a very detailed and practical way to different classes of people, specifying the 'fruits that befit repentance' which they were to bear (Lk. 3: 8, 10–14), it is at least possible that their public confession was more precise than general. This was certainly the case in Ephesus when, as a result of Paul's teaching and certain supernatural happenings, new believers 'came confessing and divulging their practices' and made a bonfire of their books of magic (Acts 19: 18, 19, R.S.V.). These two incidents are similar. It is significant that in neither case is it stated to whom the confession was made, for neither was strictly a 'confession' to an injured party (whether God or men), but rather the public 'acknowledgment' of the sinfulness of a past life. Each marks a unique occasion, not a habitual practice. John the Baptist was summoning the people to prepare for the coming of the Kingdom, and the apostle Paul was bidding them enter it. Such a new beginning involved a drastic renunciation of all that belonged to the past. It included a public confession, and at Ephesus a public burning of evil objects associated with the past, much as converts from heathenism today will express their conversion by publicly burning their idols. Similarly, Dr. B. G. M. Sundkler states that in the Zionist Church initiation ceremonies in South Africa, which he describes as 'essentially purgative', 'baptism or purification cannot take place without being preceded by confession of sins.'[3]

---

[3] Quoted from *Bantu Prophets in South Africa* (London, 1948) by M. A. C. Warren in *Revival – An Enquiry*, p. 69.

If the public confessions which took place at Jordan under the ministry of John the Baptist and at Ephesus under the ministry of St. Paul were exceptional, marking the beginning of a new life, there is only one biblical reference left which could imply the practice of habitual public confession. This is James 5: 16: 'Confess your faults one to another, and pray one for another, that ye may be healed.' I have already suggested in the previous chapter that this alludes to the duty of confessing our sins to those we have offended. That the reciprocal confession envisaged is private rather than public is further implied by the immediate mention of an individual 'righteous man' whose 'effectual fervent prayer . . . availeth much'. Nevertheless, reliable commentators have taken the verse to justify the practice of reciprocal confession in public, or at least in small groups. According to the Second Book of Homilies, 'the true meaning' of this command is 'that the faithful ought to acknowledge their offences, whereby some hatred, rancour, grudge, or malice have risen or grown among them, one to another, that a brotherly reconciliation may be had,' and our Lord's words in Mt. 5: 23, 24 are then quoted as an example. But an alternative explanation is added, 'that we ought to confess our weakness and infirmities one to another, to the end that, knowing each other's frailness, we may the more earnestly pray together unto Almighty God, our heavenly Father, that he will vouchsafe to pardon us our infirmities for his Son Jesus Christ's sake . . .'[4]

It is certainly true, if we turn from the Bible to church history, that many movements of the Holy Spirit have been accompanied by this kind of informal reciprocal confession in public. It was a feature of Methodism from the earliest days. The fourth rule of the 'bands' (into which the 'classes' were subdivided) was 'to speak each of us in order, freely and plainly, the true state of our soul, with the faults we have committed in thought, word, or deed, and the temptations we have felt since our last meeting'.[5] To John Wesley himself this custom, which characterized the class meetings, was a natural expression of 'speaking the truth

[4] *Of Repentance* in the Second Book of Homilies (1562), p. 575.
[5] *A Plain Account of the People called Methodists.* In *Works* of John Wesley, Vol. VIII (3rd edition, London), p. 258.

in love' (Eph. 4: 15). It had wholesome results. 'Many were delivered from the temptations out of which, till then, they found no way to escape. They were built up in our most holy faith. They rejoiced in the Lord more abundantly. They were strengthened in love, and more effectually provoked to abound in every good work.'[6]

Public confession of this kind continues to be a mark of the contemporary East African revival. The 'fellowship meetings' of the 'Balokole' or 'saved ones' usually follow an identical pattern, the time of corporate Bible study being preceded by singing, extempore prayer, and a period of confession with testimony. Canon Max Warren, in his *Revival – An Enquiry*,[7] points out that 'one of the dominant impulses from which revival is born is a recovered awareness of "the exceeding sinfulness of sin" '. However we would define 'revival', it is or includes a supernatural awareness of the presence of God. This brings a conviction of sin, or 'brokenness', which in its turn 'produces an impulse to confession'. A second emphasis in the East African revival is on fellowship, on 'walking in the light' with God and with each other. Only sin breaks this fellowship, and if the fellowship is to be restored, the sin must be confessed. Canon Warren quotes a missionary who allowed herself to be drawn into the movement because to hold back was 'to refuse to be identified with the fellowship of forgiven sinners'. Thirdly, it is important to know that, over the course of the last twenty-five years, the emphasis on confession seems to have yielded to an emphasis on testimony. It is not enough to confess sin; 'What is also looked for,' says Dr. Warren, 'is testimony to release from sin, to victory over sin.' And as experiences of the power of Jesus to save are shared, the fellowship meeting is interrupted by the singing of 'tukutendereza' (Luganda for 'we praise Thee'), a chorus which praises God for the cleansing blood of Jesus, the Lamb of God and Saviour of sinners. This is thoroughly biblical. It is the other kind of 'confession' found in the Bible, confession of Christ rather than confession of sin, and is in some ways greater even than testimony to Christ, for 'while witness is addressed to men, confession is addressed in the presence of men to God

[6] *Op. cit.* p. 259.
[7] pp. 67–74 and 118–121.

in a voluntary impulse of gratitude and praise'.[8] We are back in the atmosphere of the Psalms, in which a song of praise is sung in the congregation for some mighty deliverance of God: 'He reached from on high, He took me, He drew me out of many waters' (18: 16, R.S.V.); 'This poor man cried, and the Lord heard him, and saved him out of all his troubles' (34: 6); 'He brought me up also out of an horrible pit, out of the miry clay, and set my feet upon a rock, and established my goings. And He hath put a new song in my mouth, even praise unto our God . . .' (40: 2f.); 'The sorrows of death compassed me, and the pains of hell gat hold upon me: I found trouble and sorrow. Then called I upon the name of the Lord; O Lord, I beseech Thee, deliver my soul. Gracious is the Lord, and righteous; yea, our God is merciful. The Lord preserveth the simple: I was brought low, and He helped me. Return unto thy rest, O my soul; for the Lord hath dealt bountifully with thee. For Thou hast delivered my soul from death, mine eyes from tears, and my feet from falling' (116: 2–8).

There seems, therefore, to be far more biblical warrant for this kind of public confession of the Lord, than there is of the public confession of sin. Canon Warren is right to place 'a question-mark' against the practice of public confession of sin. 'Long Christian experience suggests,' he adds, 'that exhibitionism, prurience, and superficiality lurk in the shadows of this particular discipline.' The test must always be whether the church is edified by it (I Cor. 14: 26). Confession of sin may sometimes be unedifying, unhelpful; but the confession of Christ and of His power to save can encourage the downcast soul and lift the drooping spirit, provoking others in the fellowship to love and to good works (Heb. 10: 24, 25).

Certainly there is a place for the confession of infirmity leading to a request for prayer; and we are plainly commanded to 'bear . . . one another's burdens, and so fulfil the law of Christ' (Gal. 6: 2); but this is best done, as the context in Galatians implies, between individual believers who seek to get alongside one another in a time of need.

---

[8] Article *Confess* by Ch. Biber in J.-J. von Allmen's *Vocabulary of the Bible*.

The first two forms of 'public confession' which we have been considering are, strictly speaking, not public confession at all. Let me explain why. To 'confess' is 'to admit or declare oneself guilty of what one is accused of',[9] and therefore confession is rightly made to the person who has been offended and is in a position to accuse one. This is why 'secret' confession is properly made to God alone, 'private' confession to the particular individual against whom one has sinned, and 'public' confession to the church in the case of some public offence against the church. What we have so far been discussing in this chapter is really the confession of secret sins against God or of private sins against our fellow-men, which for some reason may be publicly acknowledged. But in its true sense 'public confession' can only be made to the community against whom the sins in question have been committed.

Such 'public confession' is the public acknowledgment to the church of some public offence against the church, so that the offender may be publicly forgiven and restored by the church. Without it he should be and remain publicly excommunicated. The most notable example of this in the Old Testament is Achan, whose disobedience in hoarding some booty which God had commanded to be destroyed, had brought military disaster to Israel before Ai. Joshua said to Achan: 'My son, give, I pray thee, glory to the Lord God of Israel, and make confession unto Him; and tell me now what thou hast done; hide it not from me' (Josh. 7: 19). Achan had sinned against the people as well as against the Lord. His sin had therefore to be publicly confessed and publicly punished. What Achan was to the new nation of Israel, Ananias and Sapphira were to the infant Church of Christ. Their sin was an attempt to deceive the whole Christian community. It could no more be kept secret than Achan's. It was visited upon them by a dramatic judgment of God (Acts 5: 1–11).

There were unusual, supernatural elements in both these events, and we need now to turn to the more normal administration of discipline to public offenders which was commanded by Jesus and practised by the New Testament

[9] Definition of *homologeō* in the Grimm-Thayer Lexicon.

43

church. We have already considered our Lord's instruction (Mt. 18: 15-17), regarding a brother who sins against us, that we are to go and tell him his fault privately 'between you and him alone'. If he listens to us, Jesus said, we have 'gained' him. But if he does not listen to us, we are to go to him a second time, taking with us 'one or two more', who are evidently in a position to confirm the fact of his offence, in order that 'in the mouth of two or three witnesses every word may be established'. This was the requirement in the law courts of Israel (Num. 35: 30; Deut. 19: 15); it was to be the same in the public discipline of the Church of Christ. If the offender refuses to listen to the corroborating witnesses, he is to be given a third chance. 'Tell it to the church,' Jesus said, clearly meaning the whole local congregation. But 'if he refuses to listen even to the church, let him be to you as a Gentile and a tax collector' (v. 17, R.S.V.). That is to say, he is to be excluded from the Christian fellowship. And then our Lord adds the statement: 'Verily I say unto you, whatsoever ye shall bind on earth shall be bound in heaven: and whatsoever ye shall loose on earth shall be loosed in heaven' (v. 18).

These words have been variously interpreted. The Rabbis in the Mishnah used the metaphor of 'binding' and 'loosing' for 'forbidding' and 'permitting' certain practices, so that E. A. Litton explains it of 'framing and abrogating ecclesiastical regulations'.[10] The Reformers, as we shall see in the next chapter, usually assumed that the expression 'binding and loosing' was the same as 'retaining and remitting sins', and applied it to the public preaching of the Gospel. But the context in which it is here found strongly suggests that Jesus had ecclesiastical discipline in mind. Thus Bishop Jewel gives this alternative interpretation of 'loosing': that the 'minister, when any have offended their brothers' minds with some great offence, or notable and open crime, whereby they have as it were banished and made themselves strangers from the common fellowship and from the body of Christ, then, after perfect amendment of such persons, doth reconcile them, and bring them home again, and restore them to the company and unity of the faithful'.[11] Similarly, 'we say that the power, as well of loosing as also of binding,

[10] p. 357.
[11] p. 354f. Cf. p. 361f.

44

standeth in God's word; and the exercise or execution of the same standeth either in preaching, or else in sentence of correction and ecclesiastical discipline'.[12]

It is urged by some that these interpretations are mutually exclusive, and that 'binding' and 'loosing' must refer either to precepts (which are thereby forbidden or permitted) or to persons (who are thereby excommunicated or restored). We have seen above that proper arguments may be advanced in favour of either interpretation. It is not certain, however, that we are obliged to choose between these interpretations, since in the exercise of discipline they are inevitably combined. If the church has authority to remove an offender from its fellowship and to restore him, it must have authority to determine the grounds on which it will do so. It is by 'binding' and 'loosing' certain practices (declaring them lawful or unlawful) that the church can go on to 'bind' those who disregard its teaching and 'loose' those who obey it, or, having disregarded it, repent.

This is not to claim for the Church an absolute or authoritarian rule, for the Church's authority in both ethical instruction and ecclesiastical discipline is always secondary, being subordinate to the Word of God (Article XX). Although authority to 'bind' and 'loose' seems in Mt. 18: 18 to have been extended by Jesus to each local church, it was first given to Peter and with him (we believe) to his fellow apostles (Mt. 16: 19). So the local church may only administer discipline by reference to, and in submission to, the moral teaching of the apostles.

We see in the epistles of the New Testament how this authority was exercised in the first days of the Church's life. The incestuous offender at Corinth, whose sin was evidently not a single act but that he was actually 'living with his father's wife' (I Cor. 5: 1, R.S.V.), and had not repented, was to be 'removed' or 'driven out' of the fellowship (vv. 2, 13). Such excommunication is called a 'delivery to Satan' both here (v. 5) and in I Tim. 1: 20, presumably because the church is the sphere of Christ's rule and outside the church is 'the dominion of darkness' (cf. Acts 26: 18; Col. 1: 13). We cannot be certain whether the offender mentioned in II Corinthians 2: 5–11 is the same person,

[12] Ibid. p. 362.

45

but in any case we are given there a complementary example of the forgiveness and restoration of a sinner who has been publicly punished. It is plain that during the period of excommunication, until and unless the offender has repented, confessed, and been restored, he is to be repudiated from fellowship. The Christians were not even to associate with him (I Cor. 5: 9ff.;[13] cf. Tit. 3: 10, 11).

It is important to notice the cause and the purposes of this drastic discipline. The cause was in each case serious sin wilfully persisted in. The list of grave moral offences which is given in I Cor. 5: 9–11 refers not to an isolated lapse, but to people whose lives are characterized and contaminated by immorality, idolatry, drunkenness, or greed. Similarly, it is only after admonishing a factious person once or twice (Tit. 3: 10), if he stubbornly refuses to obey apostolic teaching (II Thess. 3: 14), and resists even the increasingly solemn rebukes prescribed by Jesus (Mt. 18: 15–17), that he is to be thus rejected.

The purposes of excommunication are retributive, remedial, and deterrent. All three are implied in the passages we have considered. The biblical writers do not shy away from the concept of retribution, as many modern thinkers do. The apostle Paul could write of 'judging' and of 'punishing' an offender (I Cor. 5: 12, 13; II Cor. 2: 6). He clearly regarded it as right and just that an open offender should be openly punished. Nevertheless, the discipline which punished him was intended, where possible, to reform him too. The obstinately disobedient brother was to be shunned 'that he may be ashamed' (II Thess. 3: 14). Hymenaeus and Alexander were 'delivered to Satan, that they may learn not to blaspheme' (I Tim. 1: 20). Even if the incestuous offender of Corinth was not restored, either on the occasion described in II Corinthians 2 or at any other time, the purpose of his excommunication was positive. It was 'for the destruction of the flesh, that his spirit may be saved in the day of the Lord Jesus' (I Cor. 5: 5). The destruction of his flesh might mean his sanctification, and certainly the Reformers constantly stressed that ecclesiastical discipline was intended to help an offender 'to tame the flesh', but it probably refers

[13] In II Thess. 3: 14 the same Greek verb *sunanamignusthai* is used, but apparently the man in question is not yet excommunicated, as he is still to be warned as a brother (v. 15).

46

to his physical death. In this case, even if he died for his sin, as did Ananias and Sapphira, and also other Corinthian Christians (I Cor. 11: 30), the purpose of the excommunication was his final salvation. The third purpose was deterrent. Paul instructed Timothy to administer a public rebuke to 'those who persist in sin . . . , so that the rest may stand in fear' (I Tim. 5: 20, R.S.V.).

This administration of church discipline was continued in the primitive Church of the first few centuries. The Commination Service begins, as we have seen in an earlier chapter, with the statement that in those days 'there was a godly discipline' by which 'such persons as stood convicted of notorious sin were put to open penance, and punished in this world, that their souls might be saved in the day of the Lord; and that others, admonished by their example, might be the more afraid to offend'. Precisely how it fell into desuetude is not known. It may be that during the fierce persecutions of the third century the discipline administered to those who lapsed was too severe, or, as Hooker suggests, that the scandal of public confessions became worse than the scandal of the sins themselves. But, whatever the cause, we know that this healthy and biblical practice of public confession and public penance became gradually displaced by the unhealthy and unbiblical practice of auricular confession and private penance. In the fifth century Pope Leo the Great wrote to the bishops of Campania that public confessions should no longer be made to the congregation but to the priest as their (N.B. not God's) representative. This practice seems to have become general by the end of the following century.

The Reformers were anxious to restore public discipline for serious offences. When preaching before King Henry VIII, Hugh Latimer, oppressed by the moral laxity of the country, appealed to him 'to restore the discipline of Christ, and return to the Church the power of excommunication'.[14] The Commination service, which is a general 'denouncing of God's anger and judgments' against impenitent sinners, was offered as a substitute 'until the said discipline may be restored again (which is much to be wished)'. Meanwhile, one of the rubrics before the Holy Communion service instructs the minister to warn any 'open and notorious evil

[14] Quoted by Drury, p. 151.

47

liver', who has offended the congregation by word or deed, not to 'presume ... to come to the Lord's Table, until he have openly declared himself to have truly repented and amended his former naughty life, that the congregation may thereby be satisfied, which before were offended'. So convinced were our Reformers of the necessity of this exercise of discipline, that it was sometimes added to the preaching of the pure Word of God and the due administration of the sacraments as a third mark of the visible Church of Christ. Thus, in the second part of the Homily for Whitsunday, one of the 'three notes or marks' of the Church 'whereby it is known' is 'the right use of ecclesiastical discipline'.[15] Although this phrase does not occur in Article XIX, Article XXXIII teaches with great definiteness that any person who 'by open denunciation of the church is rightly cut off from the unity of the church and excommunicated' is to be treated by the multitude, as our Lord commanded, like 'an heathen and publican, until he be openly reconciled by penance'.

We today should share the desire of the Reformers for a restoration of this 'godly discipline', in obedience to the plain instructions of our Lord and His apostles. The Church's great weakness and ineffectiveness in our generation are undoubtedly due in part to its lack of discipline, not only in the administration of Baptism and the Lord's Supper, but in the treatment of open offenders. At present the divorcee is commonly the only person who is excommunicated. This not only gives an exaggerated prominence to divorce, but appears to minimize the gravity of other offences.[16] Of course there are many reasons advanced against the enforcement of a stricter discipline. The modern quest for the unity of the Church; the hatred of all intolerance (which fails to distinguish between a right intolerance

[15] pp. 494f.

[16] A welcome new rubric is printed before the Holy Communion Service of the Canadian Prayer Book (1959), in which the minister is authorized to 'refuse to administer the Communion' both to those 'whom he knows to be living in grievous sin', if they will not repent, and to 'those between whom he perceives malice and hatred to exist', if they obstinately refuse to be reconciled. The rubric adds that 'before repelling any from the Lord's Table ... the minister should consult with the Bishop or the Archdeacon', and that 'after so repelling any, he shall within 14 days give a written account to the Bishop. ...'

of sin and a wrong intolerance of spirit); a mistaken notion that such public discipline betokens pride, animosity, or priggishness; a horror of anything approaching the public accusation meetings promoted by Communist governments; a misinterpretation of the parable of the wheat and tares as prohibiting all attempts to separate the bad from the good in the visible Church; a fear of public scandal in these days of mass media of communication – these and other arguments are used to hinder the restoration of a proper discipline to the Church.

Let us agree that some of these arguments are not without substance, that the practice of ecclesiastical discipline is exposed to many perils, and that after many years of neglect great courage and wisdom will be needed to recover it. But the arguments in its favour are stronger and more compelling than the arguments against it. The eternal good of serious offenders is not served by lax discipline; we have seen that public discipline and excommunication in the New Testament were exercised for the reform and benefit of sinners. Again, the Church's witness is impaired by its own low standards. The secular world is almost wholly unimpressed by the Church today. There is a widespread departure from Christian moral standards, and unbelievers see no great difference between themselves and church members. So long as the Church tolerates sin in itself and does not judge itself (I Cor. 5: 12, 13; 11: 31; I Pet. 4: 17), and fails to manifest visibly the power of Jesus Christ to save from sin, it will never attract the world to Christ. And have we no vision of the purpose of Christ for His Church, that we are content with our easy-going mediocrity? Jesus Christ 'gave Himself for us to redeem us from all iniquity and to purify for Himself a people of His own who are zealous for good deeds' (Tit. 2: 14, R.S.V.). He came from heaven to seek her as His bride. He 'gave Himself up for her, that He might sanctify her, having cleansed her by the washing of water with the word, that the church might be presented before Him in splendour, without spot or wrinkle or any such thing, that she might be holy and without blemish' (Eph. 5: 25–27, R.S.V.). How can we, in the light of this purpose of His death, remain indifferent to the Church's holiness?

One last practical point. In the administration of

discipline, the responsibility belongs to the whole local congregation. The power of the keys may have been given to Peter according to Mt. 16: 19, although Bishop Jewel quoted Augustine in his *Defence of the Apology* that 'when Christ said unto Peter "unto thee will I give the keys of the king-dom of heaven" he signified thereby the whole church'.[17] At all events, a little later, this very same authority to bind and loose was explicitly granted by Jesus to each local church, according to Mt. 18: 17, 18. 'Tell it unto the church,' He had just said. It is true that the apostle Paul, when instructing the Corinthian church what they must do, indicated that his spirit would be present with them while they did it, but still it was *they* who, with the power of the Lord Jesus, were to 'deliver to Satan' the offender, and 'drive' him out from their fellowship (I Cor. 5). Of course the local church should only act in agreement with its pastor, and will in any case act through its pastor, and the pastor should consult his bishop, but biblical discipline is essenti-ally parochial and not diocesan, congregational and not ministerial or episcopal. It is the local church which has been sinned against; it is the local church to which public con-fession must be made; and it is the local church which must take responsibility to administer discipline and to use its God-given authority to bind and to loose.

[17] p. 356.

CHAPTER FOUR

AURICULAR CONFESSION

THE MINISTER'S AUTHORITY

IT was suggested in the Introduction that the existence of an indissoluble link between sin, confession, and forgiveness is common ground between Christians of all persuasions. We are all agreed that in order to receive the forgiveness of sin the confession of sin is indispensable. In answer to the question 'to whom should we confess our sins?', the Bible has been seen to teach that secret sins should be confessed secretly (to God), private sins privately (to a fellow human being we have wronged), and public sins publicly (to the local church). We are now in a position to ask the further, specific question: can any place be found in this biblical scheme for the practice of 'auricular confession', confession *ad auriculam*, 'into the ear' of a priest, or what the Reformers sometimes termed 'earish' confession? We have already seen that it developed gradually from the wholesome discipline of open confession and open penance, and that the Lateran Council of A.D. 1215 under Pope Innocent III made it compulsory for every Christian at least once a year. We no doubt also know that weekly confession is practised by Roman Catholics today, and that since the Tractarian Movement at the beginning of the last century weekly or less regular confession has become widespread among Anglo-Catholic churchmen in the Anglican Communion. Further, it is not uncommon nowadays for the practice to be commended by Anglicans who would not welcome the label 'Anglo-Catholic'.

Let me say at once that, from the purely historical point of view, leaving aside for the moment the question of biblical warrant, neither the custom of the primitive Church nor the formularies of the Church of England support or encourage the practice as a normal, regular, or healthy part of the Christian life. Some students of early church history have been too ready to find in any patristic mention of 'confession' an allusion to auricular confession to a priest. Bishop John Jewel did not hesitate to write that 'the express term of auricular or secret confession is never mentioned in the ancient fathers'.[1] Richard Hooker went further He described how what they called 'private penitency' had come to be regarded as 'a sacrament of remitting sins after baptism', and a little later wrote: 'I dare boldly affirm, that for many hundred years after Christ the fathers held no such opinion; they did not gather by our Saviour's words any such necessity of seeking the priest's absolution from sin, by secret and (as they now term it) sacramental confession.' Was this custom not primitive then? 'No, no,' Hooker replies, 'these opinions have youth in their countenance: antiquity knew them not: it never thought nor dreamed of them.'[2] Thus, the author of the homily *Of Repentance* quotes St. Augustine's words: 'What have I to do with men, that they should hear my confession, as though they were able to heal all my diseases?'[3] And Frederick Meyrick, himself an old-fashioned high churchman, collected a number of quotations from the sermons of St. Chrysostom and from his *De Poenitentia* in which sinners are urged not to uncover their sins to men, their 'fellow servants', but in secret, 'no one being present except the all-seeing God'.[4]

It is quite true that, in the earlier years of the sixteenth century, before the Reformation had reached its zenith, our Anglican divines still commended auricular confession. In the eight article of the Thirteen Articles of 1538, for instance, it is described as 'very useful and highly necessary', although even then Cranmer would have preferred 'convenient' to 'necessary' and wanted to add that it was 'not enjoined in Scripture'. The Six Articles of the following year, known as 'the whip with six strings' because by it Henry VIII tried to enforce uniformity of doctrine by the threat of severe penalties, affirmed that auricular confession was 'necessary to be retained and continued, used and frequented in the Church of God'.

The famous *King's Book* of 1543 ('The Necessary Doc-

[1] p. 353.
[2] Book VI, iv, 3, 6, 13.
[3] *Homilies and Canons*, p. 577.
[4] pp. 22–23. Some of them are quoted in Hooker's *Ecclesiastical Polity*, Book VI, iv, 16.

trine and Erudition of a Christian Man'), which belonged to the twilight stage of the Reformation, called the sacrament of penance 'the ordinary mean for penitent sinners to obtain remission of sins', and Cranmer's catechism of 1548 similarly called it a 'sacrament' and the way to receive the forgiveness of sins committed after baptism. The same year (1548), however, in his Order of the Holy Communion, the first Communion service to be written and published in the English language, the first exhortation referred to 'a general confession' and 'the auricular and secret confession to a priest' as alternatives, and urged the champions of the one not to be offended by the champions of the other, but to follow their own conscience and live in charity. This was incorporated in the first reformed Prayer Book which appeared the following year.[5] But in the second Prayer Book of 1552 the wording of the first exhortation was changed to make secret confession to God the ordinary means of preparing to come to the Lord's Table, while the private resort to a 'discreet and learned minister of God's Word' (which was not now called 'auricular and secret confession to a priest') was relegated to the exceptional case of a person 'who by this means cannot quiet his own conscience'. It is in this sense that Ridley, Latimer, Becon, Tyndale, and other Reformers mention it appreciatively, as an abnormal but legitimate means of relieving a troubled conscience, not because they believed in the necessity of regular priestly absolution; and it is in this sense that it is still permitted in the Prayer Book of 1662.

But why is the regular use of auricular confession to be deprecated? I am not going to use or elaborate any of those popular arguments which have been based on the abuse of the confessional; right-minded 'Catholics' deplore these things as much as any evangelical. Nor am I concerned so much with what greatly bothered the Reformers, namely, in words taken from the Second Book of Homilies, that 'it is

[5] The statements that 'private confession to God in prayer' and 'confession to God before a priest' are equally legitimate alternatives, and that those who practise the one should not be offended by those who practise the other, have reappeared in the alternative South African Prayer Book (1954), in the third rubric before the *Form of Confession and Absolution*, and in the second rubric before the same form in the new Prayer Book of the Church of India, Pakistan, Burma and Ceylon (1960).

against the true Christian liberty that any man should be bound to the numbering of his sins'.[6] Nor shall we spend time discussing the potential danger of this practice to the soul of the priest who hears confessions, although I must agree with Bishop J. C. Ryle that he is in 'a place which it is not safe for any child of Adam to occupy'.[7] If we are to 'hate even the garment spotted by the flesh' (Jude 23), like people afraid of a contagious disease, and if 'it is a shame even to speak of those things which are done of them in secret' (Eph. 5: 12), it seems to me very doubtful if God ever meant His ministers to have to enter thus into the secret sins of others. Nevertheless, it is neither because of the abuse, nor because of the perils, of auricular confession that I believe it should be avoided by those who do not use it, and abandoned by those who do, but because the very practice itself is misconceived. I submit that this form of confession is not the will and purpose of God either for the penitent who confesses or for the priest who absolves.

Yet it is precisely this which those who commend the practice claim. Their major arguments are first that it is a right and proper thing in itself, that it is in fact the plan of God that the priest should absolve the penitent in this way; and secondly that it is expedient, being of great practical benefit to the penitent in his spiritual pilgrimage. We shall consider the theological argument in this chapter, and the practical argument in the next. In this way we shall be able to consider both Christian ministers and the nature of their ministerial authority, and also Christian people and the means of their spiritual growth.

THE 'CATHOLIC' VIEW

The medieval schoolmen, like Duns Scotus, taught quite plainly that Christ had given the keys of the kingdom to priests, and that therefore heaven could be opened or closed to men at the sentence of a catholic priest alone. More precisely, original and pre-baptismal sins were put away by baptism, venial sins after baptism by penitence and the mass, and mortal sins after baptism by the sacrament of

[6] p. 577.
[7] p. 271.

penance, although only partially. The Council of Trent, in Sessions XIII and XIV, made the sacrament of penance, including auricular confession, a necessary condition of coming to the eucharist, and anathematized those who denied either its divine origin or its necessity for salvation. It was to be a regular practice binding on all catholics. According to Cardinal Bellarmine, the sixteenth-century Jesuit who sought to defend Rome against the Reformers, Christ had 'ordained His priests judges in such sort that no man which sinneth after baptism can be reconciled unto God but by their sentence'.[8]

This is still the official teaching of the Roman Catholic Church, which (it is important to grasp) rests on their doctrine of the priesthood. Their view of confession arises from and depends on their view of absolution. According to Ludwig Ott's book *Fundamentals of Catholic Dogma*,[9] the argument runs like this: when Jesus was on earth He forgave sins, Mk. 2: 5f.; Lk. 7: 47f. (p. 419). This very same power to forgive sins He bestowed 'on the Apostles and on their legitimate successors' (p. 417) who are not 'all the faithful indiscriminately, but only . . . the members of the hierarchy' (p. 439) – that is, catholic priests. He promised it to them in His words about the keys of the kingdom and about binding and loosing, both of which include 'the power to forgive sins' (p. 418), and then actually transferred it to them 'on the evening of the day of the Resurrection', when He said to them 'As the Father hath sent me, I also send you . . .; whose sins you shall forgive, they are forgiven them; and whose sins you shall retain, they are retained' (pp. 418f.). This 'power to forgive sins involves not merely the power of preaching the gospel of the forgiveness of sins, as the Reformers interpreted it, but also the full power of really remitting sins' (p. 417). Again, 'the Church firmly insists that the power of absolution is a true and real power of absolution, by which sins committed against God are immediately remitted. The proof derives from John 20: 23. According to the words of Jesus, the act of the remission of sins, performed by the apostles and by their successors, has the effect that sins are remitted by God. There is a causal connection between the active remitting and the passive

[8] Quoted by Hooker in Book VI, vi, 2.
[9] pp. 416–40.

55

being remitted' (p. 422). Priestly absolution 'does not merely indicate forgiveness of sins, but also effects it' (p. 436).

Moreover, 'the priestly absolution is a judicial act' (p. 423). As such, it includes 'three essential elements, (a) judicial power (auctoritas iudicalis), (b) knowledge of the state of the facts (cognitio causae) and (c) judicial sentence (sententia iudicalis)' (p. 424). The second of these three is necessary because the judicial sentence imposed by the judicial authority would be arbitrary if it were not 'related to ... the state of conscience of the sinner'. The sentence must be based on a knowledge of the facts and therefore presupposes an 'investigation of the guilt and disposition of the sinner' (p. 424). We must notice the roundabout way in which the subject of confession is reached. It is conceded that 'the Divine institution and the necessity for salvation of the particular confession of sins is not explicitly expressed in Holy Writ'; nevertheless 'it is a necessary consequence of the judicial power to forgive sins. The power of remitting sins or of retaining them can only be properly exercised, if the possessor of the power of penance knows both the sins and the dispositions of the penitent. But the self-accusation of the penitent is necessary for this'. So comes the definition of confession as 'the self-accusation by the penitent of his sins before a fully-empowered priest, in order to obtain forgiveness from him by virtue of the power of the keys'. Therefore 'the sacramental confession of sins is ordained of God and is necessary for salvation' (p. 431).

What emerges from this account of the official teaching of the Church of Rome is that its practice of auricular confession is grounded upon its doctrine of the priesthood and its unique authority to absolve from sin. If their foundation doctrine can be shown to be faulty, the confessional (at least as they describe it) will be discredited also. It is quite true that Anglican writers who commend the practice of auricular confession do not usually base their arguments on a fully developed 'catholic' doctrine of priesthood. They tend to argue their case rather from the pragmatic benefits of confession than from a doctrinaire view of absolution. Yet their position still derives from John 20: 23. Lord Halifax, at the Fulham Conference in December 1901 could go so far as to state 'that the act of absolution is not merely declaratory, but is instrumental in conveying forgiveness'.[10] He later added that 'people do not go to confession to relieve their minds, or primarily for advice, but to get absolution for their sins in the way our Lord has appointed'.[11] 'Manasses' in his little book entitled *Go in Peace* writes that 'we come to the priest in confession for absolution', and although he adds that this is 'to receive God's forgiveness of our sins', he does not shrink from expressions like 'he will then give you absolution' and 'we do receive absolution and that is the greatest of gifts in this sacrament'.[12] Similarly Wilfred Knox can write that 'the words of absolution have bestowed on him for his particular sins that pardon which was won for all mankind once and for all by the death of Jesus on the Cross', although he adds that the priest is 'the medium of a divine gift, not the bestower of it'.[13] Again, the Rev. Kenneth Ross, in his *Instruction on Confession* which he has kindly allowed me to see, begins '(1) Jesus forgave sins . . . (2) Jesus passed on the power specifically: John 20: 21–23.' He thus assumes that the two activities are identical, before he goes on to suggest that the power was exercised first through baptism and ecclesiastical discipline, and now through private confession and absolution. From these quotations it seems fair to say that, although Anglo-Catholic writers do not define the authority of priestly absolution with the precision of Roman Catholics, or make confession compulsory as 'necessary to salvation', they still regard absolution as the foremost benefit of confession and believe that the priest has unique power to 'give' it to the penitent. They would agree that auricular confession is, strictly, not *to* a priest, but 'the confession of sins to God in the presence of a priest authorized to forgive them in His name' (*Oxford Dictionary of the Christian Church*). The fundamental question remains: What is the nature of this authority?

THE BIBLICAL TEACHING

We have already noted that there are three sayings of Jesus

[10] p. 28.
[11] p. 70.
[12] pp. 84, 82, 86.
[13] pp. 79, 80.

on which the claim to a unique priestly authority to absolve is based. They concern three pairs of activities, stated positively and negatively: to lock and to unlock (implied by the gift of 'the keys of the kingdom of heaven', Mt. 16: 19), to bind and to loose (Mt. 16: 19; 18: 18), to remit and to retain sins (Jn. 20: 23). The Reformers did not dispute the Roman Catholic view that the first two pairs were a metaphorical description of the third, that what was promised in Matthew 16 and 18 was actually given in John 20, or that all three passages referred to a certain authority in connection with forgiveness and the withholding of forgiveness. They maintained, however, that this authority lay not in the priesthood but in the Gospel, not in the words of men but in the Word of God. The key which Jesus gave to His Church was 'nothing else but the holy Word of God', wrote Robert Barnes;[14] 'this is the thing only whereby that our conscience is loosed and made free from sin'. Possessing this key the apostles 'did bind with the Word when it was not believed; they did loose by the Word when it was believed: thus did they by one Word preach both salvation and damnation . . .' Becon put the same conviction in very similar terms, that Christian preachers of the Word of God 'loosen, that is to say, they preach to the faithful remission of sins by Christ. They also bind, that is, they declare to the unfaithful damnation.'[15] Even more explicitly, William Tyndale wrote: 'To bind and to loose is to preach the law of God and the Gospel or promises, as thou mayest see in the third chapter of the second epistle to the Corinthians, where Paul calleth the preaching of the law the ministration of death and damnation, and the preaching of the promises the ministering of the Spirit and of righteousness'.[16] Jewel explained in *The Apology* how the minister 'looses' when he offers 'by the preaching of the Gospel the merits of Christ and full pardon to such as have lowly and contrite hearts and do unfeignedly repent them, pronouncing unto the same a sure and undoubted forgiveness of their sins and hope of everlasting salvation', and 'binds' when he 'shutteth up the gate of the kingdom of heaven against the unbelieving and stubborn persons, denouncing unto them God's vengeance

---

[14] *The Works of Dr. Barnes* (1573), p. 258.
[15] p. 566.
[16] p. 269.

and everlasting punishment'.[17] In *The Defence of the Apology*, Jewel supported his interpretation of the keys from the fathers: 'We with Chrysostom say "they be the knowledge of the Scriptures", with Tertullian we say, "they be the interpretation of the Law", and with Eusebius we call them "the Word of God".'[18]

It must be admitted that the Reformers were a little uncritical in assuming that locking and unlocking with the keys, binding and loosing, and remitting and retaining sins were simple synonyms. Let us consider them separately. We cannot deny that the keys were given to Simon Peter personally. Unlike the scribes and Pharisees who had 'taken away the key of knowledge' and 'shut up the kingdom of heaven against men' (Lk. 11: 52; Mt. 23: 13), Peter was to use the keys to open it, and he did so first to the Jews (Acts 2: 38ff.), secondly to the Samaritans (Acts 8: 14ff.) and then to the Gentiles (Acts 10–11; cf. 15: 7). The unique privilege which the keys brought him was one of historical priority in opening the kingdom, not of permanent primacy.

Immediately after promising to give Peter 'the keys of the kingdom of heaven', Jesus went on to say to him: 'What soever thou shalt bind on earth shall be bound in heaven: and whatsoever thou shalt loose on earth shall be loosed in heaven' (Mt. 16: 19). He later extended this authority to each local church (Mt. 18: 17, 18). The use of the neuter 'whatsoever' (which seems to refer to things, not people) and the Rabbinic use of the metaphor for permissions and prohibitions in the realm of conduct,[19] tend to confirm Bishop John Wordsworth's opinion that 'on this text we may rest the validity of the canonical rules of the church, but not the ministry of penitence to persons'.[20] Further, as was indicated in the last chapter, the context in Matthew 18 suggests that ecclesiastical discipline was in our Lord's mind, namely the further authority to excommunicate an offender and to restore him when he repented. Hooker took it thus: 'The Church bindeth by the censures of her discipline' and 'the Church looseth but her own bands, the chains wherein she

[17] p. 60.
[18] p. 363.
[19] See Prof. H. B. Swete's words at the Fulham Conference. *Confession and Absolution*, p. 15.
[20] Letter to the clergy of Salisbury diocese, 1898, quoted by Bishop Drury.

had tied them before'.[21] In this sense the Church has an authority to grant an absolute forgiveness to those who have offended against her; she has no such authority to forgive those who have offended against God.

If the power of the keys and the activity of binding and loosing do not necessarily refer to the forgiveness of sins against God, the direct statement in John 20: 23 about 'remitting' and 'retaining' sins clearly does. Two questions confront us. First, to whom was this authority given? Secondly, of what did the authority consist? It is an essential part of the Roman Catholic system that the power of absolution was given only to the apostles and their successors, the priests. This cannot be proved. Quite apart from the lack of any reference to the transmission of the authority, and of any identification of those to whom it might be transmitted, and of any suggestion in the New Testament that there is a priestly or sacerdotal ministry in the Christian Church[22] or that 'absolution' is necessarily a function of 'priests', there is no evidence that the words of the risen Jesus recorded in John 20: 23 were spoken to the apostles alone. Was the Great Commission, sending them into the world as the Father had sent Him, addressed to the apostles only? Was the Holy Spirit, whose Pentecostal coming He anticipated by breathing on them in a dramatic acted parable, to be given to the apostles alone? If we are not prepared to restrict to the apostles our Lord's sending of them out or giving to them the Spirit, we cannot properly restrict His promise about remitting and retaining sins to the apostles either. Besides, if we insist that the power to absolve was given to all the apostles and to them alone, it will have included Thomas although he was absent (Jn. 20: 24), yet excluded the Emmaus disciples and others, although they were present (Lk. 24: 33ff.). There is no indication that Jesus discriminated like this. We must therefore conclude that the bestowal of authority, like the great commission and the promise of the Spirit, was made indiscriminately to all present as the nucleus of the whole Church.

What, then, was this authority? It is *a priori* improbable

[21] Book VI, vi, 8.
[22] See J. B. Lightfoot's dissertation on 'The Christian Ministry', appended to his *Commentary on the Epistle to the Philippians* (1868). Eighth Edition, London, 1885 especially pp. 248–69.

that Jesus was actually transferring to the Church the same authority to forgive sins which He had claimed and exercised Himself (Mk. 2: 7). His hearers understandably accused Him of blasphemy, since they recognized that to forgive sins is a divine prerogative. Besides, He claimed that He had this authority as 'the Son of man' (His favourite Messianic title), just as in the other controversy stories in this chapter of St. Mark He defended His actions by claiming to be the Good Physician of sinners, the heavenly Bridegroom and the Lord of the Sabbath (vv. 17, 19 and 28). Are we proposing to transfer these offices to the Church as well? No, these titles and the functions which go with them belong exclusively to Jesus because of who He was and is. We cannot forgive sins as He did for we are not the Son of Man, any more than we are the sinners' Physician, the Church's Bridegroom, or the Sabbath's Lord. This being so, we must interpret His description of the Church 'remitting' and 'retaining' people's sins as a dramatic figure of speech for a dogmatic declaration in certain circumstances that their sins are forgiven or not forgiven. This would be in keeping with other startling expressions of Jesus like 'hating' our parents, 'plucking out' our eyes, 'taking up our cross', and 'losing our life'. The interpretation of the verbs 'remitting' and 'retaining' as the verbal declaration of a truth is paralleled in the publicans' 'justifying God' (Lk. 7: 29; so Hooker) and in Jeremiah's 'destroying' and 'building up' the nation of Judah which, Tyndale argued, was 'verily by preaching and prophesying'.[23]

If it be asked by what principles we thus interpret this controversial verse, we must reply: by the two most important and reliable of all the canons of biblical interpretation, namely the comparison of parallel passages and the understanding of the original hearers. If we compare Scripture with Scripture, and especially the wording of the Great Commission as it is recorded here in St. John and in St. Luke 24: 46–49, we find similar references to the evangelization of the world, the gift of the Spirit, and the offer of forgiveness. But the 'remission of sins' which in St. John is portrayed as an activity of the disciples in St. Luke is the substance of the message which they are to

[23] Wm. Tyndale: *Expositions and Notes* (Parker Society, 1848), p. 160.

preach in His Name among all nations (v. 47). The natural explanation of the parallel is that the Johannine statement is a strikingly forceful version of the Lucan, and is to be interpreted in the same way, as a proclamation.

The second principle of exegesis concerns the understanding of the original hearers. We must always beware of imposing upon Scripture the ideas of a later age. The fatal objection to the 'catholic' explanation of John 20: 23 as the bestowal of a judicial, absolving authority is that the apostles never spoke or behaved as if they understood it in this way. There is no evidence in the New Testament that they believed such an authority had been given them. They neither claimed these powers, nor exercised them. What they did, on the other hand, was to declare with authority the terms on which God would forgive men's sins through Christ, and then to admit penitent believers by baptism into the Church (Acts 2: 38ff.; 3: 19; 13: 38f.; 22: 16; 26: 17f., etc.). Similarly, in the epistles, even in the pastoral epistles, there are no verses which can be construed as an allusion to private confession and absolution, but only triumphant affirmations that 'in Christ we have redemption through His blood, even the forgiveness of sins' (Eph. 1: 7; Col. 1: 14). Paul understood the 'ministry of reconciliation' committed to the Church as a proclamation of 'the message of reconciliation' and an appeal, as Christ's ambassadors, to men to be reconciled to God (II. Cor. 5: 18-21). As Becon put it: 'Neither did the apostles absolve any otherwise than by the preaching of God's Word'.[24]

From these biblical data we conclude that the authority to 'remit' and 'retain' sins, which the risen Christ gave to His disciples, was ministerial, not magisterial. It was not an authority to forgive, but to preach forgiveness, to proclaim 'not in word only but also in power and in the Holy Ghost and in much assurance' (I Thess. 1: 5) both the promises and the warnings of the Gospel – the promise of salvation to the believer, the warning of judgment to the unbeliever. Moreover, this authority was given by Christ to the whole Church, to whom the universal commission and the gift of the Spirit were also given. As Bishop Jewel wrote: 'Christ's disciples did receive this authority, not that they should hear the private confessions of the people . . . ,

[24] Preface, p. 560.

62

but to the end they should go, they should teach, they should publish abroad the Gospel.'[25] True, it is an authority exercised primarily through ministers duly called and ordained to preach the Word, but this limitation is one of expediency rather than of necessity. It is God who forgives through Christ; it is the Church which proclaims His forgiveness through its ministers.

THE PRAYER BOOK

But, it may be asked, is this interpretation, of an authority to declare sins remitted or retained, delegated to ministers by the Church, consistent with the Prayer Books of the Anglican Communion? In particular, is it not contradicted by the authority ascribed to ministers in the Ordinal, the first exhortation of the Communion service, and the Visitation of the Sick in the 1662 Book? Do they not imply that the priest has the power by virtue of his ordination to absolve sins? These questions are often asked and must be plainly answered. Moreover, in answering them we must be careful not to offer an explanation which is incompatible either with the Prayer Book as a whole or with the known opinions of our Reformers as disclosed in their writings, the Articles, and Homilies. We must give them credit for logical and consistent thought and not impute to them either confused minds or self-contradictory utterances.

The actual words spoken by the bishop while hands are being laid on the candidate for full orders are in three parts. First: 'Receive the Holy Ghost for the office and work of a priest in the Church of God, now committed unto thee by the imposition of our hands.' The word 'priest' is unfortunately ambiguous in modern ears, but not in the writings of the Reformers. It is an English contraction of the word 'presbyter', and refers not to distinctively sacerdotal functions in the ministry, which the Reformers had abandoned, but to the second of the three orders 'bishops, priests (that is, presbyters) and deacons' (see the Preface to the Ordinal). Secondly, the words of Jesus are quoted: 'Whose sins thou dost forgive, they are forgiven; and whose sins thou dost retain, they are retained.' These words had appeared in unreformed ordinals from the thirteenth century, but not in association with the act of ordination itself. Cranmer took

[25] p. 365.

63

them 'out of a subordinate position, and made them the actual formula of ordination'.[26] How he intended them to be understood is made clear by the charge which immediately follows: 'And be thou a faithful dispenser of the Word of God, and His holy sacraments . . .' This is further emphasized by the *traditio instrumentorum* which comes next, while the candidate remains kneeling. He is not given a paten and chalice, with bread and wine, as in the medieval services, with the words, 'Receive power to offer sacrifice to God, and to celebrate Masses for the living and for the dead . . .', nor even a Bible in one hand and a chalice in the other (as in 1550), but a Bible only, with the words, 'Take thou authority to preach the Word of God, and to minister the holy sacraments in the congregation . . .' It is this emphasis on the Word of God, in the ministry of preaching and the sacraments alike, which interprets the meaning of John 20: 23 in this context. 'If we can only get back,' wrote Bishop Drury, 'to the original breadth of that solemn commission, and read those words . . . in the large sense that the Reformers attached to them, we need not regret that our Church, in granting her commission, uses the *ipsissima verba* with which she received it.'[27] They indicate in graphic terms both the substance of the Church's message and the authority with which it is to be proclaimed.

Turning from the Ordinal to the first exhortation of the Communion service, the best way to discover what the Reformers intended by it is to compare the significant ways in which the wording of the 1549 Prayer Book was altered in that of 1552. Apart from the fact that a private resort to the minister, which in 1549 was a recognized alternative to general confession, has now become exceptional, there were two principal changes – regarding the character of the 'confession' and the means of 'absolution'. In 1549 we still read of 'the auricular and secret confession to a priest', and the invitation to the conscience-stricken penitent is: 'Let him come to me or to some other discreet and learned priest taught in the law of God, and confess and open his sin and grief secretly.' In 1552, however, the person who cannot quiet his conscience is not to confess his sin to a priest, but rather to 'open his grief' to a 'discreet and learned minister

[26] Drury, p. 248.
[27] pp. 248–9.

of God's word'.[28] The absolution is different too. In both
forms the penitent is to receive not only 'counsel' and
'advice', but absolution – in 1549 'of us (as ministers of God
and of His Church)', in 1552 'by the ministry of God's holy
word'. The authoritative message of assurance is to come
not from the words of men but from the Word of God
Himself, as, in Girdlestone's rather quaint phrase, 'whilst
the inquirer opens his grief, the minister opens his Bible'.[29]
This interpretation of private 'absolution' as authority
through the ministry of God's Word to pronounce a penitent and believing sinner forgiven is consistent with the
public absolutions at Morning and Evening Prayer and at
Holy Communion. In the former services the absolution is
plainly declaratory, the 'power and commandment' which
God has given to His ministers being 'to declare and pronounce to His people, being penitent, the absolution and
remission of their sins'. They do not 'give' absolution but
proclaim it; the gift is God's, for '*He* pardoneth and absolveth all them that truly repent and unfeignedly believe
His holy Gospel'. The minister therefore concludes by exhorting the congregation to pray that God will give us
(minister and people alike) 'true repentance and His Holy
Spirit', without which God's forgiveness cannot be received. In the Holy Communion service there is neither a
'giving' of absolution, nor even a 'declaration' of it, but a
prayer for it, grounded upon God's merciful promise of
'forgiveness of sins to all them that with hearty repentance
and true faith turn unto Him'. This reference to God's
promise is immediately confirmed by the recitation of the
four 'Comfortable Words', which are gracious invitations
and pledges of the Gospel – 'Gospel-comfort' in fact, in
the expression of Hermann's German liturgy. Thus again
the pardon of man and the assurance of it flow from the
Word of God.

A rubric in the Order for the Visitation of the Sick reads:
'*Here shall the sick person be moved to make a special confession of his sins, if he feel his conscience troubled with
any weighty matter. After which confession, the priest shall
absolve him (if he humbly and heartily desire it) after this*

[28] In 1662 Convocation rejected the proposal to replace the word
'minister' by 'priest' as in the 1549 book.
[29] p. 50.

sort.' The first point to be noted here is that both the confession and the absolution are exceptional and voluntary. The two conditional 'if' clauses show this. It is only if a sick person has some 'weighty matter' on his conscience that he is to be 'moved' (that is, encouraged, not commanded) to 'make a special confession of his sins'.[30] And it is only 'if he humbly and heartily desire it' that the minister is to 'absolve him'. What form will this optional absolution take? No obligatory form is prescribed. The words which follow may be used either as a form or as a pattern ('after this sort'). They comprise two complementary parts. The first addresses Jesus Christ as the One who has left 'power to His Church' (not just His ministers) to absolve, not 'all sinners', but all those 'who truly repent and believe in Him', and prays that 'of His great mercy' He will forgive the penitent's offences. In the second part the minister says: 'By His authority committed to me' (that is, delegated to me by the Church to whom it was originally given) 'I absolve thee from all thy sins, in the Name of the Father, and of the Son, and of the Holy Ghost. Amen.'

This phrase has been taken by some to mean that the Church of England claims for its ministers the power of judicial absolution. Certainly the formula is the 'catholic' one, *'ego absolvo te'*, but there is no justification for interpreting it in the 'catholic' way. We have liberty to understand it only in the light of the known theological position of the Reformers. We must agree with the Puritans that it is ambiguous. At the Savoy Conference they wanted the formula changed from 'I absolve thee' to 'I pronounce thee absolved'. But the bishops justly replied that the words were 'more agreeable to the Scriptures than that which they desire', since they are an echo of John 20: 23. We must balance the minister's statement of absolution with the prayer to God for it which both precedes and follows, and we must understand the statement itself as the Reformers did.[31] Hugh Latimer in a famous sermon on the petition

[30] In the 1928 Prayer Book a form of confession is supplied, and the rubric directs that the confession be made 'in this or other like form'.

[31] It is significant that the American Prayer Book omits the form of absolution, adding instead in the rubric that 'on evidence of his repentance, the Minister shall assure him of God's mercy and forgiveness'.

for forgiveness in the Lord's Prayer, preached in 1552, claimed that 'a godly minister . . . instructed in the Word of God' could absolve sinners 'in open preaching' and went on to explain what he meant: 'As many as confess their sins unto God, acknowledging themselves to be sinners, and believe that our Saviour, through His passion, hath taken away their sins, and have an earnest purpose to leave sin, as many I say as be so affectioned, *ego absolvo vos*: I, as an officer of Christ, as His treasurer, absolve you in His name. This is the absolution that I can make by God's Word.'[32] The absolution in the Visitation of the Sick is simply a personal and particular application of this general authoritative ministry of the Word. Thus Bishop Christopher Wordsworth of Lincoln wrote in a Pastoral Letter dated 1874, and quoted by Bishop Drury: 'By those words "I absolve", we do not claim for ourselves the power to give pardon, but only as heralds sent from God Himself, to certify and assure you, that He is ever ready to be gracious . . . and that if you have true repentance, lively faith, and fervent love . . . He has washed away your sins in the Blood of Christ, and will remember them no more.'[33]

With this position, of course, the formularies of the other Reformed churches of the sixteenth century are in complete agreement. To take one example, chapter 14 of the Second Helvetic Confession speaks as follows: 'All ministers, truly called, have and exercise the keys, or the use of them, when they preach the Gospel, that is to say, when they teach, exhort, reprove, and keep in order the people committed to their charge. It is thus that they open the kingdom of God to the obedient and shut it against the disobedient. . . . Rightly, therefore, and effectually do ministers absolve when they preach the Gospel of Christ, and thereby remission of sins, which is promised to everyone that believes. . . . Nor do we imagine that this absolution is in the slightest degree more effectual by being mumbled privately into some priest's ear or over some man's head; yet we judge that men must be taught diligently to seek remission of sins in the blood of Christ and that all should be reminded that forgiveness of sins belongs to Him alone.'

[32] *Sermons of Hugh Latimer* (Parker Society, 1844), Vol. I, i, 423f.
[33] p. 179.

God's way of forgiveness according to the Scriptures is plain. The authority to forgive sins He has given to Jesus Christ His Son alone, who died for our sins and whose blood of the New Covenant was shed for the forgiveness of sins. The authority which Jesus Christ has given to His Church, and which the Church delegates largely (but not entirely) to its ministers, is to preach the Gospel of forgiveness in His Name (Lk. 24: 47; Acts 13: 38, 39), and to declare with confident authority to those who repent and believe that their sins are indeed forgiven. We cannot avoid the conclusion that to go to a human priest privately, to confess our sins and to seek absolution, is not the way which God has appointed. The Christian ministry resembles that of John the Baptist. It is a signpost ministry pointing to Christ. Our constant theme must be: 'Behold the Lamb of God.' We do not, therefore, say to sinners 'Come to me' (except in exceptional cases which we shall consider in the next chapter), for those are the words of Christ. What we say is 'Go to Him'. The habitual practice of auricular confession is damaging to the penitent (since it at least confuses, if not contradicts, his God-given right of direct access to Jesus Christ); it is falsely glorifying to the minister (since it implies a judicial authority to forgive which he does not possess); and it is derogatory to Jesus Christ (since it obscures His uniqueness as our only and absolutely adequate Saviour, Mediator, and Advocate: I Tim. 2: 5; I Jn. 2: 1, 2). Bishop Ryle was right to ask what the sense or reason was of going to an earthly confessor so long as we can have access to the best of all Priests, Jesus Christ Himself: 'When His ear is deaf, and His heart is cold – when His hand is feeble, and His power to heal is exhausted – when the treasure-house of His sympathy is empty, and His love and goodwill have become cold – then and not till then, it will be time to turn to earthly priests and earthly confessionals. Thank God, that time is not yet come!'[34]

[34] p. 258.

68

CHAPTER FIVE

AURICULAR CONFESSION – 2

THE PENITENT'S NEED

THE two principal arguments by which the practice of auricular confession has been commended are first theological, that God has willed it this way (giving His priests authority to absolve) and secondly practical, that sinners need it this way (it is most helpful and beneficial to us). The Reformers certainly agreed that, rightly understood and shorn of unbiblical notions of priesthood and absolution, it should be retained for *exceptional* cases. It is, as we have seen, in this sense that the references to it in the English Prayer Book are to be understood. But modern writers of varying schools of thought, though not wishing to make it compulsory, strongly urge that it should be *habitual*. They do not think of it 'as a medicine for special cases of sickness' but 'as food for the soul in ordinary health'.[1] Thus, P. D. Butterfield commends 'the practice of regular sacramental confession as one of proven usefulness in the Christian life'.[2] To Wilfred Knox 'the value of the Sacrament of Penance cannot be overestimated'.[3] Eric James writes of his conviction that 'everything possible must be done to proclaim that the sacrament of Confession is available for all in the Church of England'.

I must honestly say that these and other modern writers seem to me to rely too much on arguments of expediency. We are all agreed about our human degradation, our sin and guilt, our waywardness and weakness. We know that 'there is no health in us'. So what do we do? Well, we are too precipitate in prescribing the remedy which *we* favour, instead of consulting the Great Physician and applying the remedies which He prescribes. After all, the first criterion by which a Christian judges a course of action is not its

[1] Drury, p. 137.
[2] p. 8.
[3] p. 93.

apparent value, but its rightness. The first question we should ask about any practice is not 'is it useful?' but 'is it biblical?' Is it part of the gracious revealed purpose of our Saviour for the salvation and sanctification of sinners? If not, then what *is* His purpose for them? I find it alarming that so few modern writers seem to stop to ask these questions and to get a satisfactory answer to them. It is this failure to begin from first principles which has led many to adopt and commend a practice which, although undoubtedly helpful to some people in special need, is not for the highest good of the average Christian, because it is not God's normal purpose for him.

Perhaps the best way to proceed will be to consider the benefits which are claimed for the practice of regular confession, and then to examine if there is some other, better way by which these benefits may be secured. The forms of confession which I have seen put into the penitent's mouth, after the enumeration of his sins and the expression of his sorrow and resolve to amend, are requests for 'penance, advice, and absolution'. We could profitably take these requests as summarizing the value said to be derived from confession: 'penance' to humble us and help us see the sinfulness of our sins; 'absolution' to assure us of God's forgiveness; and 'advice' to guide us in our Christian growth and discipline. These are certainly three great benefits. We all need to be convicted of the gravity of our sins, comforted by the forgiveness of our sins, and counselled about the conquest of our sins. The question is: what is the best and God-appointed means to secure these proper ends?

REPENTANCE

According to Roman Catholic theologians, the outward signs of the sacrament of penance are said to be 'contrition, confession, and satisfaction'. 'Contrition' is a grief and hatred of sin, with a resolve not to sin again, while 'attrition' is the word they use for an imperfect contrition proceeding not from the love of God but from fear of punishment or other lesser motives. They further teach that one of the valuable effects of the sacrament of penance is that it turns attrition into contrition. Anglican theologians do not favour this kind of subtlety but do teach the value of confession to deepen the penitent's contrition, which is a necessary sign of his repentance and condition of his forgiveness (Ps. 51: 17; II Cor. 7: 10). No one will deny P. D. Butterfield's statement that God 'calls us sooner or later to deepened penitence'; but I must question his conclusion that 'for most of us, when we have put away prejudice and fear, that means going to confession'.[4] I question this not because I doubt the costliness to human pride involved in the practice, but because I do not believe this is God's normal method of humbling and convicting the sinner.

Let us examine the arguments further. 'The sorrow is increased by the use of sacramental confession,' writes 'Manasses': 'the fact of somebody else hearing what we have to say increases our horror at what we have done, and at what we have omitted to do.'[5] Eric James suggests that as the Prodigal Son could have written his father a letter of apology but found 'owning up to his face ... more costly' and productive of a 'deeper reconciliation', so in sacramental confession we can speak to God 'face to face' more than when we are on our own. 'This sacrament enables repentance to be increasingly deep,' he writes later.[6] But it is Wilfred Knox who lays most emphasis on this point. He refers to it several times in his book *Penitence and Forgiveness*. He describes 'the Sacrament of Penance as a means of ensuring the adequacy of our personal sorrow for our sins' (p. 13). If we were to ask him how this is, he would seem to reply like this: 'It is the hardest possible thing to be conscious of God's presence' (p. 51); 'we have no such consciousness of His presence as would make it possible for us to feel any part of that sorrow which we ought to feel'; but 'the practice of Confession to another human being' produces 'an entirely new reality to our confessions of sin, which was absent before' (p. 52).

The argument is plain. We ought to be more penitent. We cannot deepen our penitence by secret confession to God because this is not real to us. So we resort to sacramental confession as a device to make it real. Mind you, some writers are candid enough to concede that the device does not by any means always work. Auricular confession is as prone to degenerate into a formality as any other

[4] p. 9.
[5] p. 54.
[6] pp. 18, 19, 39.

confession, and Jack Winslow rightly says that it can be 'an escape from honesty with our fellowmen. We can put off our mask before one who is pledged to secrecy, and put it on again amongst those with whom we live day by day'[7] and (he might have added) before God Himself.

I fully agree that the danger of unreality in secret confession to God is great, but I submit that the remedy proposed is the wrong one. What is needed is not an artificial device to make God more real, but a resort to the biblical method. Have we forgotten the promises of Jesus about the Holy Spirit, that when He came in Pentecostal fullness He would convict of sin and glorify Christ, that is, reveal Him and make Him known (Jn. 16: 8, 13)? I rather doubt if faith in the confessional to bring deep conviction of sin in the presence of God can co-exist with a strong faith in the Holy Spirit. We need to recapture our belief that one of the God-appointed functions of the Holy Spirit is to make us know, feel, mourn, loathe, and forsake our sins; and if we are conscious of a superficial view of sin our proper course of action is to cry to the Holy Spirit, not to flee to the confessional.

But how does the Holy Spirit bring conviction of sin? The instrument He uses is the Word of God. You may recall that the Commination service has been mentioned several times in this book. It begins by bemoaning the prevalence of vice in those 'dangerous days' and by desiring that public discipline will be restored to the Church. Meanwhile, the remedy for the restraint of sin which it proposes is not confession but a 'commination', that is a reading of 'the general sentences of God's cursing against impenitent sinners' gathered from the Scriptures, 'to the intent that . . . ye may the rather be moved to earnest and true repentance'. The preaching of the law and the Gospel can awaken and deepen penitence if the Holy Spirit confirms the Word. The result of Peter's sermon on the Day of Pentecost was that the crowd were 'pricked in their heart' and cried out 'Men and brethren what shall we do?' (Acts 2: 37), while the same ministry of God's Word through the prophet Nathan brought repentance and confession to King David (II Sam. 12: 1f.). If, therefore, we are conscious of a lack of conviction of sin in ourselves, or in the congregation we may have been called

[7] pp. 28, 29.

to serve, or in the Church at large (as we undoubtedly must be today), the right course to pursue is to read the Word of God ourselves, and expound it faithfully to others, with a humble, earnest entreaty to the Holy Spirit to exercise His promised ministry and stir our sluggish consciences. The remedy is less precise, less concrete, less ready-made than the confessional, but I venture to say that it is more biblical and is therefore certain to be more effective.

ASSURANCE OF FORGIVENESS

The second benefit which auricular confession is said to bestow is an assurance of forgiveness. Let us agree with modern writers on this subject that deliverance from the bondage of guilt and a certainty of divine absolution were never more needed than they are in our twentieth century. Jack Winslow quotes the head of a large English mental home as having said: 'I could dismiss half my patients to-morrow if they could be assured of forgiveness.'[8] George MacLeod handles the subject with his customary force and eloquence. 'It has been authoritatively claimed,' he writes, 'that some 60 per cent (of patients in Scottish mental hospitals) are suffering in some degree from a guilt complex', and he describes general practitioners who are 'delayed in their work by the number of quite normal patients with an overflowing need to unburden their souls'. 'We live in a world,' he goes on, 'where literally thousands of our church members are in need of ... release ... We live ... in a vacuum where men simply are not freed.'[9] He is not exaggerating. He is quite right. Men are crying out for forgiveness, and an assurance of it, for integration and release.

Once again we are agreed in the diagnosis, but disagreed about the cure. 'I am concerned with the consequence of true confession,' writes George McLeod, 'which is absolution.' He describes what he calls the 'fragrant and beautiful' system of penance which the early Celtic Church introduced, with its 'anamchara' or 'soul-friend', and urges a new synthesis of individual and corporate absolution.[10] Wilfred Knox tells us his problem quite candidly: 'How can I be

[8] p. 22.
[9] pp. 3, 4, 5.
[10] pp. 3, 7, 8.

certain, so long as penitence is regarded simply as an attitude of the soul or a psychological state, that its depth and sincerity is sufficient to obtain forgiveness?' He later answers his own question: 'The value of the Sacrament of Penance as a whole lies in the fact that it enables the penitent to express his sorrow for his sins by a formal outward action, and thereby satisfy himself that he has repented with a sufficient degree of sincerity to justify himself in believing that his penitence is acceptable to God.' But the assurance comes not only from his own confession, but from the words of absolution by which 'the penitent is assured of the fact that he has received that gift of forgiveness to an extent which justifies him in regarding his past sins as obliterated'.[11] Other writers tell of their personal experiences of sacramental confession. 'In that way, and that way alone, have we found peace,' says 'Manasses', and adds: 'indeed it is not perhaps too much to say that many have only in this way discovered the meaning of Christianity.'[12] Jack Winslow is convinced that it could be 'of rich blessing to many guilt-burdened souls'.[13]

My purpose in quoting these passages is not to throw doubt on their sincerity or even their reality, but to ask again: is this really the normal way which God has appointed, by which we sinners may find our burdens lifted, our guilt absolved, our sins forgiven, and peace? I think not. The Bible does not say it is. Nor does the Prayer Book. On the contrary, the way to receive assurance of forgiveness, like the way to receive conviction of sin, is through the Word of God as it is illumined to our hearts and minds by the Spirit of God. I certainly agree that there are psychological disorders, involving deep represssions and a guilt complex, which need medical treatment, rather than the ministry of God's Word. I fear there are also experiences of release through 'getting something off one's chest' whether at confession or elsewhere, 'making a clean breast of it' after 'bottling it up' for years, which may be psychological rather than spiritual and may not give evidence of the actual forgiveness of God.

How can we receive God's forgiveness and be assured of

[11] pp. 45, 46, 78, 79.
[12] pp. 50, 57.
[13] p. viii.

it? Forgiveness is possible and available for sinners today, as we have seen, only because Jesus Christ bore our sins on the Cross, enduring in our place their penalty and judgment. God accepts or 'justifies' those who call upon Christ to save and cleanse them, and who trust Him to do so. Forgiveness comes from what God has *done* in and through Christ; assurance comes from what God has *said* in and through Christ. He has promised to give rest to those who come to Him and eternal life to those who trust in Him (for example, Mt. 11: 28; Jn. 6: 37, 47). Can we not believe His promises? Remember not only what He has *done* and *said*, but what He *is*, eternal and unchangeable, true to His covenant, faithful to His Word. 'God is not a man, that He should lie; neither the son of man that He should repent: hath He said, and shall He not do it? Or hath He spoken, and shall He not make it good?' (Num. 23: 19). With this biblical way of assurance the Prayer Book is in full agreement. At Morning and Evening Prayer we pray for mercy and restoration 'according to Thy promises declared unto mankind in Christ Jesu our Lord'. In the absolution at Holy Communion the minister reminds us that God has 'promised forgiveness of sins to all them that with hearty repentance and true faith turn unto Him', and immediately enforces this reminder by the four great gospel promises we call the comfortable words.

Yet His Word of promise is not the only means of assurance which God has given us. He knows that our faith is 'brittle', to use Luther's word, and needs strengthening. Or, to change the metaphor, He knows how hard we find it to believe a 'naked' word; so He has graciously 'clothed' it for us to see, in the two sacraments of the Gospel. Augustine called them *verba visibilia* (visible words), and Bishop Jewel added that 'the substance of all sacraments is the Word of God'.[14] They dramatize the promises of the Gospel in such a way as to evoke and confirm our faith. Baptism, being unique and unrepeatable, is the sacrament of our once-for-all justification; Holy Communion, being repeatedly enjoyed, is the sacrament of our daily forgiveness. By them we are assured, audibly and visibly, of our acceptance and forgiveness. Once we have grasped this we can understand how mistaken medieval churchmen were to

[14] p. 353.

think of their sacrament of penance as 'a second baptism'; how wrong 'Manasses' is to write, 'we were baptized and received remission of our sins but we have sinned since; we need a new baptism';[15] and how misleading it is for Eric James to say that confession 'mediates "Justification by Faith" in sacramental form'.[16] We have baptism as our sacrament of justification and Holy Communion as our sacrament of forgiveness. Bishop Drury is right to say that 'they both convey, in their several functions, the fullest possible promise of remission to those who truly repent. There is no place for any minor sacrament' to supplement them.[17]

God's way of assurance is, therefore, by His Word, proclaimed to us through the Scriptures and the sacraments, and apprehended by faith. One of the most urgent needs in the Church of God today is a recovery of the simple biblical truth that the Christian life is a life of faith in response to God's Word. Faith feeds on the promises of God and grows healthy and strong by them. Why should we need the words of fallible men as a substitute for, or even supplement to, the infallible Word of God? A man, however experienced and perspicacious, cannot read our inner thoughts and motives. Only God knows our heart, and St. John makes this omniscience of God one of the means by which we may pacify our heart whenever it condemns us (I Jn. 3: 19, 20). Some may find it easier to believe the word of a visible man, but do we forget that God has called such to preach to us the message of forgiveness (Lk. 24: 47; Acts 13: 38) and that He has graciously made His Word visible to us in the sacraments? Kenneth Ross writes: 'If you would like to have heard Jesus say to *you*, "Son, be of good cheer; thy sins be forgiven thee", then you should make your confession . . .' But no! Jesus speaks these words of comfort and assurance to my soul every time I come to Him as a repentant, believing sinner, whether in response to the public preaching of His Word or in my private Bible reading or at the Lord's Supper. We need to meditate, in the eleventh chapter of the Epistle to the Hebrews, on the great heroes of faith in the Old Testament, to whom the Word of God came, who embraced it and staked their whole lives

[15] p. 108.
[16] p. 10.
[17] pp. 81, 82.

upon it, 'being fully persuaded, that what He had promised He was able also to perform' (Rom. 4: 21). It is God's will that we should become 'mature in Christ' (Col. 1: 28), not continually resorting to men and depending on the words of men, but 'fight the good fight of faith' (I Tim. 6: 12), hearing and receiving God's holy Word through Scripture and sacrament, laying fast hold of His promises, and refusing to let them go until 'through faith and patience' we inherit them (Heb. 6: 12). This is the biblical way of assurance. It is the Church of England way too. Hooker summed it up in these words: '*We* (s.c. of the Church of England) labour to instruct men in such sort, that every soul which is wounded with sin may learn the way how to cure itself; *they* (s.c. of the Church of Rome), clean contrary, would make all sores seem incurable, unless the priest have a hand in them.'[18]

But, it will be immediately objected, there are some people who simply cannot find peace that way. They try to lay down their burden at the foot of the cross but somehow cannot leave it there. Their conscience keeps stabbing them, nagging them, tormenting them; and however hard they try to pacify it by believing the promises of God, they fail. In such special cases confession 'is not in reformed churches denied by the learneder sort of divines'.[19] So wrote Richard Hooker, and added that its purpose was 'for the strengthening of weak, timorous, and fearful minds'. Similarly, in Ridley's words it is 'to instruct, correct, comfort, and inform the weak, wounded, and ignorant conscience'.[20] If men find their conscience 'troubled with any weighty matter' (Visitation of the Sick), or, to use Tyndale's expressive word, 'tangled',[21] they should not hesitate to 'repair to their learned curate or pastor, or to some other godly learned man, and show the trouble and doubt of their conscience to them, that they may receive at their hand the comfortable salve of God's Word'.[22] It is for this that the Prayer Book makes provision, and we should avail ourselves of it in a time of special need. The reason

[18] Book VI, vi, 2.
[19] Book VI, iv, 154.
[20] Nicholas Ridley: *Letters of Bishop Ridley* in his *Works* (Parker Society, 1843), p. 338.
[21] p. 266.
[22] *Of Repentance* in the Second Book of Homilies (1562), p. 577.

why God's promises may not previously have brought peace to the soul is neatly expressed by Calvin: 'It sometimes happens, that he who hears the general promises of God, which are addressed to the whole Church, nevertheless remains in some suspense, and is still disquieted with doubts as to the forgiveness of his sins. But if he discloses secretly to his pastor his distress, and hears the pastor applying to him in particular the general doctrine, he will be straightly assured where formerly he was in doubt, and will be liberated from every trepidation, and find repose of conscience.'[23]

This kind of resort to a minister is quite legitimate, and, of course, a minister should sympathetically welcome any person who comes to him with a troubled conscience, and should seek to quieten it by the particular application of the general promises of God. Nevertheless, it remains exceptional and should not be encouraged as a habitual practice. The Prayer Book is quite clear that the normal 'way and means' to assurance and to preparation for Holy Communion is self-examination 'by the rule of God's commandments', followed by confession of sin and trust in God's promises of mercy. It is only 'if there be any of you, who by this means cannot quiet his own conscience' that he should come privately to his minister for 'further comfort and counsel' (first exhortation). Not only should such an approach to the minister be exceptional, but, as Bullinger rightly commented, it should 'rather be termed a consultation than a confession'.[24] All notions of 'sacramental confession', 'judicial absolution', and 'penance' are inappropriate to it. The minister is exercising a pastoral not a priestly function, in soothing a wounded conscience with the ointment of God's Word. If a visit of this kind is regarded as both pastoral and exceptional in character, no possible objection can be raised to it; it is one of every minister's sacred privileges. Bishop Ryle sums it up for us in writing: 'Occasional private conference with a minister is one thing; habitual confession of sin, with habitual absolution, is quite another.'[25] We might summarize the four changes made by the Reformers in this way: what had been an obligatory

[23] Calvin: *Institutes*, III, iv, 14.
[24] p. 75.
[25] p. 257.

and habitual confession to a priest, involving the systematic enumeration of all remembered sins, became a voluntary and exceptional resort to a minister, to consult him about some special burden of conscience.[26]

SANCTIFICATION

The third argument which is adduced in favour of auricular confession concerns the penitent's growth in holiness or 'sanctification'. This is much insisted upon by Anglican

[26] A retrograde step has been taken in this matter by the Church of India, Pakistan, Burma, and Ceylon in their 1960 Prayer Book. Part III of this Book is entitled 'The Ministry of Reconciliation' and consists of an explanatory Preface, followed by two Forms for Public Use (a Penitential Service and a Renewal of Baptismal Vows) and Forms for Private Use, namely, a form of confession to be used alone and 'a form of confession and absolution in the presence of a priest'.

The Preface opens with a welcome insistence on the necessity of repentance, confession to God, and reconciliation with our neighbour. However, after reference to general confession in church and personal confession in secret, the Preface proceeds to a description of 'the Ministry of Reconciliation', a phrase which it applies to the gaining of an assurance of pardon either through the absolution pronounced in the public services or 'through private absolution given to the individual penitent'. It is immediately added that 'the pastors of the Church are authorized and bound by the commission received in their ordination . . . to exercise this ministry when required . . .'

This makes sad reading, for no mention is made of the public preaching of the Word of God, which is the normal means that God has appointed to bring forgiveness and assurance to the penitent believer. It is to this that St. Paul was referring when he first used the expression 'the ministry of reconciliation'. He meant not the pronouncement of a formal absolution, either public or private, but the proclamation of 'the word of reconciliation' by the ambassadors of Christ (II Cor. 5: 18–21). It is for this preaching ministry also, and not for private absolutions, that the priest is authorized by the words spoken at his ordination (as has been shown on page 64). Further, although there is a valuable provision in the Preface that the 'fellow-Christian' whom a penitent consults may be either 'an experienced and devout lay member of the church' or 'his own or some other pastor', there seems to be a confusion as to what this resort to a fellow-Christian is. It is said that 'the individual is often helped to full confession by unburdening himself to a fellow-Christian'. It is not clear from this whether the unburdening of oneself is regarded as itself a confession or as a help 'to full confession'. The distinction between an 'unburdening' of oneself to friend or pastor (which should be occasional, not 'often') and frequent or habitual 'confession' is unhelpfully blurred. These things are different, and need to be clearly distinguished.

writers. 'One of the main purposes of the Sacrament of Penance,' wrote Wilfred Knox, 'is to build up the character of the penitent by enabling him to gain grace to withstand temptation ... the Sacrament is normally found to be of the utmost value in assisting the penitent in accomplishing this task.'[27] It is for this reason that Eric James called his little book *The Double Cure*, taking the expression from Toplady's great hymn *Rock of Ages*:

> Be of sin the double cure,
> Cleanse me from its guilt and power.

Referring to the Parable of the Prodigal Son again, he says that 'if the cure isn't double, the Prodigal will just "pop home", make his confession and be on his way back to the far country in no time'.[28] It is because this aspect of auricular confession is regarded as so important that the person to whom, or in whose presence, the confession is made is commonly called not a 'confessor' but a 'spiritual director'.

The two means by which his help is asked and given for sanctification are 'penance' and 'advice'. The whole concept of penance is confused and unbiblical. It seems to have started with the Old Latin version of the Bible, which was followed by Jerome in the Vulgate. In these the Greek word for 'repentance' (*metanoia*) was translated by *poenitentia*, and the verb *metanoein* by *poenitere* or *agere poenitentiam*. These inaccurate translations then crept into early English versions like Wycliffe's in the misleading expression to 'do penance' instead of a to 'repent'. We have seen how in the Middle Ages penance was regarded as a painful discipline or punishment to make satisfaction for sin. Still in the Roman Catholic Church today, although 'the virtue of penance' means penitence, 'works of penance' are 'imposed on the penitent in atonement for the temporal punishment for sins which remain after the guilt of sin and its eternal punishment have been forgiven'.[29] They are regarded as a 'sacramental satisfaction' for sin. The Reformers repudiated these ideas as derogatory to Christ's perfect satisfaction for sin on the cross and replaced the words 'penance' and 'do penance' with 'repentance' and 'repent'. It is sad that any

[27] p. 91.
[28] p. 16.
[29] Ott: pp. 434, 435.

notion of private 'penance' should have been revived in the Church of England. Anglican writers who use it are careful to reject any suggestion that penance is a satisfaction for sin, but they do not speak in a united voice as to what it does mean. To 'Manasses' it is 'some small thing for you to do as a thank offering to God' or 'as a sign of gratitude for the mercy of God's forgiveness'.[30] To Wilfred Knox it is the penitent's express 'recognition of the fact that the sins which he has confessed are actions for which he was morally responsible, and not merely the results of temperamental weaknesses which he had no power to control'; it is thus an acknowledgment of 'his own guilt'.[31] To Kenneth Ross it is 'a token of the fact that you intend to turn over a new leaf'. One is left wondering whether the 'penance' is intended as a mark of guilt, gratitude, or resolution. The very uncertainty with which contemporary writers broach the subject, and the trivial nature of the 'penances' imposed, would be good reasons for its final abandonment. In any case, the biblical way of giving evidence of repentance is the performance of good works of love and holiness (Mt. 3: 8, 10).

The second means of promoting the penitent's sanctification is advice. This is the 'ghostly counsel and advice' referred to in the first exhortation at Holy Communion. There is nothing harmful here. One is only obliged to say that it is not strictly a part of 'sacramental confession', since spiritual advice is given by all ministers to members of their congregation quite independently of the confessional. It can therefore hardly be advanced as an argument for the practice of habitual confession. It is rather an argument for a faithful pastoral ministry in the vestry and the study, in visiting the homes and in meeting with small groups informally.

Although pastoral counselling should always be beneficial and not harmful, its chief peril seems to lie in the kind of situation envisaged by auricular confession, namely the regular interview of penitent with pastor. Whether it takes place in 'confession' in church or in a consultation in the study, I do not think weekly or monthly visits to the minister are conducive to the person's spiritual health. We revert to our theme and assert that God's normal means for the edification of His people in His Word, 'the word of His

[30] pp. 82, 91.
[31] p. 63.

81

grace which is able tó build you up, and to give you an inheritance among all them which are sanctified' (Acts 20: 32). There is a constant danger of clergy tying people to their apron strings, instead of encouraging them to develop a certain sturdy and healthy independence, as they rely more and more upon God Himself. It is surely to this that Jesus referred when He warned us to call no man our 'father', 'teacher', or 'lord' on earth (Mt. 23: 8–12). We are to adopt towards no one in the church, nor require anyone to adopt towards us, the dependent attitude implied in the child-parent, pupil-teacher, servant-lord relationships. We are all brethren. We are to depend on God as our Father, Christ as our Lord, and the Holy Spirit as our Teacher. The ambition of every minister for his congregation should be so to warn every man and teach every man in all wisdom as to 'present every man' not dependent on his minister but 'full-grown, mature in Christ' (Col. 1: 28). Although occasional consultations can indeed do good, I cannot see that frequent visits to the parson, whether for 'confession' or for 'conference', are productive of true spiritual maturity.

The greatest single secret of spiritual development lies in personal, humble, believing, obedient response to the Word of God. It is as God speaks to us through His Word that His warnings can bring us to conviction of sin, His promises to assurance of forgiveness, and His commands to amendment of life. We live and grow by His Word.

We have sought in this chapter to examine impartially the claims advanced for the practice of auricular confession, from the point of view of the penitent's need. We have agreed that the need is there, for a deeper repentance, assurance, and sanctification. But we have felt it right to insist that, according to the Scriptures, the remedy proposed is the wrong one. God's normal and natural way is not to send us to the confessional but to confront us with Himself through His Word. It is commonly said, with regard to auricular confession in the Anglican Church, that 'all may, none must, some should'. Of these three assertions, I can only agree with the first: 'All may', in exceptional circumstances. But I would replace the other two with 'none should', since it is not God's ideal, though 'some need'. As Dean Goulburn correctly said about the provision made in the first exhortation, it is 'not the best thing to be done, but the second best'; and this second best is like 'walking on crutches'.[32] I could not fail to be struck, when reading George MacLeod's pamphlet, to find that he employs the same metaphor. 'The whole apparatus of confession and absolution,' he admits with great candour, 'is nothing more, and has never been anything more, than a crutch for the lame.' He goes on to suggest that perhaps his reader is 'an athlete in spiritual things', but ends: 'for myself, I am lame'.[33]

None of us walks perfectly uprightly. Varying degrees of spiritual paralysis disable us. But do not let us acquiesce in our lameness! We may feel the need of crutches from time to time. But let us look forward to the day when we can throw them away, when, like the cripple at the Beautiful Gate, through faith in the strong Name of Jesus Christ, our ankle bones receive strength, and leaping up we can stand and walk, and enter into the house of God, walking and leaping and praising God![34]

[32] pp. 39, 54.
[33] p. 16.
[34] Acts 3: 1ff.

CONCLUSION

THE principle which we have sought to establish and illustrate in this book is that sin must be confessed only to the person or persons who have been offended and from whom forgiveness is therefore desired. Confession is never to a third party, both because he has not been offended, and because he is not in a position to forgive the sin. This is the simple reason why auricular confession is a practice to be deplored. It is not an answer to say that auricular confession is not 'to a priest', but either to God through the priest or in the presence of the priest, or to the church represented by the priest. Such representative confession is neither recognized nor recommended in Scripture. If the sin has been committed against God, it should be confessed to God secretly; if it has been committed against the church it should be confessed to the church publicly. Confessing such sins to a priest is not right, since it makes secret confession not secret through including another person and public confession not public through excluding the church.

This critical rejection of the practice of habitual auricular confession is not to be interpreted as due to a light view of sin or to a desire to make confession easier for the sinner. On the contrary, I believe we need to take the gravest possible view of sin, which the Bible does, as 'that abominable thing' which God hates (Jer. 44: 4), which is responsible for the sin-bearing death of the world's Saviour, the sorrows and sufferings of many people in this life, and the irretrievable ruin of others in the next. Our opposition to 'sacramental' confession is to be attributed not to our low view of sin but to our high view of Christ and the perfection of His provision for the sinner's absolution. So let me, in conclusion, issue two practical appeals.

First, we need to *take the confession of sin more seriously*. 'General Confession,' writes Eric James, 'may conceal a refusal to take sin seriously.'[1] Yes, it may. But it need not, especially if it is no substitute for the conscientious confession of sin to God in secret.

[1] p. 17.

Every biblical Christian must agree that one of the most evident symptoms of the Church's contemporary sickness is our lack of a proper sense of the fact or the gravity of sin. It is an indication that the Holy Spirit, whose peculiar work it is to convict of sin, is being resisted, grieved, and quenched. Two of the strikingly vivid pictures of conviction of sin in the Bible are 'weeping' and 'blushing'. Many men of God have wept over sin, not just over their own but over the sins of the Church, the nation, and the world. Ezra wept over the disobedience of Jerusalem (Ezra 10: 1), Jeremiah over their pride (Jer. 13: 17), Jesus Christ over their wilful blindness (Lk. 19: 41ff.). The psalmist could even write: 'Rivers of waters run down mine eyes, because they keep not thy law' (Ps. 119: 136). If we should thus weep over the sins of others, how much more should we weep over our own, turning to the Lord with all our heart 'and with fasting and with weeping and with mourning' (Joel 2: 12ff., cf. Mt. 5: 4; I Cor. 5: 2; II Cor. 7: 2)? And if we should weep over our sins because we are sorry, we should also blush over them because we are ashamed (Jer. 6: 15, 8: 12; Ezra 9: 6).

This book is a plea for more confession, not less, but for better confession, and confession of the right kind. We need to be more disciplined in secret self-examination and detailed confession to God. This should be 'habitual, thorough, compulsory'.[2] We need to be more faithful and courageous in apologizing to those we have offended and in rebuking those who have offended against us. We need to press for a restoration in the Anglican Communion, whatever the cost, of a seemly, biblical discipline in the local congregation when a public scandal has been caused.

My second appeal is that we should *take the forgiveness of sin more seriously also*. Christianity is a religion of forgiveness. God is willing to forgive sinners through Christ. We must forgive one another. The Church has absolute authority to forgive and to restore to its fellowship those who have offended against it and been suspended, but have subsequently repented and confessed their sin. We need to demonstrate the forgiveness of God to a world burdened with guilt, and to a world torn by bitter animosities the way in which the disciples of Jesus are taught to forgive one another. We need more faith in the promises of God to

[2] W. Griffith Thomas, p. 386.

85

rejoice in divine forgiveness; more love for each other to rejoice in human forgiveness. We need to exhibit before the world our Christian freedom – freedom from guilt and freedom from spite. We need to go on beyond forgiveness, and exploit the privileges which forgiveness makes possible, a great *parrhēsia*, boldness or outspokenness, both in our access to the throne of grace and in our fellowship with one another.

It is not by a revival of auricular confession, rightly discarded at the Reformation, that God wills these ends to be accomplished, but by humble submission to His Word, so that, confessing our sins and receiving His forgiveness, we may rejoice in the liberty with which Christ has made us free.

I cannot conclude better than with the words by which Dean Wace summed up the Fulham Conference: 'Let the free forgiveness of the Gospel be boldly proclaimed, let men and women be persuaded, in reliance on it, to live a life of direct confession to God, direct reliance on Christ's absolution, direct communion with the Holy Spirit, and so we may best hope to maintain and develop that strong, frank, courageous, God-fearing, and God-trusting character which is the ideal of the English Church, and the glory of English Churchmanship.'[3]

> '*O Lord, we beseech Thee, mercifully hear our prayers, and spare all those who confess their sins unto Thee; that they, whose consciences by sin are accused, by Thy merciful pardon may be absolved, through Jesus Christ our Lord.*'
>
> (*Commination Service*)

[3] pp. 108f.

APPENDIX

SOME OFFICIAL ANGLICAN STATEMENTS

1. *Convocation of Canterbury 1873 and 1877*

ON Friday, May 9th, 1873, the Upper House of the Convocation of Canterbury considered a petition which had been sent to them, signed by 483 priests. The penultimate request of this lengthy document was 'that, in view of the widespread and increasing use of sacramental confession, your venerable House may consider the advisability of providing for the education, selection, and licensing of duly qualified confessors, in accordance with the provisions of canon law.'

A full discussion took place, in which several bishops strongly asserted that the practice of habitual confession was 'contrary entirely to the spirit of our Prayer Book' and indeed 'entirely alien to the whole spirit of the Church of England'. Archbishop A. C. Tait, who was in the chair, expressed his gladness that every bishop and member present 'altogether repudiates the practice of habitual confession, and that they all state with the utmost distinctness that they consider the sacramental view of confession as a most serious error'. A committee of the whole House was then appointed to consider the matter. On July 23rd of the same year it issued the 'report on the teaching of the Church of England on the subject of Confession', which appears below. It was sent down to the Lower House on July 3rd, 1877, who on the following day resolved by 62 votes against six 'that this House concurs in the Declaration on Confession sent down to it from the Upper House for consideration'. The text is as follows:

'In the matter of Confession, the Church of England holds fast those principles which are set forth in Holy Scripture, which were professed by the Primitive Church, and which were reaffirmed at the English Reformation. The Church of England, in the Twenty-Fifth Article, affirms that penance is not to be counted for a sacrament of the Gospel; and, as judged by her formularies, knows no such words as "sacramental confession". Grounding her doctrines on Holy Scripture, she distinctly declares the full and entire forgiveness of sins, through the blood of Jesus Christ, to those who bewail their own sinfulness, confess themselves to Almighty God, with full purpose of amendment of life, and turn with true faith unto Him. It is the desire of the Church that by this way and means all her children should find peace. In this spirit the forms of Confession and Absolution are set forth in her public services. Yet, for the relief of troubled consciences, she has made special provision in two exceptional cases.

(1) In the case of those who cannot quiet their own consciences previous to receiving the Holy Communion, but require further comfort or counsel, the minister is directed to say, "Let him come to me, or to some other discreet and learned minister of God's Word, and open his grief, that by the ministry of God's Holy Word he may receive the benefit of Absolution, together with ghostly counsel and advice." Nevertheless, it is to be noted that for such a case no form of Absolution has been prescribed in the Book of Common Prayer; and further, the Rubric in the first Prayer Book of 1549, which sanctions a particular form of Absolution, has been withdrawn from all subsequent editions of the said Book.

(2) In the order for the Visitation of the Sick, it is directed that the sick man may be moved to make a special confession of his sins if he feels his conscience troubled with any weighty matter, but in such case Absolution is only to be given when the sick man shall humbly and heartily desire it. The special provision, however, does not authorize the ministers of the Church to require from any who may repair to them, to open their grief in a particular or detailed examination of all their sins, or to require private confession as a condition previous to receiving the Holy Communion, or to enjoin or even encourage any practice of habitual confession to a priest, or to teach that such practice of habitual confession, or the being subject to what has been termed the direction of a priest, is a condition of attaining to the highest spiritual life."[1]

[1] *The Chronicle of the Convocation of Canterbury* (London, 1873), p. 558.

2. Lambeth Conference, 1878

At the second Lambeth Conference, which met in 1878, under the presidency of Archbishop A. C. Tait, the bishops considered a number of questions submitted to them and then issued an Encyclical Letter which summarized their conclusions. It took the form of five Committee Reports, and the fifth report included the following Section E:

'Considering unhappy disputes on questions of ritual, whereby divers congregations in the Church of England and elsewhere have been seriously disquieted, your Committee desire to affirm the principle that no alteration from long-accustomed ritual should be made contrary to the admonition of the Bishop of the Diocese.

Further, having in view certain novel practices and teachings on the subject of Confession, your Committee desire to affirm that in the matter of Confession the Churches of the Anglican Communion hold fast those principles which are set forth in the Holy Scriptures, which were professed by the Primitive Church, and which were reaffirmed at the English Reformation; and it is their deliberate opinion that no minister of the Church is authorized to require from those who may resort to him to open their grief a particular or detailed enumeration of all their sins, or to require private confession previous to receiving the Holy Communion, or to enjoin or even encourage the practice of habitual confession to a priest, or to teach that such practice of habitual confession, or the being subject to what has been termed the direction of a priest, is a condition of attaining to the highest spiritual life. At the same time your Committee are not to be understood as desiring to limit in any way the provision made in the Book of Common Prayer for the relief of troubled consciences.'[2]

3. Royal Commission on Ecclesiastical Discipline, 1906

The Royal Commission on Ecclesiastical Discipline was set up by King Edward VII on April 23rd, 1904 'to inquire into the alleged prevalence of breaches or neglect of the law relating to the conduct of Divine Service in the Church of

[2] *The Six Lambeth Conferences 1867–1920*, (London, 1920), p. 97.

England, and to the ornaments and fittings of churches . . .'
It held 118 sittings, examined 164 witnesses, and reported
on June 21st, 1906. Chapter V of the Report is headed 'Confession'. After stating that the subject did not appear 'to fall
within the law relating to the conduct of Divine Service and
to the ornaments and fittings of churches', the commissioners
added that nevertheless they could not pass over in silence
the evidence they had received that 'the practice of habitual
confession has increased' and that 'it is pressed by some
clergymen on their congregations as a duty, especially
before Confirmation, and in some cases before receiving
Holy Communion'. The report continues: 'It would seem
to be impossible to reconcile such systematic arrangements
as have been referred to with the practically unanimous
declaration of 100 Bishops of the Church set forth in the
Encyclical Letter issued by the Lambeth Conference of
1878, that "no minister of the Church is authorized to
require from those who may resort to him to open their
grief, a particular or detailed enumeration of all their sins,
or to require private confession previous to receiving the
Holy Communion, or to enjoin, or even encourage, the
practice of habitual confession to a priest, or to teach that
such practice of habitual confession, or the being subject to
what has been termed the direction of a priest, is a condition of attaining to the highest spiritual life". The subject
was not dealt with in the subsequent Lambeth Conferences
(1888 and 1897); but we have no reason to doubt that in
substance the declaration would be approved by the Episcopate of today, although the words "or even encourage"
might, as was suggested in 1878 and subsequently, be
thought by some to need modification for the purpose of
meeting individual cases.'

Note:
  Of the 100 bishops present at the 1878 Lambeth Conference only two dissented from the statement on Confession. They took exception to the words 'or even encourage',
but to nothing else. See Minute 13270 of the Evidence taken
before the Royal Commission.

BIBLIOGRAPHY

A list of works quoted:

Thomas Becon: *The Castle of Comfort* (Cambridge, 1844) in Vol. II of Becon's Works.

Henry Bullinger: *Of Repentance and the Causes Thereof*, the second sermon in *The Decades* (Cambridge, 1851).

P. D. Butterfield: *How to Make Your Confession* (London, 1961).

T. W. Drury: *Confession and Absolution* (London, 1903).

R. B. Girdlestone, H. C. G. Moule and T. W. Drury: *English Church Teaching* (London, 1897).

Edward Meyrick Goulburn (Dean of Norwich): *Primitive Church Teaching on the Holy Communion* (London, New Edition, 1912).

Richard Hooker: *Laws of Ecclesiastical Polity* (Oxford, 7th Edition, 1888), Vol. III, Book vi, of his *Works* arranged by John Keble.

Eric James: *The Double Cure*, How to Receive Forgiveness (London, 1957).

John Jewel: *An Apology of the Church of England* and *A Defence of the Apology of the Church of England* (Cambridge, 1848), Vol. III.

Wilfred L. Knox: *Penitence and Forgiveness* (London, 1953).

E. A. Litton: *Introduction to Dogmatic Theology* (London, 3rd Edition, 1912).

George F. MacLeod: *The Church of Scotland and the Confessional* (Iona Community).

'Manasses': *Go in Peace* (London, 1958).

Frederick Meyrick: *The Confessional* (London, 1905).

Ludwig Ott: *Fundamentals of Catholic Dogma* (Cork, 1962).

J. C. Ryle: *Knots Untied* (London, 1877).

W. H. Griffith Thomas: *The Catholic Faith* (London, New Impression, 1929).

William Tyndale: *The Obedience of a Christian Man* in *Doctrinal Treatises* (Cambridge, 1848).

M. A. C. Warren: *Revival – An Enquiry* (London, 1954).

Alexander Whyte: *A Commentary on the Shorter Catechism* (Edinburgh, n.d.).

Jack C. Winslow: *Confession and Absolution*, A Short Guide for Today (London, 1960).

Confession and Absolution: Report of a Conference held at Fulham Palace in 1901–2, edited by Henry Wace (London, 1902).

Homilies and Canons (London, 1914).
Vocabulary of the Bible, edited by J.-J. von Allmen (London, 1958).

THE BODY
OF CHRIST

A NEW TESTAMENT IMAGE OF THE CHURCH

by

ALAN COLE

CONTENTS

INTRODUCTION

'THE visible Church of Christ is a congregation of faithful men, in which the pure Word of God is preached, and the sacraments be duly ministered according to Christ's ordinance in all things that of necessity are requisite to the same' (Article XIX of the Church of England).

'Forasmuch as God from the beginning would have men to be saved and to come to the knowledge of the truth (I Tim. 2: 4), therefore it is necessary that there should always have been, and should be at this day, and to the end of the world, a Church: that is, a company of the faithful, called and gathered out of the world, a communion of all saints, that is, of them who do truly know and rightly worship and serve the true God, in Jesus Christ the Saviour, by the Word and the Holy Spirit, and who by faith are partakers of all those good graces which are freely offered through Christ' (Second Helvetic Confession, ch. 17).

'As we believe in one God, Father, Son, and Holy Ghost, so do we most constantly believe that from the beginning there hath been, and now is, and to the end of the world shall be one Church (Mt. 28: 20): that is to say, a company and multitude of men, chosen of God (Eph. 1: 4), who rightly worship and embrace Him by true faith in Christ Jesus, who is the only Head of the same Church (Col. 1: 18), which also is the body and spouse of Christ Jesus (Eph. 5: 23–32); which Church is catholic, that is, universal, because it containeth the elect of all ages, of all realms, nations, and tongues (Rev. 7: 9)' (Article 16 of the Scots Confession).

'We believe and confess that there is one catholic or universal Church, which is the true congregation or company of all faithful Christians, who look for their whole salvation from Christ alone, inasmuch as they be washed in His blood and sanctified and sealed by His Spirit. Furthermore, as this Church hath been from the beginning of the world, so it shall continue unto the end thereof—as is evident by this, that Christ is our eternal King, who can never be without subjects' (Article 27 of the Belgic Confession).

'The Church is the congregation of saints, in which the Gospel is rightly taught and the sacraments are rightly administered. And to the true unity of the Church it is enough to agree concerning the doctrine of the Gospel; nor is it necessary that human traditions, that is, rites or ceremonies instituted by men, should be everywhere alike' (Article 7 of the Augsburg Confession).

'We are very members incorporate in the mystical body of Thy Son, which is the blessed company of all faithful people' (from the Service of Holy Communion in the English Book of Common Prayer).

'And I say also unto thee, That thou art Peter, and upon this rock I will build my church; and the gates of hell shall not prevail against it' (Mt. 16: 18).

'Jesus answered and said unto them, Destroy this temple, and in three days I will raise it up ... But he spake of the temple of his body' (Jn. 2: 19–21).

'And the Lord added to the church daily such as should be saved' (Acts 2: 47).

'Take heed therefore unto yourselves, and to all the flock, over the which the Holy Ghost hath made you overseers, to feed the church of God, which he hath purchased with his own blood' (Acts 20: 28).

'And hath put all things under his feet, and gave him to be the head over all things to the church, which is his body, the fulness of him that filleth all in all' (Eph. 1: 22f.).

'For the husband is the head of the wife, even as Christ is the head of the church; and he is the saviour of the body' (Eph. 5: 23).

'For this cause shall a man leave his father and mother, and shall be joined unto his wife, and they two shall be one flesh. This is a great mystery: but I speak concerning Christ and the church' (Eph. 5: 31–32).

'And he is the head of the body, the church' (Col. 1: 18).

'Now ye are the body of Christ, and members in particular' (I Cor. 12: 27).

'Who now rejoice in my sufferings for you, and fill up that which is behind of the afflictions of Christ in my flesh for his body's sake, which is the church' (Col. 1: 24).

CHAPTER ONE

THE BODY OF CHRIST –
WHAT DOES IT MEAN?

WHAT is the Church? No answer is more readily given, or more thoroughly grounded in the New Testament, than to say: the Body of Christ. No answer would command more general theological agreement, whether in the polemical age of the sixteenth century or the eirenic atmosphere of the twentieth. But what does this phrase mean? For upon our understanding of it will depend our doctrine of the Church, and this in turn will dictate our approach to many of the great problems that vex Christendom today.

Why, under God, is this particular metaphor, symbol, or image chosen? Over what areas of the life and work of the Church is it valid? Is it possible, in this sphere as in others, to be led astray by 'illegitimate extension of metaphor'? Perhaps we cannot hope to find a complete answer to all these questions at once; but certainly we cannot even begin to answer them without a close consideration of the New Testament evidence, and a willingness in its light to jettison if need be much that has seemed to be hallowed by the tradition and devotion of the past.

THE METAPHOR OF 'BODY'

First of all, it should be realized that this metaphor of the Body is but one of many metaphors used in the New Testament to help us grasp the concept of the Church. That in itself means that it is no exclusive or exhaustive picture: otherwise there would scarcely have been need for the hundred and more other images which are also used to give meaning to this same concept.* True, 'the Body' is far more than a passing illustration; it might even be described

* See Paul Minear: *Images of the Church* (London, 1961).

as a dominant concept, especially in Paul; and this means that it must be weighed carefully. But there are other 'dominating images' in the pages of the New Testament: God's spiritual temple, the bride of Christ, the flock of God, the household of God, to choose a few, are scarcely less pervasive; and he would be a bold theologian who would attempt to decide which is the most important amongst them.

Perhaps it is not unfair to say that a continual danger for the Church of God (even, perhaps indeed especially, in days when it is biblically minded) is to pursue one biblical metaphor to the neglect of the others with which the Bible balances it. Theological distortions easily follow, as the metaphor is pushed further than the direct New Testament evidence warrants. Presumably, each metaphor is designed to illustrate certain aspects of the truth, and those aspects alone: hence we may not assume that the particular word chosen can be used in all its possible meanings, and shades of meanings, to convey further theological revelations above and beyond actual biblical statements. Such extrapolations can only lead at best to analogical thinking (which is usually dangerous), and at worst to emotional thinking (which is always pernicious). The biblical exegesis of the Middle Ages, for example, is full of instances of both; we can see the error here, but it is part of the blindness native to fallen man that we do not see the corresponding error in ourselves.

We shall take it, then, that every biblical metaphor has its 'strong points', or 'area of validity'. We shall take this latter to be the area of meaning to which attention is specifically called in the New Testament, and the 'strong points' to be those which are actually invoked there for conveying theological truth. We shall take it, as a corollary of the above, that every such metaphor has also its 'weak points', or areas where its application would be invalid, and would lead us at best to a distortion of truth, and at worst into error. These latter we take to be the areas where Scripture is silent, the points where Scripture makes no attempt

12

to press the metaphor home, logical though such application might seem to be in our eyes.

The complexity of the problem of handling biblical metaphors is increased by the fact that every age has its favourite metaphors (all, of course, drawn from the common biblical 'pool') which it develops almost to the exclusion of other aspects of revelation, and – more serious – upon which it bases its theology. Further, the particular metaphors which are the favourites of any one age are usually dictated by the circumstances and felt needs of the Church in that age, although sometimes it is difficult to decide which came first, the ecclesiastical hen or the theological egg. For example, did the widespread occurrence of celibacy in the medieval Church account for the fondness of using the image 'the Bride of Christ' for the church? Or did the continual use of this image itself encourage the already widespread monastic ideal? These, however, are questions either for the Church historian or for the psychologist, and they need not detain us now.

The impulse to seek metaphors that speak to present need is, of course, very natural, and not in any sense wrong; it merely reflects the facts that, on the one hand, metaphors bring home to us the emotive power of the thoughts which they embody, and, on the other, that, in our need, the Spirit leads us to those aspects of God's Word that are, in the here and now, relevant to that need, without in any way impugning the nature and character of other aspects, or denying them an equal place in God's revelation. We can see this in the New Testament epistles, where Paul in wrestling with practical problems turns to metaphorical aspects of truth which had theological bearing on the immediate situation – compare the successive use of the 'building', 'body', and 'bride' metaphors in Ephesians, for instance (compare Eph. 2: 20ff., 4: 4–16, 5: 22–33).

All this is but a warning not to allow our theological thinking to be dominated by that which is popular or taken for granted in our own age: it may be true, but it will certainly not be the whole truth. As a late English theologian used to say, for every new book that we read, we should read two old books, to correct our perspective. We shall always remain children of our age – if we did not, we should neither be able to understand it (let alone live in it) nor to reach it with the Gospel – but if we are only children of our age, the timeless Gospel that we bring will be mangled and truncated, tailored and cut down to fit the wishes and whims of the time. If we are not constantly questioning the assumptions of our age, including current fashions of thought in the Church itself, our understanding of God's truth will certainly be lopsided, and perhaps corrupted altogether. Thoughtful churchmen of all schools of thought will agree with this in broad outline, although they may not all agree with us as to its bearing on the matter in hand.

'THE BODY': A DOMINANT METAPHOR

Nothing, certainly, is more plain than that the concept of the Church as the Body of Christ dominates our Christian thinking about the Church today, almost to the exclusion of other symbols. The greater part of our current ecclesiology is based upon it. Can we doubt, now, that our choice of this metaphor is dictated by the theological and sociological climate of our time – specifically, by the concern for Christian community that has grown up in face of modern secularism, Communism, and the world-wide break-up of long-established social units? This is not to say that the use of the metaphor is wrong (for it is clearly biblical, and equally clearly dominant), but it is to remind ourselves that the metaphor may well get out of proportion unless it is complemented.

Nor again is this to deny that it is the Holy Spirit who has directed the mind of the Church to this particular metaphor in this particular age; for that would be to deny the reality of His promised work of bringing all things to our remembrance, standing by us as our Advocate in hours of need (Jn. 14: 26, Mt. 10: 19f.). If it be true that one of

14

the great discoveries of our age has been the rediscovery of the Church, and if the Ecumenical Movement has been one of the great facts of our times, he would be a bold man who would deny that these developments have been of the Holy Spirit, and yet equally he would be a rash man who fancied that we fallible men have either heard or interpreted all that the Spirit has to say. Indeed, we may hold fast to the evident fact that here is truth revealed from God's Word by the Spirit to and for our age, and yet conclude that at certain points we have failed to understand it properly, and, in our enthusiasm for one aspect of truth, ignored a dozen more. Therefore we may accept the Ecumenical Movement gladly as being of the Spirit, and yet be very critical of certain manifestations of it, as being shallow, unbiblical, and therefore ultimately opposed to the very Spirit who is behind it; for God cannot deny Himself, and principles that are plain in Scripture must still apply today.

On the other side, lest we be accused by those who disagree with the very basis of this movement, let us make it clear at once that we are not saying that whatever exists in the Church is necessarily of God and the work of the Holy Spirit. History and our own experience have taught us otherwise, and we cannot deny such plain evidence. But likewise we cannot deny plain evidence when a movement like this is associated with a display of characteristically Christian qualities – the fruits of the Spirit, to use New Testament language. The great test that the Lord gave was, 'By their fruits ye shall know them' (Mt. 7: 20), and to ignore the evidence of this test can come near to the sin against the Spirit (compare Mt. 12: 31–33 and 22–24).

But acceptance of a truth does not bind us to every detail of current belief or practice connected with it, still less does it forbid us to say gently that the modern emphasis on this truth that the Church is Christ's Body is recurrently one-sided, not to say lop-sided, leading often to exclusive absorption in what is, after all, only one aspect of the Christian faith and message. Thus, putting the matter bluntly, it is observable some men are so earnest for re-union that they forget about evangelism. But such was not Paul's way, nor does it accord with the mind of the primitive Church. If it be retorted that they were not faced with our problems, that is of course true; nevertheless, to judge from what is contained in Scripture, we have no reason to assume that their answer would at this point have been the same as ours.

CHAPTER TWO

THE ORIGINS AND USE OF THIS METAPHOR

LET us now turn to the biblical evidence for the use of the term 'Body', and its history and development, if any, within Scripture itself. Here, one of the most helpful recent studies has been that of J. A. T. Robinson, entitled *The Body: A Study in Pauline Theology* (London, 1952), though not all his conclusions are acceptable, and much of his theology is dependent on that of Lionel Thornton, as set forth in his book, *The Common Life in the Body of Christ* (London, 1942). Nevertheless, his linguistic survey is invaluable, though James Barr has justly warned the theological world in recent years not to identify linguistics with theology.* One is tempted to add a further warning, not to confuse theology with sociology either; but treatment of this aspect of the matter can await a later section, when we consider how far it is legitimate to speak of the Church as 'the extension of the Incarnation'.†

THE OLD TESTAMENT

Unlike many of the other images used for the Church in the pages of the New Testament (Temple, Flock, Family, Wife, for instance) that of the Body seems at first sight to have no exact Old Testament analogue. Perhaps the nearest analogy, in outward form, is to be found in some of the imagery of the Book of Daniel where a body, or even parts of a body, can represent a kingdom (see, for instance, Dan. 2: 31–43).

The absence of the Body-idea from the Old Testament is not surprising, in view of the fact that the Hebrews had

---

* See his book *The Semantics of Biblical Language* (London, 1961).
† Another useful survey of the older type is K. L. Schmidt: *The Church* (London, 1950).

no one commonly used word for 'body'; instead, they had a cluster of words, each of which roughly corresponded to part of the area of meaning which the word 'body' covers. While this fact sheds interesting light on Hebrew psychology, it need not detain us here, except to show us that we shall look in vain for Old Testament linguistic roots for the 'body' concept. But this is not the whole story. Since Hebrew had deep within it the concept of 'corporate personality', with which Wheeler Robinson, amongst other scholars, has made us familiar; since, also, both the Suffering Servant (in Isaiah) and the Son of Man (in Daniel, and possibly in the Psalter) are equally capable of individual and collective interpretation – and it is doubtful if the Jew of Old Testament times would have seen or felt any cause why these figures should not be interpreted both ways together – we can hardly deny that the germ of the Body-idea exists in the Old Testament. Once the eye of faith had seen in Jesus of Nazareth not only the Christ, but also the Suffering Servant and the Son of Man, the thought of this people as a collective unity in virtue of their relation to Him was at once implicit: it needed only to be expressed. Thus, while it is formally true to say both that Hebrew has no proper word for 'body' (in biblical times at least), and also that Paul's use of the Greek *sōma* to mean a group or collection of people, is a linguistic novelty, yet it is also true that the novelty was devised to express an existing idea.*

THE GOSPELS

But is this a strictly Pauline revelation or insight? At what point does that which is latent in Old Testament become patent in the New? Certainly, the Synoptic Gospels show no sign of the Body-concept. In the Synoptic Gospels, the Lord's disciples are already a coherent whole, a group with well-defined limits: a man either 'follows' or he does not.

* For the linguistic evidence, see Arndt and Gingrich: *Greek-English Lexicon of the New Testament*, (Cambridge, 1957), under *Sōma*, and the excellent books and articles quoted there.

The disciples are constituted such a group by the call of Christ and their response to that call, which is a personal response to Him. Thus we might even say that they are constituted as a group by their faith in Him, inadequate though this faith must have been in its initial stages.

The 'crisis' of the Synoptic drama is Peter's confession at Caesarea Philippi, with Christ's reply, recorded in Mt. 16: 16–19. In this passage, it is made plain that 'foundation membership' in the Church of Christ is dependent on a confession that expresses faith in the enigmatic Jesus as God's Messiah. This faith is itself the gift of God, mediated through the revelation of the Holy Spirit. The concept of the Church that is linked with so rich a notion of faith will certainly be no shallow one. But the only metaphor for the Church that is used here is an architectural metaphor. 'Rock', 'build', 'gates', 'keys' – these terms all belong to this world of architectural ideas. Why is there no reference to the 'Body of Christ', if such a concept existed before Pauline times? For traces of most of the other New Testament categories for describing the Church appear in the Synoptic Gospels, although it is only fair to say that in most cases they are seen more clearly in John. Sharpening our question, we may ask: why is it that, in the Synoptic Gospels, the thought of the union of Christ with His people finds virtually no expression, Christ being almost 'set off' against His embryonic Church? Why are they kept so distinct? Why this absence of the thought of the close connection, almost identification, that the Body-metaphor implies, and the rest of the New Testament asserts?

The answer surely lies in the fact that the Synoptic Gospels, whatever the actual date of composition or compilation in their present form (that is almost irrelevant for our present purposes) are nothing if not 'pre-Pentecost' gospels. That their doctrine, over so many areas, is 'pre-Pentecost' doctrine is a plain guarantee of their good faith. True, it is fashionable in some circles to consider even this story of Peter's confession as Post-Pentecost in origin, an imaginative product of the later life and faith of the Jerusalem Church, with its orthodox 'Christian Judaism'; but this is a critical hypothesis which cannot be proved, and has no more intrinsic probability than the position of those who see in Christ's words to Peter, as Matthew records them, a genuine dominical pronouncement. It seems gratuitous to take exception to statements which are as thoroughly grounded in Jewish life and thought as this one is, and so full of Old Testament echoes. If it be argued on these very grounds that this exchange between Peter and Jesus would be a typical invention of the ultra-Jewish Church of Jerusalem, it may with reason be replied that the Lord was a Jew Himself, after the flesh, and that the later Church of Jerusalem, in recalling this incident, was but recapturing the strongly Jewish atmosphere of the days of the 'peripatetic Church', the little group who followed Him while He was on earth.

Further, the passage is not Jewish in a merely conventional way; it is strikingly original, even revolutionary, in its content, and to anyone who has pondered the lack of originality of the Jerusalem Church in later days, and its manifest reluctance to take any new step whatsoever even where it was conscious of a word of command from the Lord (as in the case of evangelizing the Gentiles), it will seem inconceivable that this Church could have invented the story of Peter's confession. But it is not at all hard to believe that such a church would have cherished in its memory the account of Peter's great spiritual 'revelation' and 'discovery', with Jesus' solemn and dramatic words confirming it, once the story had been told them.

But granted all this, we still have not answered the question: why, in the Synoptic Gospels, does Christ, as it were, stand apart from His Church, so that no use of the metaphor of 'the Body' would have seemed appropriate? The answer is simple. He stands apart, because as yet He still is apart; it is still the Christ-in-the-flesh who is the focus of the life and activity of the band of disciples. Here we have followers of Jesus, not yet fully the Church of Christ. The Spirit is not yet given as He will be given, for Jesus is not yet glorified. Jesus' death is yet to come, and His followers cannot begin to understand the true nature of His Messiahship until after that, for even Peter's new-found faith in it is defective here (Mt. 16: 21–23). Still more important, the Resurrection is not yet; and it is only in the light of the Resurrection that they will understand many half-forgotten sayings of Jesus about their life in Him, which the Spirit will then call to mind.

But if the years of our Lord's earthly ministry were in this way an 'interim period', a bridge between the days of the old and new covenants, a period when the two peoples of old and new covenant were living side by side, and when, indeed, it was still possible that they might have become identical, until Israel after the flesh, in her blindness, finally rejected that which was her right and due – is it not conceivable that there may have been some sayings of Jesus which suggested by anticipation the Body-metaphor, just as there were undoubtedly sayings that suggested by anticipation some of the other dominant metaphors?

It is hard to resist the conclusion that Jn. 2: 19–21 preserves a saying of Jesus ('Destroy this temple, and in three days I will raise it up') that is at one and the same time a bridge between the Body-metaphor and the Temple-metaphor, and a dominical justification for the later use of the Body-metaphor. Certainly it would seem from II Cor. 5: 1 that Paul knew of a dominical saying about the destroying and rebuilding of the Temple, from whatever source. If Paul knew it in its Synoptic form as quoted by the suborned witnesses at our Lord's trial (see Mk. 14: 58 and parallels), it is just as likely that he knew it in its Johannine form, where in John's explanation the link with 'his body' is specifically brought out. This then would mean that the Pauline use of the Body-metaphor is but a further conserving and developing of dominical tradition, instead of being the startling innovation that it is often said to be.

Rightly considered, there was very little of the innovator about Paul; for he was able to appeal with assurance to the Jerusalem gospel against that of the Judaizers, knowing it to be the same as his own (Gal. 2: 6). The one thing that he did claim for himself in connection with the doctrine of the Church was that, by divine revelation, he had come to see the 'mystery', hidden from past ages of God's children, but now revealed, that it was not necessary for a Gentile to become a Jew first in order that he might be saved (Eph. 3: 1–6). It is clear, however, from Acts that Peter knew this as well as Paul – and also by revelation (see Acts 10: 9–17 and 15: 7–8) – and had the Jerusalem Church heeded the words of the Lord that they themselves treasured, for example St Matthew 8: 11, they might all have grasped this truth from the start.

It is interesting to note that although this saying about the destroying and rebuilding of the Temple appears in the Synoptic tradition, the link with the Body of Christ only appears in John. This we would expect, for John is in its point of view a 'post-Pentecost' Gospel. By this is meant, not that its date of composition is later than that of the Synoptics (recent scholarship has shown that the late date for John is not as certain as was once thought), but rather that it is deliberately written in the light of the Resurrection and Pentecost. In no Gospel do we find so frequently such remarks as: 'These things understood not his disciples at the first: but when Jesus was glorified, then remembered they . . .' (Jn. 12: 16; compare 2: 22, 20: 9). It is a commonplace to say that in John 'glorified' and similar words refer to the Cross; but it would be truer still to say that they refer to the complex of events consisting of Cross–Resurrection–Ascension–Pentecost. Thus what John is saying in his allusive fashion is this: 'We, the eye-witnesses, only understood these things after the Resurrection, when long-forgotten sayings suddenly recurred to our mind because at last they had taken on relevance and meaning.' Which indeed was the promised work of the Spirit for that unique apostolic first generation (Jn. 14: 26).

22

If it be argued that it was impossible for Christ to have entertained in His mind the substance of the Body-concept, though possible for Paul, then we shall have to say that this is a wholly arbitrary position. We have seen that, once Jesus of Nazareth was identified not only as Messiah, but also as Son of Man and Suffering Servant, then the 'raw material' of the concept – the idea, that is, of solidarity between Jesus and His people – was there. According to the Gospels, both these equations were made by Jesus of Himself; indeed, it was thus that He interpreted His mission and work. If He had already made both of these equations, there is no reason why He should not have broached the theme of the oneness of His people in union with Himself in a way which would have underlain the whole Pauline development and elaboration of the Body-concept. There is no reason to assume that here more than anywhere else the servant was greater than the master; we are on very dangerous ground indeed if we assume that the trained mind of the rabbi of Tarsus could rise to heights that the carpenter of Nazareth could not reach – if, indeed, Jesus be the Christ.

There are elsewhere in the Gospels several pointers to show that this thought was indeed in Christ's mind. For instance, when He said to the disciples (Mt. 10: 40; Jn. 13: 20), 'He that receiveth you, receiveth me', and similarly in Luke 10: 16, 'He that heareth you heareth me; and he that rejecteth you rejecteth me' (RV), it is not enough to dismiss this as just a rabbinical form of speech referring to the reception of a disciple 'in the name of' that disciple's master, that is, in a way that declares one's respect for his master. In the light of other sayings such as St Matthew 18: 5, 25: 40, and in the light of the later Pauline theology, these words could equally well be interpreted as implying a species of identity between servant and master – regardless of whether or not the disciples grasped the full idea themselves at the time. Most scholars would admit that this was the meaning of the phrase for the early Church; their one query would be – could Jesus Himself have said it and meant it in this way? Again, the simplest answer of all is the question – why not? There is nothing inherently improbable here on any ground, if the Temple-saying be admitted as dominical, and John's interpretation of it is correct.

'THE BODY' IN PAUL'S WRITINGS

Thus we do not come to the Pauline use of the Body-idea regarding this metaphor as wholly a Pauline creation; it has had a general pre-history in the Old Testament (though of a theological, not linguistic sort), and it seems to rest on an authentic saying of Christ, misunderstood and therefore half-forgotten at the time, which only became meaningful later in the light of the Resurrection.

There is also, however, an important further 'interim period' which ought to be considered seriously as a factor in the situation we are analysing, even if we cannot argue with certainty from it. This is the 'forty days' that elapsed between the Resurrection of Christ and His Ascension, when we are specifically told that He was giving His disciples further instruction, and that the content of His teaching was 'the things pertaining to the kingdom of God' (Acts 1: 3). We may assume that here again the Christ was the centre and focus of the little community; He was not yet the Christ resident in their hearts through the Holy Spirit, as He would be after Pentecost: but He was now the Risen Christ, not any longer the Christ 'after the flesh'. Therefore we might assume that His teaching to them would be a stage further along the road of their spiritual education; and it is hard to see how His teaching about the 'kingdom' could avoid all reference to His new covenant-people, the Church, even though we may not equate Church and Kingdom completely.

Now of course it would be dangerous to use this period as a sort of theological 'hold-all', into which to put the promulgation of all doctrines which are not clear in the gospels, but are clear in the epistles; yet, on the other hand, if we accept the evidence of Scripture, here is a period of teaching which we are bound to take into account. Short it may have been, but it marked a distinct stage in Christ's ministry of revelation. However, hard though we may work labouring to piece together the scanty evidence at the end of the gospels and the beginning of Acts, it remains very difficult to penetrate the disciples' thought-world at this period, and more difficult still to reconstruct their views at that exact time. We may hazard guesses, but we can have no certainty. We shall therefore content ourselves with saying that, if we find a change of attitude or advance in understanding between the dominical and apostolic periods (to use a convenient though inexact distinction) it does not necessarily mean that the change did not come about till the days after Pentecost.

As the Body-metaphor itself is not used in the book of Acts, we may go straight on to Paul. It should, however, be noted that all the essential ingredients of the metaphor as Paul uses it do occur in Acts: the headship of Christ, the collective unity of the believing fellowship and their 'belongingness' to one another, the mutuality of service, and the indwelling of the Spirit within them. The one point less clearly brought out is that of 'identification' between Jesus and His people. The reality of the Body is clearly there (although this name is not used), but it is not yet characterized as Christ's Body. What comes nearest to this, as J. A. T. Robinson points out in a different context, is the Risen Christ's equating of persecution of the Church of God with persecution of Himself, in Acts 9: 5; but this does not really go any further than the similar identification of Christ with His servant in the gospels – for example, in St Matthew 18: 5. Indeed, it is exactly the same thought; so that if we should say, with many, that Pauline theology stems from this point, it seems that we should also say that Pauline theology stems from the Synoptic tradition of teaching.

When Paul uses 'the Body of Christ' as a description of the Church, does the genitive 'of Christ' imply identification, or possession? Surely, despite some scholars, the dominant thought is the latter. And is it really necessary to study together the glorified Body of the Man Christ Jesus, the 'mystical' Body of Christ that is the Church, and what is sometimes, though misleadingly, called the 'eucharistic' Body of Christ'? Are these really three modes of existence of the same reality, just as water, steam, and ice, are three modes of existence of the same chemical compound, H_2O? Robinson, E. L. Mascall, and others think so; but in fact this is to confuse issues. The third of these should be interpreted in a manner very different from that of those who assimilate the three together, while simply to identify the first with the second will lead us into other errors. To suggest, for instance, that Paul's experience of the Risen Christ should be understood as an experience of the Church is to put the cart disastrously before the horse.

Paul's use of the Body metaphor is so many-sided that we cannot hope to do more than survey a few of his characteristic emphases. The basic thesis to which they point is this: the Body-metaphor is for Paul an image of the Church which refers primarily to our common dependence on Christ, joint partaking of His Spirit, interdependence on one another, unity in Christ, and responsibility for mutual service. In saying this we do not deny that the concept of a 'body' and its 'parts' was widespread at the time, especially in Stoic cosmology, nor that Paul may well have met it in that context (though, as we have said, it seems to have roots in dominical teaching); but we assert that what was determinative for Paul in his development of the metaphor was the thought of believers' common, or rather collective, relationship to their Head, Christ; and this makes his use of it distinctively Christian.

The bulk of the relevant Pauline materials is to be found in Romans, Corinthians, Ephesians, and Colossians, though traces of the same lines of thought can be found in most of Paul's other epistles. In all his epistles, his doctrine of the Church is not thought out in the abstract, in a quiet study as

26

it were, but in the bustle and whirl of Christian life.* It is in the context of strife within the Church that the doctrine of the unity of the Church is brought forward; it is to deal with a lack of discipline that the doctrine of the headship of Christ is stressed, and it is in face of the false mysticism of a speculative-minded Asia Minor that Paul's highest expression of the doctrine of the Church's union with Christ is attained.

We may therefore take I Corinthians 1: 13 as a starting-point: 'Is Christ divided? was Paul crucified for you? or were ye baptized in the name of Paul?' This is said with reference to the quarrels at Corinth, which had resulted in divisions, though not yet, it seems, in any open schism, for there is nowhere any hint that the various groups met separately for worship. To Paul this is utterly anomalous, just as it is utterly inconceivable that Christ Himself should be divided. Christians are a unity; Christ died for all, and all are baptized into Him. ('One Lord, one Baptism' was to be used again by Paul as a great Christian rallying-call in Ephesians 4: 5.)

Christians, then, have shared a common transforming experience; they have a unity resulting from a common loyalty to the Lord who bought them (compare I Cor. 6: 19f.). This, in its turn, issues in self-giving, all to the Lord and each to the others; all who have shared in that 'death to self' which is symbolized by baptism henceforth form part of one whole, bound together by a common allegiance and a mutual love. Although the phrase 'one body' is not used here, the idea is inherent, and later in the Epistle it is expressed clearly, in I Corinthians 12: 13–27 '. . . by one Spirit are we all baptized into one body . . . ye are the body of Christ.' (I Corinthians 6: 15 expresses a slightly different thought.)

It is interesting to review the various ideas brought out in this context by means of the use of this metaphor. The

* For the best recent study of the background and controlling factors in this process see C. F. D. Moule: *The Birth of the New Testament* (London, 1962).

first is clearly that of *unity* (I Cor. 12: 13); the body is one. The second is that of *diversity* (I Cor. 12: 14); the one body has many members (limbs). The third is *mutuality* – the mutual need that the limbs and organs have of one another (I Cor. 12: 15 and onwards); there are duties of ministry one to another within the body. It is observable too that the thought of 'body' brings with it, to Paul, the correlative of 'Spirit'; and thus the thought enters of the common life of Christ that is shared by all members of this body, through the common gift of the Spirit, the life-giver. I Corinthians 12: 1–13 is a development of this theme.

In this particular context, there is no development of the thought of the relationship between Head and Body; but this is worked out elsewhere. It is possible that the imagery of the book of Daniel provides the background here, although the details are somewhat different. Paul tells us that as husband stands to wife in a position of headship, so Christ stands to the Church (I Cor. 11: 3, with Eph. 1: 22 and 4: 15). The first of these references shows how quickly the 'body'-metaphor can pass into the 'bride'-metaphor, as we have seen it passing into the 'temple'-metaphor elsewhere.

The last reference (Eph. 4: 15f.), with its thought of growth ('grow up into him in all things') and its further thought of the Head as the One from whom the whole body is 'fitly joined together', comes very close to the Johannine picture of the branches abiding in the vine (Jn. 15: 1–8). Once again, the thought is that life and growth are only possible by maintaining a faith-relationship with the One who is our Head and the source of our life.

Another major passage to be considered is Ephesians 1: 22f.: '... and gave him to be the head over all things to the church, which is his body, the fulness of him that filleth all in all.' For the various interpretations of the final phrase, the standard commentaries on Ephesians must be consulted. Here, it is enough to say that the main subject of this statement is not the Church, but Christ. The mention of the Church is almost incidental here, coming amid a string of clauses designed to show the superior position of Christ as Lord of all created things. Moreover, the term 'the fulness' (the meaning of which is disputed) has to be understood in this context in the light of its other uses elsewhere in the Epistle. If, as is likely, it is a word deliberately taken from the Gnostic terminology of those who were disturbing Paul's readers by their false teaching, it is also likely that the purpose of its use in every case is to show the finality and fulness of the revelation and grace given in Christ – of which, of course, the Church is the recipient. In Colossians 1: 19 and 2: 9, the term 'fulness' is applied directly to Christ Himself, as the One who embodies and expresses the whole of Godhead directly; the term is therefore primarily Christological, but here in Ephesians 1: 22 it is applied, in a secondary sense, to the Church as indwelt by Christ through His Spirit. If all of God is in Christ, and all of Christ is, by His Spirit, present in the heart of the one who believes, then all of God is present there; and that which is true of one believer is doubly true of the believing group. In this sense, the Church is the fullness of Christ, who is Himself the fullness of God.

This thought is confirmed by Christ's special promises to His followers dating from the days of His earthly ministry, such as '. . . where two or three are gathered together in my name, there am I in the midst of them' (Mt. 18: 20). That is a church-promise, found in what is often called the church-Gospel, Matthew. Paul in Ephesians is but giving this truth wider expression in the light of the fuller understanding of the meaning and nature of the Lord's abiding presence with and in His people that came after Pentecost.

CHAPTER THREE

HOW DO I BECOME A MEMBER OF CHRIST'S BODY?

IF 'the Body of Christ' is of this nature, how do I become a member, a limb, of it? We cannot find an answer to this question within the terms of this particular metaphor. No doubt, if Paul had lived in our modern days of 'transplanted kidneys', he could have used some such illustration, but, in his days, while a limb could be amputated from the body, it could neither be added nor replaced. In the closely allied image of the olive-tree, the simile of 'grafting' is used (Rom. 11: 17ff.). Similarly, Paul pictures stones being added from the outside to an existing building when he is developing the temple-metaphor (Eph. 2: 20–22). So it is probably only the limitations of his metaphor itself that hindered Paul from describing the process of initial union with Christ in terms of it. With the thought of subsequent growth there is, of course, no problem; the metaphor of the human frame lends itself to this as readily as does that of the plant or the temple (Eph. 4: 15f.).

If, then, we wish to know the answer to our question, we must enlarge our terms of reference. There are two ways of doing this: first, by considering what is said of the point of entry in totally different metaphors, and, second, by considering separately a parallel and complementary metaphor which is concerned, not with our collective relation to Christ as body to head, but with our individual relationship to Him, whereby we 'put on' Christ, Gal. 3: 27, or 'put on' the 'new man', as in Eph. 4: 24. With this parallelism of metaphor we may compare another pair of parallels, a double use of the Temple-metaphor, by which we are not only collectively the temple of God, but individually these mortal bodies of ours are temples of the Holy Spirit (I Cor. 3: 16, 6: 19).

Resolved into modern terms, the question is, what makes a man a Christian? Is it baptism, or faith, or both? and if so, in what relation do these stand to each other? Ultimately, the nature of the Church, the nature of the ministry, and the nature of the sacraments are all involved here. The question is one of fundamental importance, and one to which the Reformers of the Church of England gave much careful thought. Unhappily, their views, and the essentially biblical nature of their position, are not always understood today – often because we fail to understand the 'sacramental' nature of their language.

We cannot do better than look back once more to the event whereby Simon Peter was marked out as the 'foundation member' of the Christian Church (Mt. 16: 13–18). We say '*foundation* member' advisedly; for, while in one sense Christ Himself is the Foundation Stone, in another the apostles and prophets themselves are regarded as foundational, as, so to speak, the 'lower courses' of the building (compare I Cor. 3: 11 with Eph. 2: 20, Rev. 21: 14). The apparent point of the reference in such cases is to the peculiar place in the providence of God of the first apostolic generation, who had the unique task of witnessing to, and recording, the words and deeds of the Christ-in-the-flesh.

In St Matthew 16: 16ff., Peter voices a confession of Christ, expressive of faith in Him, a faith which involves an apprehension of His true nature and deity. To Peter, the confessor, the first great 'Church-Word' is spoken by Christ, and to him, as confessor, the great 'Petrine Promises' are given – which, be it said, we would interpret very differently from our friends in the Church of Rome.

It is important to note, in connection with this 'confession', that it is nowhere said that the 'confession' in itself made Peter the first member of this new society. Jesus' point in verse 17 is that ability to make such a declaration from the heart shows what later theology would call the prior working of the Holy Spirit in the heart –

Peter believed, and therefore Peter spoke. It was not the voicing of his faith, but rather the faith which he voiced, that constituted Peter a Christian. In the terminology of the passage before us, ability to make this heartfelt declaration is a sign of the divine 'blessing', and it is a token of Peter's having received a direct revelation from the Father, in contrast with a mere acceptance of some human tradition, with reference to the true identity and vocation of Jesus of Nazareth. This spiritual insight alone gives the key to understanding the ministry of Jesus. Other views of His significance there are, but they are mere human misunderstandings of Him, based on a comparison of Him with the known past (John the Baptist, Elijah, Jeremiah, a prophet: speculative 'christology' outside the realm of the Spirit was as varied then as it is now). Since according to Scripture it is always the special task of the Spirit to reveal God we are not wrong, although there is no direct reference to the Spirit here, in identifying at this point His presence and His work in Simon Peter. Jesus' word thus shows that it was not the confession as a vocal utterance, but the inward, Spirit-given faith which it expressed, that gave Simon his 'foundation member' status in the Church of Christ.

Peter, then, to put it bluntly, is here marked out as the first 'Christian' (as distinct from 'follower of Jesus') because he first realizes and confesses that Jesus is the Christ, God's Messiah. The reception of this revelation is proof of the presence of God's Spirit within his heart, and it is this that makes a man, Peter or any other, a Christian, a member of the Body of Christ. Now Peter shares in the very life of the Head, that common life into which others will later be introduced and grafted, by sharing a common faith and a common Spirit. Before Pentecost, however, these things could not be fully enjoyed. Indeed, they could not become full realities before the Cross, and the Cross was still to Peter a stumbling-block (v. 23), from which we see how shallow and superficial his 'Christian faith' as yet was. And yet it was upon such faith that the Lord declared He

32

would build His Church; and the powers of Death and Hell would not be able to overcome it. (If this is, in the first instance, a reference to Christ's own resurrection, then there is here another concealed link between the Temple-metaphor and the Body-metaphor.)

Now, in spite of the presence of individual and non-recurring factors in this story, it is obviously given to us as a pattern-in-outline of all true Christian experience in its initial stages. Here is a transforming new 'discovery', which proves to be evidence of prior working of God. It is an insight which Peter has not had before, and which he does not lose later, for all the stormy period when Satan sifts him and the rest like wheat; Christ prays that his new-born faith may not fail (Lk. 22: 31–32), and Christ's prayer is answered. Peter's later experience ('when thou art converted', or more accurately with R.V., 'when once thou hast turned again') is one of forgiveness and restoration (Jn. 21: 15ff.). But here there is no word about baptism from beginning to end; indeed, while Peter had probably received John's baptism, in company with other of his fellow-apostles (Jn. 1: 35), there is no evidence that he or they ever received specifically Christian baptism.

This is all the more remarkable, in view of the fact, stressed in John 4: 2, that these very apostles baptized others during the earthly ministry of Jesus (presumably 'into Christ,' that is, to enrol men as Jesus' disciples, whatever formula they used), and were commanded after the Resurrection, according to St Matthew 28: 19, to baptize all those who, through them, should subsequently become disciples. While, therefore, baptism appears to have been made the rule for others at a later stage, there is no evidence that it was thought indispensable either in the case of Peter or any other of the original band. (It is true that Paul 're-baptized' one group, who had already, as it seems, received John's baptism (Acts 19: 5); but the context indicates a special reason for this, and there is no hint in the New Testament that this rule was applied in the exactly similar case of Apollos (Acts 18: 26).)

If it be affirmed that Peter's subsequent spiritual enlightenment gave meaning to the original baptism that he had already received from John, as nowadays one's subsequent spiritual awakening gives meaning to the baptism one received as an infant, this is of course true in a wide sense, inasmuch as John's baptism was forward-looking to the Messiah and His gift of the Spirit. But John's baptism was essentially different from Christian baptism (even in the presumed form which the disciples used during the earthly ministry of Christ) in that it was purely a baptism of repentance, with a view to remission of sins (Acts 19: 4). Though it was forward-looking, it was also inadequate theologically, because it was incapable of effecting by faith that which it symbolized. It knew as yet no way by which this forgiveness could be gained, and so guaranteed to the one baptized. It held out no promise of the power to live the new life which made such searching moral demands – except in the most general of terms, in connection with the Coming One, who would baptize with the Holy Ghost and with fire. Yet it is evident that in the case of the apostles Christian baptism was not regarded as necessary to salvation; John's baptism, though palpably inadequate, was apparently held by Jesus Himself to suffice.

BAPTISM, CONFESSION, AND FAITH

Thus, it is faith in Christ that constitutes a man a Christian; and this faith, if it is living faith and not merely an intellectual assent, will issue in 'confession' of Christ, by lip and life (compare Rom. 10: 9 with Jas. 2: 6 – is this another unsuspected reference to 'the Body'?), just as Peter's faith has already done in the Matthaean context before us. John's congregation had been exhorted to 'bring forth therefore fruits meet for repentance' (Mt. 3: 8), but had found this impossible to perform; henceforth, however, the transformation of Peter himself and those who shared his faith would be proof positive of the existence of the new tide of life within the Body of Christ.

34

But many scholars would say that the very introduction of the concept of 'confession' is in itself an implicit allusion to baptism; the fact that Peter makes this kind of 'confession' at all makes this passage a 'baptismal context'. In commenting on this, first let us gladly admit that 'confession' of Jesus is indeed in the Bible often associated with the physical act of baptism, and presumably was its regular accompaniment in the primitive Church. It is clear that the early Church demanded some such confession as 'Jesus is Lord' (I Cor. 12: 3) as a sort of 'baptismal creed', on the profession of which a man might be baptized. This was because they judged, presumably on the basis of Peter's confession and other Gospel instances (for example John 1: 49), that such illumination could only be brought by the Spirit of God ('no man can say that Jesus is the Lord, but by the Holy Ghost'); and they knew that where the Spirit was, there Christ was. The Authorized Version of Acts 8: 37 may be an interpolation into what Luke wrote, but it certainly shows what was the practice of the early Church.

I Timothy 6: 13 takes us further still. In a passage where Paul is apparently reminding Timothy of his own baptismal 'confession' (v. 12) he specifically refers to Christ Jesus 'who, before Pontius Pilate, witnessed a good confession'. In this connection we should recall that Jesus Himself spoke of His death as His true baptism ('I have a baptism to be baptized with . . .' (Lk. 12: 50). Stephen witnessed the same sort of good confession in Acts 7, and Jesus predicted that one day Peter himself was to do the same (Jn. 21: 19). Baptism, the token of discipleship, symbolizing death to the old, may prove to be a commitment to death in the most literal sense of the word; for Jesus' own Messiahship was itself a commitment to death, as in the context under discussion Jesus went straight on to show (Mt. 16: 21ff.).

But all we have admitted in this is that this story of the 'confession' of Peter contains many elements that will occur again in baptismal contexts; and as physical water-baptism does in fact symbolize and assure us of these same truths, that is scarcely surprising. But the important thing is the spiritual truth in either case, not the rite which is its sign, seal and pledge. It is clear that water-baptism is the normal sign of entry into the Christian community in the New Testament; but it is also clear that that which is held to make a man a member of Christ is the faith which in baptism he confesses.

It is unnecessary to quote in detail the numerous passages in Paul where baptism is closely linked with what elsewhere in the New Testament is called the New Birth (in Jn. 3, for instance). We may refer the reader to such passages as Romans 6: 3f., I Corinthians 12: 13, Galatians 3: 27, Titus 3: 5, as examples; and there are many more. But these texts do not mean that Paul ascribed the gift of the Spirit, and the new life in Christ, to the mere act of physical water-baptism accompanied by the correct formula, any more than the Reformers did; it is just that he continually speaks of the physical act in language which more properly applies to the spiritual reality symbolized and expressed by it – and indeed vice-versa. For it is clear that, as he does not contemplate an 'unbaptized Christian', so he did not conceive the thought of a 'baptized pagan' (even though mistakes were made in the apostolic Church, as in other Churches since, over the question as to who were fit candidates for baptism – think of Ananias, Sapphira, and Simon of Samaria!).

It was not until events in the Roman Empire, two centuries after the apostolic age, had made Christianity fashionable, if not actually profitable, so that people began to ask for baptism from other motives than Christian conviction, that the danger of treating the physical act as automatically conveying the symbolized reality assumed its modern form. In the absence of this danger it was easier for Paul to use 'realistic' language than it would be for us. As any missionary will understand, it was also much easier to speak in this fashion in what was virtually everywhere a 'first generation church'.* In the light of these facts, we can

* It is this fact, incidentally, which explains why the New Testament is so vague on the question of infant baptism, which certainly

36

understand why Paul felt no inhibitions about using 'sacramental' language; why, indeed, he thought it so appropriate and fitting to use baptismal imagery when appealing to the spiritual reality of which baptism is both the outward sign and assurance.

THE EXPERIENCE OF PAUL

The simplest way of seeing Paul's own view of the matter is to study his recorded experience of becoming a Christian, as set forth in Acts 9, and in his own autobiographical references to it.

Acts 9 depicts Paul's spiritual experience in outline as follows. From an initial position of knowledge of the facts about Jesus (compare II Cor. 5:16) but of unbelief of the Gospel and bitter opposition to both Jesus and the groups of His followers, Paul came to trust in, and submit to, the One whom once he had opposed. So much is patent. But how did he arrive at this volte-face? It is clear from the story that it was by a personal encounter with Christ; it was by the same sort of revelation from God's Spirit as Peter had had (or John, beside Jordan: compare Jn. 1:29, 35), enabling him to recognize this enigmatic Person, despised by the world, as God's Chosen One. True, this knowledge and revelation did not come to him without the witness and ministry of the Christian community; and it seems true to say that what this vision of Christ brought directly was only 'death to self' (or conviction of sin, as our forefathers would have phrased it). Its immediate consequence was three days of darkness that must have reminded Paul of the time spent by the Lord in the tomb, before His Resurrection took place.

But it seems unwarrantable (with Robinson) to see the vision of Christ as itself a vision of the Church, simply because of the words 'I am Jesus whom thou persecutest'

---

was the rule very soon after; normally in any heathen area, all the first baptisms are of adults, and the question of infant baptism only enters where an entire family wishes to turn to the Lord.

addressed to the one who styles himself elsewhere 'perse-cutor of the church' (Acts 9: 5, and Phil. 3: 6). It was because Paul had opposed the Christ that he was opposed to the Church of Christ; that is not at all the same as say-ing that he was opposed to the 'Christ-of-the-Church' be-cause he was the foe of the Church. Once again, that would be to put the theological cart before the horse; it was not faith in the Church that saved either Paul or his later con-verts, but faith in Christ.

Nevertheless, in Paul's hour of darkness, through Brother Ananias there comes to him the word which discloses the full meaning of the vision (see Acts 9: 10–18). The spiritual experience is now doctrinally explained, and, apparently through a laying-on of hands, Saul at once receives both physical and spiritual sight, the gift of the Holy Spirit (Acts 9: 17). On the basis of this, he is baptized, and thereafter enters fully into the life and fellowship of the Christian group at Damascus, preaching to others the transforming revelation that he has himself received (v. 19f.).

There is in this account no hint that baptism in itself is the door to the new life, though it is certainly part of the complex of events that marks its beginning. If it be objected here that this is but a 'third-party' account by Luke, then we may turn to two accounts in the first person, in Acts 22 and 26 respectively. (This frequency of narra-tion in Acts must surely reflect a habit in Paul of explaining his present action by appeal to his own past spiritual ex-perience.) In the first of these passages, baptism appears in the mouth of the careful Ananias – '... why tarriest thou? arise, and be baptized, and wash away thy sins, calling on the name of the Lord' (22: 16). But this language is closer to the Johannine baptism of repentance, full of Old Testa-ment echoes. In any case, Paul's position was similar to that of those in Acts who, on hearing Peter preach, were 'pricked in their heart' (2: 37); and in reply to their anxious inquiry Peter gave them virtually the same advice regarding the next step as Ananias here gives to Paul. And if we allow that Paul, habitually and without risk of being misunderstood, used 'sacramental' language, we ought not to doubt that Ananias and Peter could use it too, in just the same sense. Indeed, the evidence would indicate that, so far from 'sacramental' language being Paul's invention, it was established in the Church before ever Paul arrived on the scene.

Thus, to put it in modern terminology, Paul's appeal when explaining his position as a Christian is not to his baptism, but to his conversion: his great cry is not 'I am a baptized man', but 'I am a converted man'. On the other hand, when he appeals to Christians for moral living, it is often on the grounds of the symbolism of baptism that he does it. Had they really understood all that baptism stood for? had their spiritual experience truly been that which baptism signified? – then they simply cannot act as they now seem to be doing, but must henceforth walk 'in newness of life' (compare Rom. 6: 1ff.).

That the principle of salvation through faith as such, rather than by baptism as such, runs through the great body of Pauline thought, is sufficiently shown by Paul's various autobiographical references to his conversion in different epistles. Galatians 1: 15f., for instance, shows the same concentration on God's revelation, rather than on any outward rite, important though that might be ('. . . when it pleased God . . . to reveal his son in me, that I might preach him among the heathen . . .'). Nor is this to base all on a private and possibly delusive experience, for this revelation is the will of God and the work of the Spirit, and the subject of it is the Christ of history, who is also the Christ of faith and of theology (compare also I Cor. 15: 3–10; Phil. 3: 7–12; I Tim. 1: 12–16).

CHAPTER FOUR

THE FUNCTION OF MEMBERS
WITHIN THE BODY

THE following questions might be asked with reference, not only to the Body-image, but to any of the other church-metaphors of the New Testament – What is the relation of the part to the whole? It belongs, yes: it has some form of cohesive relationship, but is this relationship active or passive? Is the mutual relation of the fellow-members of the Body essentially different in any way from their common relation to the Head? Are there a group of members who stand in a position of 'limited headship' over the others? What justification is there for our modern division into 'clergy' and 'laity'? Is this an absolute distinction? and if so, on what is it based?

CLERGY AND LAITY

First, it is quite clear that our common use of the words 'clergy' to denote those set aside for the ordained ministry within the Church, and 'laity' to denote the rank and file, is quite without scriptural warrant. The words 'clergy' and 'laity' come from the Greek *kleros* (lot) and *laos* (people) respectively. In the Bible, God's 'kleros', the 'lot' that falls to Him as His peculiar possession, is the whole of His people, not a small section of them, while the 'laos', the people of God, is again the whole company of His chosen ones. So, all clergy are laymen, and all laymen are also clergy, in the biblical sense of these words.

But this is, after all, purely a linguistic point, and we have often been reminded in recent years that the quest for theological truth is more than mere linguistic archaeology. Yet the point is not without importance; for the fact that we have thus misused a pair of biblical words, differentiating what was once one and the same concept into two complementary but mutually exclusive ones, and then setting the one against the other, suggests at once that our modern thinking about Christian ministry is insufficiently biblical.

In the Bible there is no such absolute contrast as we often assume between ministers and the rest. The Old Testament, to be sure, knows a sharp division into 'priests' and 'people', but in the New Testament we are all priests alike. There is no priestly caste any longer, for no job remains for such a class of men to do. The New Testament knows nothing of any offering or sacrifice that only one small section of the Church may and should perform on behalf of the rest. Since the all-sufficient atoning sacrifice of Christ was offered and accepted, there is no longer any cause or room for vicarious offerings of any sort. Apart from 'general' sacrifices, to be offered by all God's people (such as praise, thanksgiving, and the presenting of our bodies in self-dedication to God), the only 'special' sacrifice mentioned in the New Testament is the offering-up of the Gentile converts to God, spoken of by Paul in Romans 15: 16. On the basis of this test, if any group within the Church exercises a particular sacrificing 'priesthood', it must be the soul-winners, the evangelists; and since evangelism is a Christian duty which falls equally on every member of the Body (though some members are peculiarly gifted by the Spirit for the task), this line of thought would again in effect generalize the concept. The New Testament thus provides no basis for attributing to any Christian a priestly and sacrificial office that is not shared alike by all.

But this is not to deny a distinction in the New Testament between the general body of Christians and those called by God to a particular kind of ministry within the Body of Christ, persons whose prior calling has been outwardly recognized by the Body, which thus gladly identifies itself with the loving purpose of God. As we shall see, all members of the Body have some ministry, though not all have the same ministry; but there are some types of ministry which, by their very nature, and for their proper exercise, demand the type of public recognition and acknowledgment which we call 'ordination'. There is a special word in the New Testament for those in this group, the word presbyter (elder). Had we clung closer to the philology of the New Testament, the modern clergyman might have been called a 'prester' (as in 'Prester John'), and the non-clergyman might have been called an 'idiot' (*idiotes*, a word which in the New Testament meant 'private individual', a person not holding an official position). 'Idiot', however, has changed its meaning for the worse, like 'silly', which once in Old English meant 'blessed'. For obvious reasons, it would not be ideal to use 'idiot' for a non-presbyteral Christian today! Perhaps 'church member' will serve our turn (although it is symptomatic of our muddled thought that those whom Paul called members of *Christ,* we call members of a *church*). For 'prester', however, we are better served; we have either 'presbyter', a transliteration of the original Greek *presbuteros*, or 'priest', which is the same word in more modern dress, 'old presbyter writ small'. As Hooker tells us, whether we say 'priest' or 'presbyter' or 'minister' makes no difference; we are in every case thinking of the 'elder' in the Church of God. These 'presbyters' or 'priests' (it is very unfortunate that to our minds the word 'priest' suggests sacrifice, while the word 'presbyter' suggests a particular form of church polity) are in the pages of the New Testament identical with the 'episkopoi' or 'overseers' (regularly translated 'bishops' in our English versions). By what ways in post-biblical times *presbuteros* and *episkopos* came to be differentiated, we need not discuss now; we would merely note that in the New Testament both names apply to the same local church officers (see Acts 20: 17 and 28; Phil. 1: 1; Tit. 1: 5–7, etc)

But now let us turn directly to two great passages where Paul discusses the doctrine of ministry in terms of the metaphor that lies before us. It is noteworthy that, while in general outline Paul's line of thought is the same in both,

42

there is no detailed point by point correspondence. This is what we should expect of the fertile many-sided brain of Paul. But it is also a warning to us that, while the theological principles involved are plain and constant, the detailed pattern is by no means as set as we should like to have it. In days when all men are discussing the differing forms of ministry in various areas of the Church of God, this is not without its import. I Corinthians 12 and Ephesians 4 are the two scriptures in question; let us then see them in their context.

VALID AND INVALID MINISTRY

In I Corinthians 12, it is important to note that Paul is not primarily dealing with the doctrine of the ministry at all, but with the question of spiritual gifts – a very real problem in the exuberant church of Corinth. (Their problem was more that of 'anabaptism' than of deadness; there was abundant life, sometimes taking strange forms, with little sense of restraint and order. A similar problem to Paul's faced the Reformers in dealing with the 'left wing' of Protestantism.)

First, Paul points out (v. 3) that the roots of Christian ministry lie deep in Christian experience; or, rather, that an experience of the revelation of God, through the Spirit by Christ, is the threshold of the Christian life. It is only by the Spirit that we can see who Jesus is; it is only by the Spirit that we can make that confession of Him which we have seen to be fundamental. Christian ministry is but an extending of this 'confession' to those outside and inside the church. When directed to those outside it is evangelism (nowadays often called more technically *kerugma*, the herald's proclamation of his King's message). When directed to those already inside, it is pastoral instruction (often again referred to by its technical name *didache*, 'teaching', after the Greek word).

Thus to Paul, the true test of the presence or absence of the Spirit in the individual (that is, whether or no he is,

43

as we would say, a Christian) is whether or not he bears authentic testimony to Christ. And though Paul is here thinking primarily of verbal witness, his position at this point is not essentially different from that expressed in the great canon of the Lord, 'by their fruits ye shall know them' (Mt. 7: 10); for the witness of the changed life is itself an essential part of the 'confession'.

To Paul, then, the acid test of the 'validity' (strength, stability, authenticity, reality) of Christian ministry is the nature of the testimony that it bears to Jesus Christ. If it bears true testimony, then its source is the Holy Spirit, and it is not only valid, but will be effectual also. If it bears false witness to Christ, then it cannot have the Spirit as its source. This does not, to be sure, mean that Paul did not take steps to assure order and continuity in the ministry of the local churches which God had used him to found; but 'order' and 'validity' are very different concepts.

VARIED MINISTRY

Second, in I Corinthians 12: 4ff., Paul goes on to point out that the ministry of the Spirit in the Church, through the individuals whom He has gifted for the task, is an infinitely varied thing; yet its variety does not in any way deny the underlying unity of the Spirit. Perhaps there has been no greater folly in the Church down the ages than the steady attempt to 'standardize' the ministry, leading to repeated refusal to make room for those to whom the Spirit has given gifts that do not fit into our tidy ready-made patterns. If the patterns themselves are of a theologically doubtful nature, then our dangers are multiplied tenfold. It is true that in the New Testament, we can isolate a set of spiritual qualities and say 'these befit the elder', or 'these befit the deacon'; in fact, Paul does precisely this for us in the Pastoral Epistles; but what we have done is to confine ministry to one or two of the Spirit's channels, instead of enjoying the many-sided richness of His giving.

Our limiting of the idea of 'ministry' to the regular work of ordained office-bearers is indeed calculated to quench the Spirit in our churches.

Thirdly, Paul points out that spiritual gifts are not confined to some spiritual aristocracy, nor even to a spiritual 'middle-class'! They are in fact universal within the Church of God (vv. 7, 11f.). We need not concern ourselves now with the exact nature of the spiritual gifts listed in verses 8–10 and 28–31. Doubtless the list reflects the particular circumstances of the Church of Corinth at that time, and there is no hint that Paul considered it exhaustive; he is simply picking out typical and apposite examples.

Fourthly, Paul is clear that the function of these gifts of the Spirit is 'to profit withal' (v. 7). Were we to take this out of its context, we might suppose it means that a spiritual gift is given to a man that he might grow spiritually; but this is not Paul's notion, as the immediate context makes clear. In view of the doctrine of 'mutuality' or 'belongingness' inherent in the simile of the body, and made explicit by Paul in the second half of the chapter, it is clear that what he means is that the gift is given to the one for the profit of the many, and must so be exercised. Indeed in verses 28ff. Paul is not so much listing 'orders' of the primitive Church as instancing ways in which the early Church recognized these spiritual gifts, isolated them, named them, and perhaps allocated to them spheres of function – although even to say this is to tread on dangerous ground and to risk limiting the sovereign freedom of the Spirit.

Fifthly, Paul shows in verses 14–26 that the Church has need of the right exercise of all these gifts alike, if the Body is to grow and be healthy. He deals in whimsical fashion with the possibility of organs of our physical body being 'arrogant' or 'bashful' (a sort of parable so common in the thought of the day that it is quite unnecessary to seek any special source for it, or to see in it any specifically Greek, as distinct from Hebrew, influence). He does not mean us to take his physiology seriously; but the illustration is arresting, for the two dangers that hamper and hinder the right exercise of Christian ministry by every member of the Church are either self-assertive pride (often on the part of the man with ten talents), or diffident shrinking back (usually by the man with one talent). The striking thing is that Paul sees both of these as dangers; we see the first, but usually ignore the second.

As to the actual list of functions, Paul is vague; apostles he mentions – but who are they? Paul certainly does not restrict this title to the Twelve; he claims to be one himself, for instance (see Rom. 1: 1, I Cor. 9: 1f.). If 'prophets' are distinct from 'teachers', what are they? Are we, for instance, to think of some temporary group (men like Agabus in Acts 21: 10) who could foretell the future, rather like Old Testament prophets? And where are the 'elders' and 'deacons', the only two ministries in the New Testament that sound at all familiar to us? They appear nowhere at all – unless the teaching function of the elder appears here under 'teachers', and their ruling function under 'helps and governments' in verse 28. If so, then Paul puts ruling in the Church at the end of the list – lowliest of all, except for the gift of 'tongues'. However, the order in the text may have no intrinsic significance; it may simply be the order of the images that, as a matter of psychological fact, the phrase 'spiritual gifts' called up in Paul's mind. But even if the presbyterate does appear here, it is rapidly pushed into insignificance again by the crowning gift of love, which is the subject of the whole next chapter, and is probably intended as the true definition of all Christian ministry, as being based on the pattern of the life and death of Christ Himself.

It would seem therefore on the basis of this passage as if Paul was much less concerned with details of Church order than we are; witness the way in which, for all his theological exploration of the richness of the symbolism of Christian baptism, he dismisses a baptismal question with the remark 'Christ sent me not to baptize, but to preach

46

the gospel' in 1 Corinthians 1: 17. This is not, as is often held, an impatient aside; it is a full and deliberate expression of the Pauline sense of proportion and values. Had Paul thought it essential for every church to observe the same system of church order, surely his epistles would have contained much clearer indications than they do as to its form.

Ephesians 4: 4-16 adds little to this. Once again, the root of all Christian ministry is seen to lie in the calling of God, and to be an expression of love. Again, mutuality and interdependence are stressed; and the gifts of ministry are associated with the sovereign Spirit, for they are described as flowing from the risen and glorified Christ (v. 8). Here the detailed list is apostles, prophets, evangelists, pastors-and-teachers (presumably, one group). The ultimate aim is the growth of the whole body, which will involve Christian maturity for every member, and will show itself in stability when faced with heresy. Once again, while apostles are mentioned, they are not defined; and the other 'orders' are named more for their part in inaugurating the Church (the work of evangelists), or maintaining it (the work of pastors), than for any value or relative importance that they have in themselves.

ORDER IN THE CHURCH

In the light of this consistent attitude on the part of Paul, it is quite clear that he cared more for spiritual realities than for outward forms. This is brought out most clearly in his own robust claims to be an apostle, claims based not only on his 'calling' by Christ (Rom. 1: 1) and his encounter with the Risen Lord (I Cor. 9: 1), but also on the spiritual results produced amongst them by his preaching of the Gospel (I Cor. 9: 2). And yet, in this very context, it is striking to see his concern for order in the churches, not only in worship (I Cor. 14: 40), but also in administration and government (Acts 14: 23). It appears to have been part of the regular Pauline practice to set apart with prayer,

47

and apparently laying on of hands (in which it would seem that the other elders joined, I Timothy 4: 14), those who had been chosen from the main body of the Church, as possessing those spiritual qualities which marked them out for the presbyters' task. This is the only possible interpretation of the lists of qualifications to be found in the Pastoral Epistles (I Tim. 3: 1–13, Tit. 1: 5–9).

Such, at any rate, is subtantially the practice of every Reformed Church at least, including the Church of England. It is not from a denial of the priority of spiritual qualification, but from a concern for church order, and that the rest of the Church should have the opportunity of setting its Amen to the prior calling of God, that we normally restrict public ministry in the Church to those whom the Church has duly set apart for that purpose. There is no thought of any special new powers being regularly conferred by the act of ordination, though no man will wish to limit God in His sovereign freedom from giving fresh graces corresponding to fresh needs; and I Timothy 4: 16 suggests that some special gift was in fact given to Timothy at his own ordination, although its exact nature is unspecified in the context.

This attitude of Paul is precisely that of the still earlier Church in Acts. At first the Twelve are its natural leaders, though gradually the Jewish feeling for the importance of family relationships places James, brother of the Lord – never one of the Twelve – at the centre. But soon alongside of them we find a larger group of 'elders' (see Acts 15: 4; it seems unlikely, if not impossible, that the two groups were coterminous). Likewise, we find in Acts 6 the origin, at least in Jerusalem, of a group of men who correspond to the later 'deacons' of the Pastoral Epistles – younger men, in charge of the practical arrangements of the congregation; a type of duty which, like the office of the elder, had a long history both in orthodox Judaism and in heterodox Judaism of the type found on the shores of the Dead Sea. In Acts 6: 2ff. we learn that the chief reason for the setting apart of the new group of 'deacons' was so that the original apostolic group might be the more free to devote themselves 'to prayer, and to the ministry of the word' (Acts 6: 4).

It had by that time become clear that, if the apostles devoted themselves in this way to prayer and preaching, ordinary work would be impossible for them, and they would have to depend for their support on the gifts of God's people – as indeed the Lord and His disciples had already done during the years of Jesus' earthly ministry (Lk. 8: 3). In the days of Acts this presented no problem, because of the primitive 'collectivism' by which men gladly and freely (though, perhaps, incautiously) pooled their property and resources. By the time of Paul, however, when most members of the Gentile churches were 'working men' (and were expected to be so, I Thess. 4: 11), the problem had become more acute, and Paul needed all his resources of pastoral delicacy to handle it. While Paul jealously guarded his own independence, and was always ready to 'work for his keep' if necessary (Acts 20: 34), he did not ever glorify a 'part-time ministry' as something good in itself. Indeed, he always accepted gifts for his support from the Churches, though, so far as we know, he never solicited them for himself – in contrast to his continual endeavour to raise funds for the 'poor saints' at Jerusalem. Indeed, Paul maintained it as a biblical principle (from Deut. 25: 4) that elders, especially those who both ruled and taught, should be supported by the gifts of the congregation (I Tim. 5: 17f.). Thus we have the outline of a recognized, full-time, 'salaried' ministry, by the end of the age of the New Testament.

Further than this we cannot go. How, or by what means, the concept of a universal monarchical episcopate arose, we may guess, but cannot prove, most certainly not from the New Testament. Therefore, we may be content to accept the Anglican form of church government as one possible variety, without condemning brethren who feel differently.

To recapitulate: of 'apostolic succession', in the now usual sense of the expression, we find not a trace in the New

49

Testament. There are apostles, yes, but their circle is far wider than the Twelve. Membership of the apostolate depends, not on human recruitment, but on divine calling. Paul and James, two of the most important who came to occupy this position, were completely outside the original circle of Jesus' Palestinian disciples. Paul exercises powers roughly analogous to those of a modern missionary bishop; he has been the evangelist, and the converts are his spiritual children; he has been their pastor, and he agonizes over them, yearning for their spiritual growth. This prior calling of God to Paul is recognized by the Church at large (Gal. 2: 9 – although apparently by a handshake rather than by imposition of hands), rather as we might consecrate a man as bishop because of his obvious spiritual qualities. In turn, from within his own circle, Paul chose men like Timothy, Titus, Tychicus, and no doubt others, to bear this sort of comprehensive pastoral responsibility over a wider area. They were tried and proven men, selected for their spiritual qualities, but there is no hint that any kind of further ordination was necessary, in the sense of any 'tactile succession', before they undertook this ministry. So again we see Paul content with the spiritual reality, rather than being a stickler for outward form, and yet with a strong sense of church order.

We have seen that each local church has elders, drawn from its own members, and solemnly set apart for their task, which includes ruling and teaching. While we cannot prove from the New Testament that such men had any particular duties to perform at the Lord's supper or baptism, it is highly likely that they would preside at such functions. If this were so it would come under the heading of order, not faith, and would correspond to the Jewish concept of ruling elders in the local synagogue. But it would be most unwise to build a theology of the ministry on such a foundation. Teaching and ruling we can prove, and it is highly probable that the duty of maintaining order in the Church would involve presiding at the sacraments as it did later. But, probable though it is, we cannot prove it. It is hardly necessary to say that there is no thought in the New Testament of the presbyter having any quasi-priestly powers of absolving' or 'blessing', and the context shows that Jesus' words to the apostolic circle in John 20: 23 have to do with Gospel proclamation in the Spirit's power.

CHAPTER FIVE

THE UNITY OF THE BODY

UNITY is one of the most pressing questions that faces the Church today. Is the Church one? Week by week we profess our faith in 'one Catholick and Apostolick Church', but where is it? Is it purely an object of faith, not to be apprehended by sight? or something hidden in the future, and yet to be realized, or at least manifested? Or are these qualities only to be predicated of the Church as known to God, while remaining hidden in the Church as known to man? Are we justified, on these grounds, in distinguishing between a 'church visible' and a 'church invisible' or 'mystical church', to use phrases beloved by our forefathers? What are we to think of 'the denominations' of modern church life—*our* denominations, which involve us all in the dividedness of the Church? Is the quest for unity so evident on every side today, both within and without the Church of Rome, just another 'movement', a mere fashionable hobby, or is it, as its advocates claim, simple obedience to the mind of Christ as expressed in the Gospels, and the theology of Paul as found in his epistles?

We cannot hope to answer these questions directly from the New Testament, for the simple reason that many of the situations which evoke them did not exist in the first generation of the life of the Church. All we can do is to examine the Church of the New Testament and endeavour to find out wherein its unity lay. Thus we should be able to recover broad theological principles which we can apply to the present situation; though if Church history has shown anything, it is that different men come to different conclusions, even when they apply the same biblical principles to apparently identical situations.

The unity of the Body is directly involved in the metaphor itself. Paul cannot conceive of anything else; the Body is and cannot but be one, inasmuch as there is but one Spirit, one hope, one faith, one Lord, one baptism, one God and Father of all (Eph. 4: 4f.). Like so much of Pauline doctrine, this unity is not so much proved as assumed. It is to Paul axiomatic, the basis of all subsequent thought. How, for instance, could Jew and Gentile become 'one in Christ', unless there was 'one body' in which to be united (I Cor. 12: 13)? Does this therefore mean that the unity is 'revelational'? Is it grasped by a flash of spiritual insight, brought by the Spirit? This is so, in the sense that all those who are brought by faith into a new relationship with Christ find themselves thereby brought into a new relationship with countless others. The sense of being Christ's brings with it, immediately and inseparably, a sense of oneness with all Christ's people. On the broad scale, this is a *confessional* unity, for it is based on a common confession, made by lip and life, that Jesus is Lord. On a narrower scale, it is a *local* unity, for they find themselves actually meeting together with those living in their vicinity who profess this same 'faith-loyalty' to Jesus Christ.

When New Testament writers speak of 'the Church' (the *ekklesia*) they always do so in one or other of these two senses. It would perhaps be wiser if we had followed their example, instead of using the term 'Church', as we do, chiefly of buildings and denominations. The local church is an experience more than an object of faith, for that which is an object of sight can hardly be one of faith as well. Yet there is one standpoint from which it is an object of faith, for in this poor struggling group of sinners, the eye of faith sees God's saints. What the individual Christian does feel towards them, the product of the work of the Spirit within his heart, is 'love' towards 'the brethren' (I Jn. 3: 14). He cannot look at the man in the next pew without seeing him as 'thy brother . . . for whom Christ died' (Rom. 14: 15).

Here, clearly, is the local expression of the Body of Christ; here is where we must 'keep the unity of the Spirit in the bond of peace' (Eph. 4: 3). This is the unity that was being endangered by party strife at Corinth ('schisms' – AV 'divisions': I Cor. 1: 10) though the 'parties' clearly continued to function together as one church; there is no hint of any 'breakaway meeting'. Paul meets this situation simply by his incredulous 'Is Christ divided?' of 1: 13. It is, to him, just as unthinkable that the local church should be divided. The New Testament assumption throughout is that men will not leave a group like this unless they fail to share the common faith: indeed, to John's mind, the fact that some 'went out' (like Judas, Jn. 13: 30) indicated clearly that they never really belonged (compare I Jn. 2: 19) – they had not shared in the 'one Spirit' (I Cor. 12: 13), who alone makes men Christ's (Rom. 8: 9).

This unity of believers was fittingly symbolized by the partaking of the Lord's supper together, and even by the 'one loaf' normally used on such occasions ('one bread', I Cor. 10: 17). We often forget what a real test this was of true spiritual unity, in days when it was forbidden for Jews to eat with Gentiles, lest they unwittingly incur ritual defilement (Acts 11: 3). Indeed, even to keep company with them rendered an orthodox Jew suspect (Acts 10: 28). So the supreme recognition of Gentile Cornelius as a full brother in Christ was that Peter was willing to have 'table-fellowship' with him; and it was for this very reason that Paul attacked so furiously Peter's vacillation at Antioch in face of James's emissaries (Gal. 2: 12). To refuse to eat with fellow-Christians (presumably the Lord's supper, but the point is not directly important here) was to refuse to recognize them as full brethren. Areas where 'caste' enters into church life, whether East or West, face virtually the same problem – or where a colour bar tries to re-establish a distinction blotted out in Christ (Col. 3: 11).

Today most Christian people deplore such social 'apartheid', but what of the theological apartheid that we erect in our denominations today, forbidding the inter-communion which our spiritual ancestors allowed? Is it possible to do this without impugning our brother's position in Christ? In point of fact, we do not know definitely of a single place in New Testament times where there was more than one 'church' (though there may well have been within the fellowship of that one church several local places of meeting); nor do we know of any place where the local Christians were not prepared to gather together to eat the Lord's supper together (although they may frequently have been in the habit of eating it in private houses). The situation when the Jerusalem deputation came to Antioch is the nearest approach in the whole New Testament to 'two Lord's tables' in one local area; and we have seen how roundly Paul deals with that problem.

So far, so good; here we have the local church, locally organized with its presbyters and deacons, and normally dependent, in the New Testament, upon some founder-evangelist, like the apostle Paul (although there is no reason to assume that all new churches were founded by apostles even in the wider sense; had it been so, there would have been no possibility of certain churches later boasting of having been founded by apostles, as against others, who were saved from this temptation by the undeniable facts of history). We cannot, however, take the question of unity further without considering the Church in the wider 'confessional' sense. Indeed, we have incidentally drawn near to the heart of this question already, for the great danger in the Antioch dispute was not at Antioch itself, but in the parent Jerusalem church that might so easily, but for the grace of God, have stood behind those who 'came from James' (Gal. 2: 12). Here we have the nearest thing in the whole of the New Testament to the emergence of two 'denominations', a Jerusalem-style church and an Antioch-style church, each with its numerous 'branches'. And yet, even in that event, the most

55

that could have happened would have been the rise of two different 'usages', not two different faiths; as is shown by the confident way in which Paul could appeal to the confessional position of the Jerusalem Church, as against the Judaizers, his foes. Paul knew that the Gospel of the Gentile churches was the same as the Gospel of the Hebrew-Christian churches. How could there be two Gospels? Either they preached the Gospel, or they preached a false man-made substitute. And, by definition, if they preached the one eternal Gospel, it was because they had received the same illumination of the one Spirit, and were thus members of the one Body. To Paul, there was no need to prove this; it was a self-evident fact, thought at times men's actions might seem to be a denial of this truth. So Paul's appeal to Peter at Antioch, and his continual appeal to every 'man in Christ', was to realize the implications of the position in which, by grace, he had come to stand, and to 'walk' accordingly.

The Christian churches of the Pauline age (by which we mean the various local groups, not 'sects', as in modern usage) were by no means isolationists in relation to each other. They had a consciousness of belonging to a collective whole, not just numerically, as 'the churches of Judaea' (I Thess. 2: 14), or 'the churches of Galatia' (Gal. 1: 2), which we could easily understand, but as 'the Church of God' (Acts 20: 28). This was something distinct from any geographical sense of unity (although such undoubtedly existed, as the first two quotations show), and distinct too from the focus of unity given by a common evangelist (as in the case of the Pauline churches). It came directly from their knowledge that they were one body in Christ. This is what we mean by saying that this was a 'confessional' unity; it sprang from spiritual truth, directly perceived. We should distinguish it from the later type of 'confessional' church, where full membership is made dependent on the acceptance of a narrow range of formulated biblical doctrines. It was a spiritual unity: it was, so far as we know, not 'organizational' in any sense of the word whatsoever. It is precisely this sort of unity that the Book of Common Prayer has in mind when it defines Christ's church as the 'blessed company of all faithful people' (Collect of Thanksgiving, Service of Holy Communion).

It is important to realize this lack of organizational unity in the days of the New Testament, not so that we may glorify it as an ideal (that would be foolish), but so that we may see how total the contrast is between the attitude of the New Testament and the attitude of the 'Catholic Church' of some centuries later, when the bishop has become the local centre of unity (as Paul might have been to a group of his converts), and organizational linkage with the rest of the Church, and especially with the bishop of Rome, has become the decisive test of orthodoxy. The emptiness of this position can easily be seen by contrasting Paul's attitude to the Church at Jerusalem.

JERUSALEM AND THE YOUNGER CHURCHES

It appears that for quite a time, in the period of the Acts, the title 'the Church' was restricted to the physical group meeting at Jerusalem, or to members of this group temporarily scattered throughout Palestine or neighbouring places by persecution (Acts 8: 3). That is of course natural; indeed, it seems obvious that in the early days 'the Church' as such can only have existed at Jerusalem itself, though 'disciples of Jesus' or 'disciples of John' may well have existed elsewhere. For it was at Jerusalem that the Spirit descended at Pentecost; and we do not even know that the Pentecost crowds necessarily all returned home after their transforming experience. It would seem reasonable for those who could to remain as members of this new group. The fact that the simple title 'the Church' in later days, when used without further qualification, applies to the Jerusalem Church, appears to derive from this period, when Jerusalem was the only place where there was a group to which the name 'church' could properly be applied.

Even when scattered groups existed elsewhere (as, for example, at Damascus, Acts 9: 2), there was hardly a problem of 'churches'. The first signs of a change probably came when some 'overseas Jews' preached to Gentiles as well as Jews at Antioch (Acts 11: 20), and a body so distinctive arose that the local wags had to coin a new name for its members (Acts 11: 26). It is natural that the name *ekklesia* was also used of the group at Antioch. Right through the Book of Acts the Antioch fellowship appears the most active of the churches, apart from Jerusalem. Certainly the name 'church' is later used of it with no sense of strangeness or even novelty (Acts 13: 1). Yet this Antioch church stood in no known organizational relation to Jerusalem. It certainly shows no signs of coming under its jurisdiction in any sense; it seems, rather, to deal with Jerusalem as an equal (compare Acts 11: 29 and 15: 2).

But our problem was only really high-lighted after the first missionary journey of Paul. Then, for the first time, multiple groups, recognizably the same in faith as the already existing groups in Jerusalem and Antioch (and who knows where else?) had been called into being by the same word of the Gospel. From the first, Luke quite naturally uses for them the title *ekklesiai*, 'churches'. What else can he call them? They share in the same Spirit as the Jerusalem church, therefore they belong to the same Body. Peter uses a rough and ready version of this argument himself, when explaining his conduct in the house of Cornelius to the carping Jerusalem elders (Acts 11: 15ff., 15: 7ff.). Moreover, these are largely, if not exclusively, Gentile churches, whereas even Antioch had been, at worst (to Jewish eyes) a 'mixed' church – as can be seen from the list of their 'ministers' in Acts 13: 1. That might have been thought to make some form of inclusive organizational unity even more imperative; for their whole outlook would certainly be quite different from the existing Hebrew–Christian groups further south. In point of fact, many of the problems faced in epistles like Corinthians or Romans stem from this basic difference in attitude. But how does

Paul deal with them? He does not try to resolve them by organizational means – laying down rules and regulations and a detailed code for church life – instead, he wrestles with them in terms of principles; and his method of wrestling with these problems springs from his basic conviction that Jew and Gentile are one in Christ (Col. 3: 11). It would, for instance, have been an easy move to set up at Corinth one church which allowed the eating of sacrificed meat, and another which forbade it. That is undoubtedly what we should have done; and both parties could then have remained serenely conscious of their 'rightness'. But Paul would not dream of taking such a line. Christians were one in Christ, and must learn to live together.

What then is the relation of these Gentile local churches to Jerusalem? They obviously did not consider her as a 'mother church'. If they had had any such filial feelings, one would have expected them to be directed rather towards the Church of Antioch. But, in point of fact, there is not a hint even of this. Such filial feelings as they have seem rather directed towards their evangelist, and thus their 'father in God', Paul (Gal. 4: 15). True, Judaizers followed Paul about the Roman world. We know that they impugned Paul's position as an apostle (I Cor. 9: 1f.), and it is therefore also possible that they were scandalized by the failure of the Pauline churches to look up to the 'genuine apostles' at Jerusalem (II Cor. 11: 5). But the whole point of Paul's counter-attack is that such men do not represent the mind of the Jerusalem Church – and with this James agrees (Acts 15: 24).

Paul's own relations with Jerusalem are too well known to suggest any dependence. Indeed, the whole point of Galatians is the complete independence of his Gospel from that of Jerusalem, which proved the genuineness of both, as alike spiritual revelation; for the Gospel was to Paul not so much a set of public historical facts about Christ – though naturally these were assumed and involved – as the divine interpretation of these facts, which is given by the Spirit alone.

But in two matters Paul's recorded attitude to the Jerusalem Church raises the question whether the relation of the Gentile churches to Jerusalem was not one of conscious dependence, as at first sight it would seem to be. The first such matter is Paul's collection for the poor saints of Jerusalem. The second is the so-called Council of Jerusalem, and the circulating of its decisions or decrees, whichever they were. Do these episodes imply on the part of the Gentile churches recognition of the supreme position of the Twelve in Jerusalem, and an acceptance of the 'precedence' of the Jerusalem Church? For, if so, we could argue for at least some measure of organic dependence of the one group on the other, and hence some organizational relationship between them. But neither of these can we actually prove from the context.

THE CORINTHIAN COLLECTION

Take, for example, the attitude of the Church of Corinth to the Jerusalem Church in this matter. It is clear that Paul taught the Corinthians, as he did others, that they had a plain Christian duty to give generously for the support of the church at Jerusalem (I Cor. 16: 1) – or perhaps it would be fairer to say, to relieve the financial needs of the church members there, for we must not think in modern terms of a Jerusalem church programme with estimated 'running costs', still less a formal 'budget'! This is much more a matter of inter-church aid, comparable to famine relief or a 'world refugee year'. (And it is a real question whether the unity of the Church will not be more convincingly displayed to the outside world today by general participation in such activities than by any great world councils, with their solemn pronouncements of faith.)

Why, then, did the Corinthians give? Was their contribution some Christianized 'temple-tax', some form of 'Peter's pence', continuing into new covenant conditions the practice, general under the old covenant in its later days, whereby pious Jews overseas contributed to the upkeep of the temple at Jerusalem, and, by so doing, confessed it to be the centre of their religious life? No: it must be acknowledged that a frank reading of the New Testament leaves us with the impression that the chief reason for these Gentile gifts was the persistence of Paul, who, while scrupulously refraining from demanding anything for himself, was a shameless beggar on behalf of others. He begged from his Gentile converts, as he himself explains, because 'giving' was for their good; and, further, because they had a spiritual responsibility to care for the physical needs of those who, however unwittingly, had been the human means of meeting their own spiritual needs. Looked at from one angle, the giving for which Paul pleaded was a recognition of how much the Gentile Christian owed to the Jew (Rom. 15: 2). Seen from the other side, it was a specific instance of the universal Christian duty to feed and support those who have ministered to one (compare I Cor. 9: 11).

Even wider principles were involved. When one member of the Body suffers every member suffers with it (I Cor. 12: 26), and giving to relieve need is a practical expression of such fellow-feeling. Moreover, it is natural to the wealthy Christian to give to those in need; for his heart is full of the consciousness of God's great gift to him (II Cor. 9: 15). All of these aspects of the situation Paul brings out again and again in his letters, but there is never any thought of ecclesiastical subservience to Jerusalem. If it be suggested on the basis of Galatians 2: 10, 'they would that we should remember the poor', that this duty of almsgiving was specifically enjoined on Paul by James (possibly after the so-called Council of Jerusalem, if that is what Galatians 2: 1 ff. refers to, though whether this is so is neither agreed nor important), then it must be pointed out in reply that in this very context Paul indignantly denies that this 'duty' of almsgiving differed in any way from his established practice already. ('The poor', in this context, is practically a technical term, corresponding to 'the saints', and it refers to the local Jerusalem church).

It should not be forgotten that, as Acts 11: 29 shows, the

Church of Antioch, of which Paul was for years a member and a minister (see Acts 13: 1), had set the example for this type of 'inter-church aid' long before, when famine threatened the Church of Judea; and in view of Antioch's vigorous later reaction against teaching, emanating from Jerusalem, which seemed to them to run counter to the Gospel (Acts 15: 4), it is hard to treat this poor relief as in any sense evidence of conscious dependence and subordination.

In passing, it is probably true to say that not even James himself regarded this gift of aid as conferring any superior position on Jerusalem; it was but an application of the general Jewish principle of 'almsgiving' (one of the traditional four pillars of Judaism). By requesting and being ready to accept such gifts from Gentile believers, however, James was showing that he recognized them as 'brethren', and it was this recognition, rather than any claim to headship, that made his plea for poor relief so significant. So, too, Paul's great concern was, not that he would not be able to persuade the Gentiles to give – that was fairly easy – but lest he should fail to persuade the Jewish-Christian church to accept (Rom. 15: 31). Once they had accepted, it was not just that the reality of the faith of these new Christians had been proved in a way which the most suspicious or hardheaded Jew could not but see; it was a virtual admission of brotherhood, and it was this supremely that Paul sought.

THE COUNCIL OF JERUSALEM

Let us turn now to the 'Council of Jerusalem' itself. If the events that precede the 'Council' are carefully scrutinized, it will be seen that the mission of Paul and Barnabas to Jerusalem was rather like the 'confrontation' of Peter by Paul at Antioch (compare Acts 15: 1–2 and Gal. 2: 14). So far from involving a confession of inferiority, it was an assertion of equality in Christ. The 'truth of the Gospel' was the norm to which either side might appeal against the other, since to it both together must bow; but under its authority both sides stood on an equal footing. If it then be asked why Paul and Barnabas bothered to go to Jerusalem at all, instead of issuing some manifesto from Antioch condemning their sister-church of Jerusalem for 'heresy', the answer is obvious. They did not believe that what they had heard in Antioch, what these peripatetic rigorists were teaching, was in point of fact the faith that was held and taught at Jerusalem. It was in this confidence that they went there. Paul was neither in doubt about the Gospel itself (how could he be, who had received it by revelation? Gal. 1: 12) nor about the faith of the Jerusalem Church.

And indeed, even if Jerusalem had supported the Judaizers instead of condemning them roundly, as it duly did, it still would have been unthinkable for Paul and Barnabas, instead of going up to Jerusalem, to fire theological salvoes from Antioch, condemning the Jerusalem Church as apostate. Paul knew enough about the Jerusalem Church to know that it was founded firmly on the one Gospel. Paul opposed Peter's practice adopted at Antioch, because he knew it to be contrary to Peter's own beliefs, utterly inconsistent with the revelation that he had already received (Acts 10: 15). We need not doubt but that he would have dealt in the same way with the whole Jerusalem Church – to their face, in sorrow and love – had he felt it necessary. But the basis and presupposition of such dealing would have been Paul's firm conviction that he and Jerusalem were actually in full agreement as to the substance of the Gospel.

What Paul thought of outward 'pillars of the church' in the shape of apostles, we know from Galatians 2: 6. Paul was no respecter of persons, not even apostolic persons! But the use in Galatians 1: 18 of the verb *historēsai* (which probably should be translated 'to make inquiries of' rather than 'to visit') in connection with Peter, suggests what to Paul's mind may have been the true and unique value of the Twelve; namely, that they were unique eye-witnesses of the sayings and doings of Christ. In the nature of the case, there was no power here that could be transmitted to others. There was only eye-witness testimony that had to be borne, a testimony which, as the original 'witnesses' died, was recorded for subsequent generations in permanent form in the pages of the New Testament.

What the Jerusalem Church itself thought it was doing when James and the elders issued the 'decree' of Acts 15: 28–29 is an interesting question, but not strictly relevant here. Did James think that he was thus exercising the power of 'binding' and 'loosing', permitting and forbidding, as some Jerusalem rabbi might decide a point of Torah (compare Mt. 16: 19)? Was this his interpretation of the promised apostolic prerogative of 'sitting on twelve thrones, judging the twelve tribes of Israel' (Mt. 19: 28) – always assuming that James thought of himself as among the Twelve? We cannot say, but we ought to note that neither of these promises had in fact been made to him, who was no member of the first Twelve, nor indeed a disciple at all, it seems, until after the Resurrection (cf. Jn. 7: 5). Indeed, his claim to apostleship was no stronger than Paul's. We say that the attitude of James here, even if we could reconstruct it, would not be determinative, for we know of too many other instances where the Jerusalem church held views, or displayed attitudes, which were logically inconsistent with the very sayings of the Lord that they treasured (compare Mt. 28: 19 with Acts 11: 20); to take one example, it was not members of the Jerusalem Church who began the Gentile mission!

But the position is still further complicated by the fact that we are not even sure of the terms of the 'decree', still less of its interpretation (the manuscripts vary considerably here, as often in Acts, where we seem to have virtually two editions of one book). Was the decree dealing with moral matters, or only with ritual prohibitions? (For the details of this problem see the standard commentaries on Acts.) And was the issue viewed as a matter of faith, or only one of order? Were the regulations of the decree purely *ad hoc* arrangements to facilitate intercourse between Jew and Gentile in 'mixed' churches? To judge from the crisis at Antioch (Gal. 2: 12), this would be a very real problem in any 'mixed' church that met for frequent fellowship meals, whether or not these were specifically linked in men's minds with the Lord's supper.

Perhaps Paul may have wished in his heart that the Jerusalem church had gone even further than it did – although, as far as it went, even from their point of view, this decree was a 'loosing' rather than a 'binding'. But we know from Acts to what lengths Paul would go rather than antagonize this painfully slow and conservative body of people. (Were they in his mind when he wrote to the Corinthians about the 'weak brother'?) Nevertheless, it must have been with real joy that Paul and Barnabas went back, bringing the good news of the decision reached at this council of the local church of Jerusalem – for this was (it ought not to need saying, but it does) in no sense an 'ecumenical' council (Acts 15: 30f.). Yet the decision seems rapidly to have become a dead letter. Paul never refers to it in any of his Gentile correspondence. It seems, therefore, that, while he may have been prepared to use it in Jewish–Christian areas ('unto the Jews I became as a Jew', I Cor. 9: 20), he quietly ignored it elsewhere. Therefore he cannot have regarded it as having any real universal or permanent authority. It was not part of the word of the Gospel. Had he quoted it in the Epistle to the Galatians, it would have been a king-pin for his whole argument; but he does not even mention it. (This, however, may be because the epistle antedates the Jerusalem council, as some hold; so this argument is not entirely conclusive).

There was, then, no thought of any Gentile church being 'under Jerusalem'; and indeed, within a very short time, there was no longer even a possibility of this, for Jerusalem was sacked, and the old Jerusalem Church was gone for ever. The new church of Aelia Capitolina, the town that the Romans built where Jerusalem had stood, though interested in ancient rites and ways, was as Gentile as any. All the more is it strange, therefore, that scarcely more than a century later Rome should be claiming for herself a position that Jerusalem had never had, nor even, so far as we know, claimed; and, worse still, that she should be claiming for Peter a position that neither he, nor even James, had ever held in the period covered by the Acts.

CHAPTER SIX

THE CHURCH AS 'EXTENSION OF THE INCARNATION'

IT is probably true to say that the two most significant theological movements in our modern age have been those that are often called 'the rediscovery of the Bible' and 'the rediscovery of the Church'. Whether these two movements are in conflict at any point will be considered below. Enough here to say that both are natural reactions to the atomistic individualism and subjectivism of the age that immediately preceded, with its barren critical approach to the Bible and its humanistic concepts of the Church. There is perhaps a further reason for their emergence in the felt loneliness of modern man, in his sense of weakness and inadequacy with great destructive nuclear forces poised in uneasy equilibrium about him. He desperately craves for love, for fellowship, for security, for belongingness, all of which he feels that he has lost in our modern society. Even the old and deep stability of the family unit is threatened. Here, above all, in the midst of a harsh, impersonal, ruthless world that counts population in hundreds of millions, man longs to find another world where the individual can still matter.

All these things are commonplaces, which are mentioned here for neither praise nor blame, but purely in order to analyse our situation and explain why men's thoughts should in our day have turned back to the concept of the Church as they had not for centuries before. It is but a further illustration of the fact that, while all theological doctrines are eternally relevant, yet different ages become conscious of different doctrines as having special relevance to prevailing needs. What is true of doctrines is also, as we said earlier, true of biblical images and metaphors; each age of history has found particular relevance in one or another facet of the truth.

Now, we have no reason to doubt that this process is of God, who prepared the way for Christ's coming by ordering the historical circumstances and moulding the thought-life of the first-century Graeco-Roman world. But we need to remember the inevitably one-sided nature of this present-day emphasis, and to correct it carefully by the other aspects of the many-sided teaching of Scripture, lest we mistake part of the truth for the whole; as we said before.

DANGERS OF THIS DOCTRINE

Further, while the movement for rediscovering the Church may thus be of God, that does not guarantee that fallen man (and all churchmen are such) will not move in the wrong direction. He feels intensely that he needs a doctrine of the Church, and this is true; but what if he should embrace wrong doctrine, doctrine which, for all its use of Scripture, is unbiblical in substance? Then his last state is worse than his first, for he has fled for security to error, not truth. That there is such a possibility should not surprise us – if we take the doctrine of the Fall seriously. We are all in continual danger of misinterpreting the guidance of God, and there is no such effective enemy of the best as the good, or the not too bad. What if the Church itself today become a 'graven image', and men bow down and worship it? What if frightening new circumstances make men forget some of the deepest spiritual insights of the Reformation? What if some at least of the modern readiness for reunion with unreformed churches springs from a faulty doctrine of the Church? (That there is also a 'reforming movement' within Rome, we do not deny; but the thoughtful reader of, say, Hans Küng's books will realize that this movement within Rome springs from the revival of biblical studies, not from ecclesiology, though it may yet make its greatest impact there. We wait to see.)

In one sense, there is nothing new in the modern movement; it but expresses the craving of the human heart for a voice of authority. We all believe in the voice of God, and the authority of God. But where may we hear it? He who will not have a Bible must needs have a church to guide him. Now, of course, the Bible will always point to the Christ of the Bible (and the Church of the Bible too); but will the Church always point to the Christ of the Bible? History and experience say 'no' – and many modern scholars would also say 'no', quite deliberately. The Church, they say, will point to the Christ of the Church; for He is the only Christ we have. If we ask whether there is not a possible conflict between the Christ of the Church and the Christ of the Bible, they will deny it at once; there is no possibility of any contradiction, they say, because the Church gave us the Bible, and we cannot now see Christ for ourselves, but only through the primitive Church's eyes. If we object that this might at the last lead to idolatry, to the worship of the Church instead of the Christ, they say in reply: but the Church is His Body, the continuation of the Incarnation.

Nowadays, there are scholars who quarrel with this, not because they feel it goes too far, but because they feel that it does not go far enough (John Knox, for instance, in his book *The Church and the Reality of Christ*). The Church they tell us, *is* the meaning of the Christ-event, whole and entire; when we say 'we have only the Church', that is all we need to say.

A HOUSE OF STRAW

From this, the evangelical turns away bewildered. It seems to him another faith. The underlying reason he sees clearly enough; whether it be the result of following Bultmann or only Dibelius, their rejection of the evidence of Scripture (or their re-interpretation of it in such 'mythological' terms that it becomes merely a medium for recording insights and attitudes of the early Christian Church, rather than an account of what Jesus really did and taught), leaves such men with no other alternative to unbelief. But it is a house of straw; all that is now needed is to question the authority of the Church, to question the reliability of its 'memory' and view of things, and there is nothing to shelter us from the bleak winds of change, by which we shall soon find the remains of our faith wholly blown away. This straw-house theology is nothing other than the twentieth-century equivalent of what Mahaffy used to call, with reference to Hellenism, 'failure of nerve'. To trust in a church, whether early or contemporary, is neither safe nor biblical.

Let us look briefly at the supposed biblical nature of this claim that the Church is the 'extension of the Incarnation', for, once it is allowed, it is a closed world. All arguments are circular, and, since this is a 'position of faith', nothing save loss of faith in the object of faith (which in this case is a wrong image of the Church) can lead men out of it. Any who have dealt with Roman Catholics who have had religious questionings have witnessed something of the agony involved in such a 'way out', and the casualties too.

This is, in fact, a good example of illegitimate extension of metaphor. True, the New Testament again and again (most clearly in the Pauline epistles) describes the Church as the Body of Christ, as we have seen. But it never describes the Church as the continuation of the Incarnation (which it sees as unique and once-for-all), still less as part of the Incarnation, or as the Incarnation itself. In the New Testament the use of the metaphor of 'the body' is carefully limited in its application.* We are the Body, in relation to Christ's headship. We are the limbs of the Body in relation to one another, and in functioning as a corporate whole. We are His Body, as indwelt by the Holy Spirit. But Scripture goes no further than this; and therefore neither should we. The Bible nowhere says that he who has seen the Church has seen Christ, though it does say that Christ may and must be manifested in and through the Church to the world around. But this is a different point.

The final result of this erroneous approach is to identify

* See E. Best: *One Body in Christ* (London, 1955).

the Church with Christ. When we enter the realm of the Atonement, this becomes particularly mischievous; for it leads to the notion that we in Christ may atone for our sins by something that we ourselves do. This is nothing other than the old error from which, by the grace of God, our spiritual forefathers broke free at the Reformation; and are we to be entangled with the same 'yoke of bondage' again?

As for saying that the Church gave us the Bible, and that therefore Bible and Church cannot be opposed to one another, this is plain nonsense, unless we redefine 'church' in such a way that it utterly loses its meaning. True, the New Testament represents the witness of the first apostolic generation to the sayings and doings of Christ. But to this generation unique promises had been made by Christ with this end in view (Jn. 14: 26). It is as witnesses of the event of Christ, not as a Church, that the apostles are significant (Acts 5: 32). True, we, like the crowds at Pentecost, must believe 'through their word' (Jn. 17: 20): we must accept the apostolic testimony to Jesus. But we accept it because we believe it to be true, and because we believe them to be credible witnesses; not because they are apostles, still less because they are the Church. Further, all believers since then have been dependent on the unique witness of this one apostolic generation, the one generation whose members were contemporaries and eye-witnesses of Jesus. This is so greatly and so often stressed in the New Testament that it should hardly need emphasis again (see for example, Acts 2: 32).

At the end of the New Testament period, there was a felt need to commit this irreplaceable evidence, so fragile in its nature now that the first generation was passing away, to the permanent record of writing (II Pet. 1: 15). That the whole of the subsequent Church recognized this is shown by the very existence of the Canon of the New Testament.

This was not the result of an arbitrary decision by the Church, but the fruit of a scrutiny based on the one question: which books can be shown to have been written by apostles, or at least to have emanated from the inner circle of this unique first generation? Other books there were in plenty, written within the Church and from the midst of its common life, with no taint of heresy (as for example the Epistle of Barnabas, or 'The Shepherd'). But, though they might enjoy a fleeting popularity in local areas, they could not pass this searching test, and so were dropped into obscurity. The Church, in point of fact, was already scrutinizing itself in the light of what we may now call the Scripture. That which was written in the apostolic documents was the preached word of the Gospel, the spoken, creative, word that had called the Church into being. If the Church was to be true to itself, it must not transgress that word. But the history of the early Church is that it did transgress it. Many of its developed practices and attitudes were contrary to the great principles of the Bible to which it paid such ready lip-service. This again may grieve, but should not surprise us, if we remember the doctrine of the Fall. And we are a Church of fallen men still.

Even the personification of the Church as a 'she' can be dangerous, for it can bring with it a whole cluster of false (though sentimentally attractive) ideas. If we speak of 'Mother Church' for instance, we are on very dangerous ground. II John 13 is far too slender evidence to justify a concept that finds no clear statement in the New Testament. What is this Church that stands above and over against us, functioning as our spiritual Mother? We who are joined to Christ are the Church. Besides us, there is at the moment on earth no other Church of God. A healthy commonsense attitude of this kind is not only more in accord with the biblical facts, but will also keep us from many forms of false mysticism.

It is interesting that it is the concept of the Body that has dominated our age, and not that of the Bride (which was perhaps the dominant image in the Middle Ages), or the Temple, or the Vine, or any of the other biblical images. Doubtless any other of these would have had its own inherent dangers; but, as these dangers are not actual, we need not dwell on them. Perhaps one reason why the Body metaphor appeals to us so much is that we are living in a highly complex society, where we realize more and more the utter impossibility in our modern world of any man 'living unto himself' (Rom. 14: 7), even in the sociological sense. Undoubtedly, however, a major factor is that the pioneers of the modern revival of the doctrine of the Church have been Roman and Anglo-Catholic theologians, to whom the thought of the Church as organically one with Christ is of fundamental importance. Such theologians treat the Body-metaphor, not as an image on the same level as other images, but as having ontological status, and therefore as admitting of extension and extrapolation beyond the biblical limits, and witnessing to the participation of the Church in various qualities and actions of its Lord which the Bible regard as peculiarly His, not shared by any sinful men. So Roman theologians argue that the Church, as Christ's body, possesses infallibility in its teaching, and both Romans and Anglo-Catholics argue (in different senses) for the Church's participation with Christ in offering to the Father the atoning sacrifice of Calvary, through the Eucharist. The latter of these unhappy aberrations is permeating a great deal of sacramental theology even in the churches of the Reformation at the present time.

CHAPTER SEVEN

SOME SPECIFIC PROBLEMS

So far we have dealt in theological generalities, but what are we to make of the situation immediately before us? What are the implications of the present divided state of Christendom? The late Archbishop Temple is reported to have said that he believed in one catholic and apostolic church, and sincerely regretted that it did not at present exist! The remark was of course jocular, but it expresses a real problem. Where is the Church of God, of which we have been talking? Where does our own particular church fit into the above analysis?

First, we shall gladly recognize in our local church or congregation the local expression of the 'Body of Christ' as far as we are concerned – without, however, denying the equal right of our Christian brother of another denomination to feel the same about his place of worship, or rather about those who meet there. We shall not regard the existence of separate places of meeting as in itself a breach of unity, any more than the numerous 'house-churches' of the New Testament were regarded as a breach of the total Christian body in one place. Mutual recognition is clearly the first need; we shall think more of this in the next chapter. At this local level, then, and within our own particular congregation of Christ's flock, we shall endeavour to keep the unity of the Spirit, to avoid schism and division, and to live in mutual love, tolerance, and forbearance.

So far, so good; the bond of unity is one of new life in Christ, shared together. But it is also a 'confessional' bond, based on the common acceptance of biblical truth. What, then, if the teaching in our local group does not correspond to the biblical pattern? This is a vexed question; the Bible does not give us any direct help here. All we can say is that, in the New Testament, there is no thought of the Christian leaving his local church because he disagrees with its doctrine. That is not because, in New Testament days, they felt – as we often tend to do – that differences of theology are nothing more than difference of 'emphasis'. To read Paul's violent explosion in face of Peter at Antioch (Gal. 2: 14) is to realize how far the New Testament Church was from our 'eirenic', and often, indeed, compromising, approach. John was the 'apostle of love', but he tells us trenchantly that those who fail to share the common faith of 'Christ come in the flesh' must be shunned (II Jn. 11). Paul's language to and of the Judaizers is stronger still (Gal. 5: 12, Phil. 3: 2). Yet all these, on both sides, claimed to be fellow-members of the Body of Christ. Peter was of course a 'foundation member', and the reason that Paul attacked him so violently was that he knew him to be a brother in error – which was bad – and a brother acting against his own conscience and spiritual knowledge – which was even worse. But when Paul denies that the Judaizers are preaching the Gospel at all (Gal 1: 6f.), that comes perilously near to denying them a place in Christ. Paul thinks of Christian unity as a unity in the common enjoyment of the fruits of a common Gospel. It is quite clear what John thought about those who were deep in christological heresy; they did not 'belong' to the Body, any more than did Simon Magus (see Acts 8: 21; I Jn. 2: 19).

All of this we say, not because we wish to sit in judgment on any of our brethren, but to show that the New Testament pioneers cared intensely for theological orthodoxy; they had no slipshod easy approach that minimized differences. The reason why the apostolic church was able to remain 'united' did not lie in doctrinal compromise, wherever else it lay.

Nor was it the case that the churches of New Testament days were so perfect in morals that there was no temptation to leave them on that account. How many modern Christians could have endured the appalling immorality present in the Corinthian Church? or the moral blindness that not only condoned, but actually boasted of such things (I Cor.

5: 1f.)? For the matter of that, how many Anglicans could have endured their forms of worship, week by week? or attended their Lord's Supper with an easy conscience? Yet, while we find vigorous protest and reaction, on the basis of evangelical truth, while we even find Christian controversy, there is no mention of any separatist group 'hiving off'; that is unthinkable, if the Body is one. Again, the description of the churches of Asia in Rev. 2 and 3 is a picture of almost unrelieved gloom. Not only are there moral outrages, as at Corinth, but there is heresy, too, even in the teaching of the local church. Again, there is strong protest. There is no acceptance of Gnostic speculation as 'another emphasis', from which the rest may learn something! But there is no thought of leaving the church. The word of God to those in difficult circumstances is simply hold fast (Rev. 2: 25).

Now (if I may illustrate from an Anglican viewpoint), we all know with our heads what is ordinarily the duty of the Anglican churchman, once he sees his regular place of meeting, his parish church, as being the local expression of the Body of Christ; he must attend it. The New Testament knows nothing of 'liking' a church; but it does know of 'love of the brethren' (I Jn. 3: 14). This is something great enough to cover a multitude of personal likes and dislikes. But what if it is felt that biblical truth is being compromised by what is being taught in the parish church? Scripture again is plain; one may and should protest, but one is given no encouragement to leave. To fail to make one's own position clear is not, of course, love; it is rather lack of faithfulness to the truth, and a wanton condoning of error. But one can protest without packing one's bags.

But, in point of fact, we all know what usually happens in such cases in every large centre of population. The person or family involved will leave and join forces with some other local Anglican church, where the worship conducted and the doctrine taught is of a different character. And yet he or she will not have left the Anglican fold, as such.

What are we to make of this anomalous situation? It is

true that in New Testament times there seems to have been no uniformity of 'use' in worship. But we have seen that Paul appeals again and again to unity of doctrine. Can we honestly do this, faced with such a divergence? And, if not, in what sense do these two places of worship envisaged above (both Anglican) possess unity at all? They have an organizational unity, to be sure, but what have they more? They share a common life in Christ (for this we can at once admit gladly without introducing questions of correctness and error in doctrine, or at any rate in secondary matters of doctrine). But do not all those who are in Christ already share this, from Roman Catholic to Plymouth Brother, if truly born again into an enjoyment of Christ's salvation? Is it that the Anglican Church is a 'local' rather than a 'confessional' group? This idea will not do for several reasons, even if it was originally true. (In any case, there is no reason why the 'local' concept should be in conflict with the 'confessional'.) Let us explain just why this view is inadequate.

THE ANGLICAN COMMUNION

Firstly, we have taken the Church of England overseas, at first by chaplaincy work among British people, then by missionary outreach. What, now, of the Anglican churches of Asia or Africa? We cannot explain them simply as 'local expressions' of Christ's Body. Secondly, there are other denominations who meet in England and elsewhere, and are equally 'local expressions' of the Body of Christ. The small group of original English Roman Catholics (as distinct from immigrant acquisitions later) have just as good a claim as we have here.

Are we then a 'confessional' church in the narrower sense, not just as 'confessing' Christ (for all Christians everywhere do that), but as being bound together by certain confessional formulae, a group of biblical insights which we feel to be basic? We would gladly believe this. Evangelicals yield hearty assent to the Thirty-Nine Articles,

77

for instance, as being biblical and Reformed, and yet (or, therefore) catholic, preserving universal truth. We find the understanding of ministry, church, and sacraments, which they offer, to be perfectly in accord with biblical teaching, and we assent to it with our whole hearts. We freely recognize their limitations of language and range, but they seem to us to express well the mind of the 'Reforming Fathers' of the Church of England, and we judge that in these matters our Reformers had the mind of Christ. We have no doubt that the Articles were intended to, and in fact do, set forth the 'confessional position' of Anglicanism. But, for a long time now, we have witnessed in Anglicanism a steady retreat from Reformation insights. Many of our brethren have given only reluctant 'general assent' to the Articles; and now there is a growing move to abolish or at least modify them. But what then will have happened to our 'confessional unity'?

Is it that we are a church that has uniformity of worship? This was undoubtedly in the mind of the Edwardine and Elizabethan Reformers, and the Caroline divines did not intend anything different, whether their motive was purely theological or partly political. Here again, we yield hearty assent. We find in the Prayer Book of 1662 nothing that is not capable of a biblical interpretation; and we wish nothing more than that our fellow-churchmen would abide by its services and regulations. But we find bewildering variety of use, with continual innovations; and, while we are no foe to innovation, it seems to us that many of these are further deliberate retreats from the spiritual insights of the Reformation, and thus, in our eyes, from Gospel truth. Again, what has happened to our 'Confessional' Anglican Church? For, if both Prayer Book and Articles are now gone, how can we define Anglican doctrine as being the same everywhere? Indeed, how can we define it at all? If it be but that of the historic creeds, then that is the doctrine of all Christians, and we have left the narrower 'confessional' area altogether.

78

When we approach 'Pan-Denominationalism' the position is even more confused. What, for example, is this 'Anglicanism' to which Episcopalians are nowadays often asked to pledge their loyalties? If the term meant the position of all Christians who lived in England, it would at least have meaning. If it meant the position of a group of Christians with a common 'Confession' in the narrower sense (like the Thirty-Nine Articles) it would at least make sense. If all used a common Prayer Book, the term would have some descriptive content. But now all that can be said is that Anglicanism is a group of 'churches' over the world, connected by a common historical origin, all having set forms of worship (though these differ greatly) and all having bishops (though Angelicans differ greatly among themselves in their understanding of the origin and significance of this office). As for the Articles, they mean little to some Anglican churches outside of England, and they now have virtually nothing to do with this common bond.

The only other possible explanation of 'Anglicanism' would be to say (as is often said) that all Anglicans have 'sacramental unity'. But a little thought will show that this is a descriptive statement of a fact, not a theological pronouncement. It is but to say that – although I disagree with another, and he disagrees with me; although I believe his views to be unbiblical and he believes mine to be untraditional – we yet meet together at the Lord's Table as redeemed sinners. But what is there *Anglican* in this? Is not this in the Bible the pattern for all Christians? If Anglicanism already contains a breadth of doctrine that stretches virtually from Rome to Geneva, and if Reformed and Anglo-Catholic can meet together now in the Church of England at a common Lord's Table, why cannot Presbyterian and Anglican enjoy inter-communion at once? Why wait for some form of 'organic' church union, which, after all, is only administrative? If it be answered that it would be impossible for the Presbyterian to do this, until his theology was in full accord with Anglican theology, the question could be asked: which Anglican theology? There are already men within the Anglican Communion whose views on ministry and sacraments are essentially his, and whose views on episcopacy would not differ much, if at all, from those of the great Reformed theologians. What is virtually being said to non-Anglican Protestant brethren is: when Anglicans communicate together, it is all right; but if you were to communicate with Anglicans and Anglicans with you, it would be wrong. But does such a position make sense?

AN EVANGELICAL ANGLICAN VIEW

No: there is no logical or theological criterion whatsoever that we may use to discern the bounds and limits of the so-called 'Anglican Communion', other than the words of the old song that ran 'We're here because we're here'; and there we must leave it. And this is not something that we either may boast of, or need repent of. It is simply a fact that must be accepted, as the basis on which we must live and work. We do not glory in the 'comprehensiveness' of the Anglican Communion at all. We grieve at the unbiblical understandings of episcopate, church, ministry and sacraments that we see creeping in more and more. Worse still, we find that we are now asked, as 'good Anglicans', to assent to things which our conscience denies; and we find that statements of the 'Anglican position', put forward in the course of reunion negotiations, do not correspond either with historic 'confessional Anglicanism' or with our own convictions. Is it any wonder that we feel at times far closer to our likeminded brethren in other denominational bodies than we do to some of our fellow-Anglicans?

The New Testament speaks of 'members of Christ'. It is we who speak of 'church members'. There is a world of difference. We are prepared to recognize Anglicans who differ from us as brethren in Christ. In many places, even as it is, with variety of usage, we are prepared to see them worship in ways which we cannot approve as biblical. But we cannot accept their worship as the 'norm'. Further, we think it retrograde that men, in their desire for unity, should urge us to be 'more Anglican first'. Which sort of Anglicanism do they mean? and why should they try to intensify cleavages which to us seem to rest on non-biblical interpretations of episcopate and ministry? Why should they try to destroy what measure of unity is there already, created by the common life in Christ, in the bond of the common Spirit? Why should Christians ever be 'denomination-conscious'? But this we shall consider briefly in the next chapter. Enough to say here that it is folly to assume that every member of the Anglican Communion is Anglican because he thinks Anglicanism the 'best of all ways'. Such a thought was far from the mind of the Reformers. To them, Anglicanism was a biblical way, but neither they nor their successors for centuries ever condemned Continental Reformers who took different ways.

Most men are Anglicans, in the Old World at least, simply because of the accidents of birth and circumstance – just as all Christians at Corinth were members of the Corinthian Church, and most Scots are Presbyterians. True, a man's later spiritual experiences commonly come to him through the church in which he grew up; and no doubt he comes to love its forms of worship, and even its characteristic styles of church architecture. But these are not theological fundamentals. He is there: God has set him there, by overruling his circumstances; and there he will live and work in the fellowship of the local expression of the Body of Christ. Here he is, and here he will stay, though he will not be silent when he feels the truth of the Gospel is at stake. But to ask him to glorify and sing the praise of 'Anglicanism' in its present state is to ask him to do what is spiritually unrealistic, and theologically impossible.

CHAPTER EIGHT

THE REUNION OF THE CHURCH

Now, if what we have said so far is true, the Church as the Body of Christ has never been divided, and cannot be divided. Its unity is a gift of the Spirit. But it must be preserved, in large as well as in small (Eph. 4: 3), by our living at peace with our fellow-Christians. Its unity is a unity of faith, a unity of loyalty to one Lord, a unity of recognition of one another as brethren. It is something that, by the gift of the Spirit, we feel within our hearts now, and express by 'unfeigned love of the brethren' (I Peter 1: 22). It is not, in the New Testament, expressed in any form of organic connection. Nor does it imply identity of outlook or practice, or even like forms of worship. Even the system of rule in the Church seems to have been fluid in those days: it was not till centuries later that uniformity of government and worship became a 'canon'. It is, we presume, for this sort of unity that the Lord was praying in John 17: 11–21. He was asking that the same inner unity of thought, will, and purpose, as exists between His Father and Himself in the essential unity of the Godhead might be realized among the little group of His disciples. This was the inner spiritual unity which would convince the world, as nothing else would do, that Christ's mission was indeed of God (Jn. 17: 21).

Put in a nutshell, the truth is this. We have no need to show God the unity of the Church, for He created it. We should have no need to convince the Christian of the unity of the Church, for he experiences and knows it by the working of the Holy Spirit in his heart. But the world outside needs to know and be shown it, lest it should mistake the Church for just one more human society, with its quarrels and splits and divisions and all else that marks that which is thoroughly earthly.

Further, in case we do not yet understand the nature of this unity which will convince the world, the Lord in a very similar saying defines it as love: 'By this shall all men know that ye are my disciples, if ye have love one to another' (Jn. 13: 35; the thought is expressed frequently elsewhere in both John's Gospel and his epistles). This is the unity that will convince the world – a oneness of love, that springs from a sense of mutual 'belongingness' to Christ. This is precisely the love that was manifested among the believers in Paul's day, in and under and through some of the cross-currents and differences of view to which we have called attention above. This was the love which manifested itself, for instance, in the 'inter-church aid' sent by the Gentile churches to Jerusalem, or in Jerusalem's genuine joy to hear that the Gentiles were turning to God, even if they found it hard to agree with, and utterly impossible to understand, the fiery little Apostle of the Gentiles.

For the Lord's words in John 17 were clearly, from the context, not spoken with reference to the small immediate circle of the Lord's disciples alone: otherwise we might restrict their reference to local churches in our day, and find refuge from the problems of denominationalism in some form of congregationalism (using that word in an isolationist sense). 'Neither pray I for these alone, but for them also which shall believe on me through their word; That they all may be one', is clearly a reference to the whole Body of Christ. Therefore, this same inner unity, expressing itself in love, was to be the mark, not only of the local congregation, but also of the whole Church of God.

So far, all would agree; but now comes a divergence of views. How should this love, this inner existent unity, be best expressed and manifested to the world?

We have already observed that our age has been described as the age of both the 'rediscovery of the Bible' and the 'rediscovery of the Church', and we can be profoundly grateful for both of these movements, in so far as they mark a healthy reaction against the humanistic liberalism and optimism of the generations immediately preceding. The rapid spread of ecumenical ideas, the great concept of a united 'world Church', is also a new phenomenon of our days. The change in attitude, both outside and inside Rome, has been stupefying. Most of us in the Protestant world have grown up in the midst of an ecumenical age, and therefore we are not conscious of any change in traditional Protestant attitudes, unless we have chanced to read controversial 'denominational' books of a century ago. But to realize the distance travelled one has only to read a book like *From Uniformity to Unity* (edited by Geoffrey Nuttall and Owen Chadwick: London, 1962). And *The Council and Reunion* by Hans Küng (Eng. tr., London, 1961) will be an eye-opener to those who have not been following the 'swing' within Rome. What is really happening? Clearly, some aspects of this move are conditioned by the age in which we live. But, equally clearly, the circumstances of the world are in the hand of God, so that, in saying this, we are not saying that this is not of God. Furthermore, instead of hate and suspicion in many places, there has come love and an attempt to understand. Love, patience, and gentleness in dealing with each other are aspects of the 'fruit of the Spirit', and the Lord pointed to this as an infallible test of the presence and working of the Spirit (Mat. 7: 16). There is a new atmosphere everywhere; this thing is clearly of God.

Or is it? Not all Christians would agree that it is – or rather, they might agree that this impulse is of God without agreeing that every form that it takes is therefore also of God. For the question is: in what way should the Church of God express its real unity? Is this unity denied or obscured by the existence of the 'denominations' or no? If it is, then we must clearly work for the abolition of all denominational barriers. If not, then we must find other means and areas of life for expressing this truth.

One group of Christians will say that they cannot see that denominations in themselves are sinful, though, certainly, they may make for administrative confusion; and if administrative efficiency is really one of the marks of the Church, then we had better work for the abolishing of denominations, in the interests of efficient centralized administration, at once. But if organizational unity has nothing to do with the unity of the Church, why should we worry? Why should it be thought a stumbling-block that we have various methods of church government and various forms of worship? Are not these all different expressions of the manifold richness of the Gospel, a guarantee that different souls will find in different places that for which they crave, and at the same time a safeguard, lest in our human folly we tie the grace of God to set forms of our own choosing? Christians holding such views will often point out that, as it is, we have not attained a spiritual unity within our respective denominations. They may also say that, in point of fact, we are even now closer to like-minded Christians in other denominations than to some folk in our own. How then, they will ask, can the union of great denominations promote the true inner unity of the Spirit?

Such Christians may already be perfectly ready to recognize their fellow-Christians in other groups as brethren, to receive them at the Lord's Table, and to interchange ministry with them: although they may find themselves restricted in the actual practice of all these things by the slower working of ecclesiastical authority. But, so far as they are concerned, there is no barrier between them now. What more can 'physical' reunion give them? They will point to great movements like the Keswick Convention in England, or the great campaigns conducted by Dr Billy Graham, in which Christians of every denomination cooperate, as examples of the present enjoyment of spiritual unity, and the manifestation of Christian love to the world. Countless other projects, both on the evangelistic and the social side, could be instanced. Christians taking this view of things may well wish that such activity could be extended and continued, but this is usually as far as they will go. Overlapping of any kind, whether in evangelism or pastoral responsibility, they deplore, and would gladly welcome any arrangements that would obviate it. But to their mind this seems to be an argument for 'comity' more than for organic union.

Such men are suspicious lest we try to realize a spiritual goal by fleshly methods – lest endless great conferences lead to the production of some vast administrative machine, the effect of which will be to quench the Holy Spirit by bureaucracy. Few of them now fear the emergence of some steam-rollering 'super-church' which might attempt to exercise repressive powers over minorities. But they do fear the opportunities created by large-scale unions for the ambition of sinful man, and for 'power politics' in theology and church life. Those who feel thus normally regard much of the discussion about organic reunion as waste of time, a turning of men's minds away from the primary duty of the Church, the duty to evangelize and teach, and a diverting of their interest and energy to a secondary concern.

Now, the thoughtful man will realize that there is much truth in all that they say, and take it into account in his own deliberations. But it is not the whole truth; for, while it is perfectly true that to join two sickly denominations together will not make a healthier group (though it may make a group comparatively more efficient in administration, and to that extent just a little more effective in evangelism and pastoral ministry), yet the whole concept of the 'denomination' is palpably something quite foreign to Scripture, as well as to the life and experience of the Church of the New Testament.

A 'FEDERATION' OF CHURCHES?

There does not seem to be anything wrong with there being a 'Church of England' – in England. It does, however, seem wrong that there should be a Church of England and a Methodist Church, and a Presbyterian Church, and so forth, all in England. Nor does it seem right that there should be a Church of England – or of Scotland, for the matter of that – in other parts of the world. The need to eliminate this anomaly is a cogent reason for seeking union of some sort. This is, of course, quite distinct from the question of whether the combined church would be more efficient or not, or even whether it would necessarily be any more spiritually minded than its present components, taken individually, are. What relationship such a united church would later have to the churches of other areas is another question, which can well wait; there certainly seems no need that there should be any form of organic union between united area churches, still less subservience of any one to another.

Why there should not be some kind of federation of independent local churches, mutually recognizing one another, and with no necessary uniformity, is a question as yet unanswered. The western idea of church union has always been much more rigid than the eastern, which, as it seems, would be satisfied by some such system. Provided the great biblical principles of episcopacy (oversight), and theological balance of worship, are accepted in principle, there is no reason to expect or require that these should necessarily be embodied in our Anglican type of bishop, or even our Anglican type of Prayer Book.

Clearly, the Lord's prayer for unity for His followers, and His injunction that we show ourselves to be His disciples by the display of love to one another, are not answered and fulfilled in the present system of denominations – although it could be argued that it is not 'denominations' that are to be deplored, but rather the 'denominationalism' that thrives in these circumstances, with all its attendant evils. It is true that the Lord may have directed His words on unity specifically to the petty personal quarrels of the disciples. It is also true that the words were spoken long before the rise of anything even remotely similar to 'denominations' in the Church. But he would be a bold man who affirmed that the Lord did not have such divisions in mind. For it is undeniable that such divisions do give sin more scope.

This, however, is far from meaning that reunion is so

important that we must have it at any price. Outward union is only of value if it corresponds to a true spiritual unity in the Gospel. In other words, there are times when truth is more important than union. We may not sacrifice biblical principles for some sort of 'shotgun marriage' of denominations. In particular, it is important that any proposed union take place on the ground of biblical truth, and be based on confessional statements which express that truth as adequately as, in their day, the Thirty-Nine Articles and the Book of Common Prayer expressed it for Anglicanism. It is important too, that those of other than Anglican background should not be given a false idea of 'Anglican' views of episcopate, ministry, and sacraments. We do not deny that unreformed interpretations exist, and are more common today than they were; but they cannot claim either to be the historic Anglican views, as expressed in our formularies, or to be anything like universally held. For these interpretations to masquerade as normative 'Anglicanism' can only create the acutest of difficulties both for Anglicans themselves and for those of other bodies with whom they converse and negotiate.

With regard to the wider issue of relations with the Church of Rome, it is perhaps too early to speak, although all will welcome the evident change in Rome's attitude. Yet it would seem as if any hope of further steps is still distant, although nothing is impossible to God. What we witness in the Church of Rome today is a very complex movement. No doubt, there is in it the striving of the Holy Ghost, as amongst us. There is also the revival of biblical studies within that church, the full impact of which is only reaching the main body of seminaries now, and will therefore only reach the average church member in the next generation. But there is also alongside of this an impatience with authority, and, in biblical studies, a reaction towards that 'liberalism' and 'modernism' which popes might condemn, but could not repress. As in the sixteenth century, so today, movements of 'reformation' produce their corresponding 'antinomianism'.

Thus, perhaps like our own sixteenth-century Reformation, what is going on is a very complex business, and we find it hard to see or say that every aspect is of God, though we know that God will overrule. At present, it is hard, in spite of Küng, to see that Rome visualizes those outside as more than 'separated brethren' and reunion as anything more than their 'returning to the Church'. Admittedly, there are Roman Catholics who are prepared increasingly to reform their church; and perhaps one of the most significant battles of its history is being waged within the Roman Church at this time, over the question as to the exact relation between Scripture and Tradition. We wish them well. We pray that they may be rightly guided into a truly biblical position. But, until they are, we may not compromise and sacrifice biblical truth by talking lightly and foolishly of 'reunion'.

What further grieves us is that there is a real danger of Protestants actively seeking a 'reunion' with Rome on other than biblical grounds. If such a reunion were seriously contemplated by the majority, our position would indeed become grievous. We see and hear those who are 'pillars of the church' in men's eyes making statements which are not, to us, in accord with Scripture. If they think that they describe our position, they are deceiving themselves, as well as those of the Church of Rome, who doubtless note such statements. Until and unless the Church of Rome is prepared to subject all tradition, however hallowed and venerated, to the scrutiny of God's Word, and jettison that which is plainly repugnant to it, we have no desire for reunion whatsoever. We will gladly acknowledge them as brethren in Christ, if their faith is in Christ alone for salvation. But we must bluntly say (as we might feel we had to say of some in our own 'communion', to use another biblical word in a non-biblical way) that we consider them grievously mistaken brethren, and we think that their teaching is not only erroneous, but is also leading others into error. More, we see their error to be growing progressively worse. New unbiblical doctrines are one after another being introduced.

When and how is this to end, save in full submission to the Word of God? We live in great days, yes: and God is at work. But let us be sure that any union envisaged is the outworking of the unity of the Spirit, and not some expedient of man which justifies error, and glorifies organizational tidiness, rather than honouring God's truth.

CALLED TO SERVE

MINISTRY AND MINISTERS IN THE CHURCH

by

MICHAEL GREEN

CONTENTS

CHRONOLOGICAL GUIDE

to some of the Patristic material mentioned in this book

Clement of Rome: wrote his letter to the Corinthians *c.* A.D. 96.

Ignatius: bishop of Antioch, wrote to several Asian Churches, and was martyred in Rome *c.* A.D. 107.

The Didache: a short early Christian treatise on morals and church practice. Although the author, date and place of origin are unknown, recent scholarship favours a date in the later first or early second century A.D.

Polycarp: bishop of Smyrna, wrote a letter to the Philippians, and was martyred in Smyrna A.D. 155.

Justin: a Christian philosopher and apologist, martyred *c.* A.D. 165 in Rome.

Hermas: an early second-century Roman writer.

Hegesippus: a Jewish Christian of the second century who wrote church history; known only in quotations.

Montanism: a prophetic movement led by Montanus and two prophetesses towards the end of the second century; it provided a serious challenge to catholic Christianity.

Clement of Alexandria: distinguished theologian and author, died *c.* A.D. 215.

Origen: succeeded Clement at Alexandria, died *c.* A.D. 254.

Tertullian: a Roman African lawyer and prolific author, died *c.* A.D. 220.

Cyprian: bishop of Carthage, died *c.* A.D. 258.

Pseudo-Clementines: writings of the second or third centuries A.D. wrongly ascribed to Clement of Rome.

Eusebius: bishop of Caesarea and 'father of church history', died *c.* A.D. 340.

Apostolic Constitutions: a manual of church order of the fourth century, but incorporating earlier material.

Epiphanius: bishop of Salamis and dogmatician, died A.D. 403.

Chrysostom: bishop of Constantinople and theologian, died A.D. 407.

Jerome: ascetic and learned biblical scholar, died A.D. 420.

Augustine: bishop of Hippo, theologian, and author, died A.D. 430.

CHAPTER I

THE MINISTRY OF JESUS

JESUS' whole ministry was one of service. This is clearly shown both by the general tenor of the Gospel narrative, and by many specific utterances. Thus, when approaching the climax of His ministry at Jerusalem, Jesus declared: 'The Son of Man came not to be served but to serve, and to give His life as a ransom for many' (Mk. 10: 45). He made it very clear, in the verses immediately preceding these words, that service was to be the hallmark of all Christian ministry. In contrast to worldly rulers, preoccupied with status and authority, 'It shall not', He said, 'be so among you; but whoever would be great among you must be your servant, and whoever would be first among you must be slave of all.'

This lesson of the royalty of service must have been indelibly imprinted on the minds of the disciples by what happened at the Last Supper. In the Middle East, feet quickly get hot and dusty, and it was the job of the household slave to wash them. At the Last Supper there was no household slave. None of the apostles was willing to lose face by doing the slave's job, so they ate with unwashed feet. We can imagine their amazement when Jesus 'rose from supper, laid aside His garments, and girded Himself with a towel . . . and began to wash the disciples' feet' (Jn. 13: 4, 5). He was introducing them to a revolutionary idea of greatness—measured in terms of service. Relentlessly the moral is pressed home. 'Do you know what I have done to you? You call me Teacher and Lord; and you are right, for so I am. If I then, your Lord and Teacher, have washed your feet, you also ought to wash one another's feet. For I have given you an example, that you also should do as I have done to you. Truly, truly, I say to you, a servant is not greater than his master; nor is He who is sent greater than He who sent Him. If you know these things, blessed are you if you do them' (13: 12-17).

There is, I think, a hint in St. Luke's account that this action of Jesus arose out of a quarrel among the disciples over precedence and status. Although he does not record the actual footwashing, Luke does tell us of this devastating question which Jesus asked them at this meal: 'Which is the greater, one who sits at table, or one who serves? Is it not the one who sits at table? But I am among you as one who serves.' Once more Jesus makes it crystal-clear that what is true of Him, must be true of His disciples: 'The kings of the Gentiles exercise lordship over them . . . but not so with you; rather let the greatest among you become as the youngest, and the leader as one who serves' (Lk. 22: 24–27).

The Christian Church has found this a very hard lesson to learn. Almost all consideration of different types of Christian ministries begins with a discussion of the validity of the orders in question, of their regularity, their authentication, their apostolicity. That is very natural. It is the way of the world. But it is not the way of Jesus Christ. He saw ministry not in terms of status but rather in terms of function. The pattern for Christian ministry which He set was one of service. Of course, the very word 'ministry' means 'service'. But for Jesus this was no idle euphemism. It is no accident that the term 'ministry' is used to describe the whole of His public life and work. He was supremely, and in everything, the Servant of the Lord. This was His glory; He looked for no other. And so it must be with any ministry which claims to be truly Christian.

A. JESUS, THE SERVANT

If we ask how Jesus came to think of Himself in this light, the answer is plain enough. He found it in His Bible, and in particular in Isaiah 40–55. Here it is made very plain that the whole nation of Israel is called to be the Servant of the Lord; service is the corollary of election (Is. 41: 8–20). The particular elements of service that are asked of the nation of Israel are obedience (Is. 44: 1, cf. 65: 12), witness (43: 12) and endurance (43: 1–6). But the nation refused to obey, recoiled from suffering, and instead of witnessing to the Lord gave way to idolatry. And so the task of the servant of the Lord devolves on a faithful remnant within Israel, who accept its implications. In the four Servant Songs of Isaiah (42: 1–4, 49: 1–6, 50: 4–7 and 52: 13–53: 12) the great themes are obedience, witness and endurance. The Servant is utterly obedient to God's voice (42: 1, 50: 4, 5), witnesses both to the lapsed among Israel and to the Gentiles (49: 6), and suffers ignominy and pain

(50: 5, 6). Indeed, although innocent, he bears the sins of the people (53: 6, 11, 12), and God will accept his sacrifice, and vindicate his cause (53: 10–12).

We may never know just how the prophet thought his words would be fulfilled, but it is certain that Jesus saw in them the foreshadowing of His own ministry, at any rate after the Baptism, when the voice from heaven addressed Him as 'My beloved Son, in whom I am well pleased' (Mk. 1: 11). These words are a composite quotation from Psalm 2: 7 and Isaiah 42: 1. Jesus the Messianic *Son* is hailed as the *Servant* of the Lord in whom His soul delights. The point is made equally emphatically at the outset of St. John's Gospel where Jesus is greeted by the Baptist as 'the Lamb of God who takes away the sin of the world' (Jn. 1: 29, 36). This title would, of course, have taken his Jewish hearers back to the sacrificial system they knew so well. But it would have done more. It would have pointed them to the Suffering Servant of Isaiah 53, for *talya*, the Aramaic word for 'lamb', is also the word for 'servant'.

The three themes of utter obedience, fearless witness and innocent suffering, which marked the Old Testament conception of the Servant of the Lord, run through the ministry of Jesus. And so, when at Caesarea Philippi Peter makes his great confession that Jesus is the Messiah, the long awaited deliverer of Jewish expectation, Jesus 'charged them to tell no one about Him' (Mk. 8: 30). If they were thinking in terms of status and position they were entirely missing the point. So Jesus reinterpreted Peter's confession. He would not allow the term 'Christ' (or 'Messiah'), which suggested earthly pomp and military might. Instead, He joined together two utterly diverse concepts, and in effect asked Peter to see Him in terms of them. 'He began to teach them that the *Son of Man* must *suffer* many things and be rejected . . .' Professor Cullmann is not exaggerating when he says: ' "Son of Man" represents the highest conceivable declaration of exaltation in Judaism; *ebed Yahweh* (the Servant of the Lord) is the expression of the deepest humiliation. This is the unheard-of new act of Jesus, that He united these two apparently contradictory tasks in His self-consciousness, and that He expressed that union in His life and teaching.'[1]

The concept of the Servant was never far from Jesus' mind, as can be seen from a whole page full of references and allusions

[1] *The Christology of the New Testament*, S.C.M., p. 161.

13

gathered by Professor Jeremias.[2] Moreover, it is clear that this became the dominant theme towards the end of Jesus' ministry. By word (for example Lk. 22: 37) and deed (Jn. 13: 4 ff., Mt. 26: 28) Jesus demonstrated that He was fulfilling the task of the Servant to the bitter end. Peter understands this (I Pet. 2: 21 ff.), so does Paul (Phil. 2: 6, 7). Both of them, in fact, make specific reference to Isaiah 53. Two of the early speeches in Acts refer to Jesus as God's Servant (3: 13, 26, 4: 27, 30; so, too, 8: 32 f.), and there are other New Testament allusions, such as Romans 15: 7–12. Of course, this title gave way to others after His Resurrection, notably 'Lord'; but it cannot be denied that the pattern and the glory of His ministry was service. It was, therefore, entirely in character when Jesus knelt to wash the disciples' feet. The Servant of the Lord had shrunk from the nation of Israel, from the faithful remnant, to a single person who fully embodied it. Later, it was to expand again in His followers. They are called to serve.

B. THE CHURCH OF THE SERVANT

Jesus is *the* Servant. He is *our* Servant. No man can be a Christian, let alone a Christian minister, until he lets Jesus be his Servant. Peter discovered this, though at first he rejected the notion outright: 'You shall never wash my feet.' But Jesus replied: 'If I do not wash you, you have no part in me.' Peter learnt his lesson, of course, and his first Epistle is full of the theme of the Servant. 'Submit' is the word that comes again and again; it is applied to husbands and wives, to young and old, to slaves — and to Christian leaders. In I Peter 5: 5 he uses a rare word for '*Clothe yourselves*, all of you, with humility', which suggests he had in mind the way Jesus took a towel and girded Himself. It is Peter's way of saying that the Church is to be marked with this characteristic of Jesus. It must be the Church of the Servant. Christian life begins when we allow Jesus to be our Servant. It continues as, incorporated into Christ, we share the role of the Servant which He made so much His own. Of course, we cannot share the atoning work of the Servant. He, and He alone, took responsibility for the sins of the world. But we can and must make His pattern of

[2] *The Servant of God*, S.C.M., pp. 98 f. See Mark 9: 31; 10: 33; 10: 45; 14:21, 24, 41. It is interesting to see how Jesus, in Mark 10: 45, dramatically reverses the specific destiny of the Son of Man according to Daniel 7: 14. He does not come to be saved, but to save.

ministry our own. Indeed, He commissions us to do so. That is made very plain in the two mission charges, to the Twelve (Mk. 6: 7 ff.) and to the Seventy (Lk. 10: 1 ff.). We meet the same characteristics of service that we saw in Isaiah and in the ministry of Jesus. They are to obey the instructions of Jesus in going out on this mission; they are to bear witness to the break-in of the kingly rule of God, and to urge men to change their minds and accept it. They are to serve those to whom they go by healing and casting out demons. They must be prepared to face suffering and rejection. Their ministry, in fact, is an extension of their Master's. It is conceived in the same terms, whether it be the Twelve or the Seventy. For apostles and for Church alike the pattern is the same. On this passage T. W. Manson comments: 'They justify their existence and earn their keep by the service that they render'; and he concludes: 'In the Kingdom of God, service is not a stepping-stone to nobility: it *is* nobility, the only kind of nobility that is recognized.'[3]

As the counterpart of this, Jesus warns His disciples against that preoccupation with status and succession that bedevilled the Jewish rabbinical schools. 'They love the place of honour at feasts, and the best seats in the synagogues, and salutations in the market places, and being called "Rabbi" by men. But you are not to be called "Rabbi", for you have one teacher, and you are all brethren. And call no man your "Father" on earth, for you have one Father, who is in heaven. Neither be called "Masters", for you have one Master, the Christ. He who is greatest among you shall be your servant' (Mt. 23: 6–11).

Such is the pattern for ministry set by Jesus. And He was the One who 'taught with authority and not as the scribes' (Mk. 1: 22), the One to whom 'all authority in heaven and earth' had been committed (Mt. 28: 18). It was the Christ, the Son of God, the Son of Man, who took upon Him the form of the Servant. He had irrefragable credentials had He wished to rely on status and authority. But He resolutely turned His back on any such suggestion. To Him the authority of the Servant lay simply in the fact of His service. The divine call, the divine equipment with the Holy Spirit, were demonstrated by obedience, by faithful witness, by patient endurance. These, and not some ecclesiastical counterpart to Gentile hierarchy (Lk. 22: 25) or Jewish succession (Mt. 23: 7, 8),

³ *The Church's Ministry*, Hodder & Stoughton, p. 27.

were to be the authenticating marks of the Christian ministry.

When we reflect on the history of the Church, are we not bound to confess that she has failed to follow the example of her Founder? All too often she has worn the robes of the ruler, not the apron of the servant. Even in our own day it can hardly be said that the 'brand-image' of the Church is of a society united in love for Jesus, and devoted to selfless service of others.

If the Church as a whole has failed, the ministry has failed even more signally, to exhibit the character of the Servant. Even when we leave the past out of account, where pope and pastor, bishop and minister, priest and synod have all alike at times domineered over those in their charge instead of being examples to the flock (I Pet. 5: 3), the present is nothing to be proud about. Does the vicar give the impression of being the servant of his people? Does he not rather behave, as too often the missionary has behaved, like a little tin god, loving to be recognized and looked up to, anxious that nothing shall go on in his parish without his personal supervision? Is it not an astonishing reversal of the pattern left by Jesus when a bishop, a chief pastor of the flock, is glad to be called 'My Lord'?[4] Even today, in the ecumenical debate, *does* the ministry seek to commend itself by the marks of the Servant, or are not the issues quite different? When Rome insists on submission to the Roman pontiff as 'altogether necessary to salvation for every human creature' (the Bull *Unam Sanctam*). when the Anglican Communion insists on episcopacy as a *sine qua non* for reunion — is this the way of Jesus?

The question is vital and urgent. It is a nettle that must be firmly grasped. In England today there is an increasing unwillingness on the part of young people to accept authoritarian or traditional pronouncements on either doctrine or ethics. In the ecumenical field, greater *rapprochement* is threatened by heavily entrenched doctrines of the ministry which appear to

---

[4] One cannot help feeling that the whole gamut of ecclesiastical courtesy titles, 'the Venerable', 'the Very Reverend', 'the Most Reverend' and so on, are a hindrance rather than a help in the work of the ministry. They tend to build an invisible wall between their bearer and the world at large; much more important, they tend to make him just a little proud, just a little pleased with himself, just a little further removed than he was before from the role of the Servant.

be entirely uninfluenced by the example and precept of Jesus; while in almost every diocese in the churches of Asia and Africa there is a real desire for help from the older churches, *provided that* such new-style missionaries come, like their Master, 'not to be served but to serve'. Unless more than lip service is paid to this pattern of the Servant, the prospects of advance in any of these three fields is lamentably small.

CHAPTER TWO

THE MINISTRY OF THE EARLY CHURCH

DID the early Church follow up the ideals of service laid down by Jesus ? In order to answer this question we shall examine first the ministry of all Christians as we find it in the New Testament, then the ministry in the specialized sense, and finally their relationship to one another.

A. THE MINISTRY OF ALL CHRISTIANS

There is no suggestion in the New Testament that one could possibly be a Christian without having a call to some form of ministry within the Church. The Christian is indeed 'saved to serve'. St. Paul, for one, could never forget that the voice of the ascended Christ at his conversion had said: 'Rise and stand upon your feet; for I have appeared to you for this purpose, to appoint you *to serve and to bear witness*' (Acts 26 : 16). It is hardly surprising, therefore, that the whole point of his argument in Romans 12 and I Corinthians 12 is that every member of the Christian body has his part to play in the service of God. He knew that ministry is the inalienable duty and privilege of every Christian. We, on the contrary, have so lost this conception of the universal requirement of Christians to serve their Lord, that we tend to understand ministry not in its New Testament sense of service, but of communication, administration. So anxious are we to transfer the plain duty of all to the sole responsibility of a church official!

Three words in particular are used to describe the devoted service of the man who knows himself to be forgiven.

1. The first is *doulos*. It means, quite baldly, bondslave. And it comes scores of times in the New Testament. It was a word which Paul sometimes used of his relation to his converts (1 Cor. 9: 19 f., 2 Cor. 4: 5), but most frequently of his own relation to Jesus. He was the 'bondslave of Jesus Christ' (Rom. 1: 1, etc.). He spoke of wearing the chain of a slave (II Tim. 1: 16), of being branded with the marks of a slave (Gal. 6: 17). He saw such dedication to Jesus as the only

fitting response of the redeemed. 'You are not your own,' he writes, 'you were bought with a price' (I Cor. 6: 19, 20). Peter makes the same plea for utter obedience to God, on precisely the same grounds: 'You know that you were ransomed . . . with the precious blood of Christ' (I Pet. 1: 14–19); and he describes those who do not give God this service as 'denying the Master who bought them' (II Pet. 2: 1).

This metaphor of the slave was particularly relevant in the first century. The Roman slave belong entirely to his master. He had no rights at law, and could demand no privileges, though often, of course, under a kind master he would get excellent treatment. His money, his time, his future, his marriage were all, strictly speaking, at the disposal of his master. That is what it meant to be a slave. And that is the metaphor which the New Testament writers deliberately took over.

Peter and Paul apply it to themselves, apostles though they were; James and Jude, though, it would seem, blood half-brothers of Jesus (Mt. 13: 55), delight to call themselves His *douloi* (Jas. 1: 1, Jude 1: 1). It is, in fact, a characteristic description of Christians (Rev. 1: 1, I Pet. 2: 16). Could anything show more graphically their loving devotion and total dedication to Christ? Should this not shame into silence our arguments about the status and validity of ministries? The highest ministry of all is open to all—to be bondslaves of Jesus Christ.

2. The second word often used of Christian service is *leitourgos*, whence we derive our term 'liturgy'. If *doulos* speaks particularly of Christian devotion to Christ, *leitourgos* speaks of Christian worship of God. This is the word used of the angels in heaven (Heb. 1: 14) and of men on earth (for example Lk. 1: 23) as they ascribe worship to God and place themselves at His disposal for service (Acts 13: 1 ff.).

Sometimes the Jewish background of the term is uppermost, as in the Epistle to the Hebrews, where it is made very plain that the Old Testament priestly offerings, though ineffectual in themselves, are filled with meaning when seen in the light of Christ's work. They are, as it were 'fulfilled' in the self-offering of Jesus (8: 2, 6; 9: 21; 10: 11).

On the other hand it is from the imagery of pagan worship that Paul draws when he calls the faith of the Philippians a 'liturgy' (Phil. 2: 17). Similarly when state officials administer justice with a due sense of what they are doing, they can be described as 'ministers' of God (Rom. 13: 6).

More than once sacrificial Christian giving is described in this way; when Gentile churches make a collection for impoverished Jewish Christians (II Cor. 9: 12; Rom. 15: 27), this is *leitourgia*, a practical outworking of their genuine worship of God — nothing less would have induced them to do it! And for Epaphras to give himself, for the Lord's sake, to the service of Paul, was no less worthy of the name (Phil. 2: 30). Finally, when Paul, by God's enabling, preaches the Gospel to the heathen, this too is *leitourgia* (Rom. 15: 16) because, through it, converts are 'offered' to God. In short, this word speaks of the service of God in worship and in work. Once again, it is brought before us as the duty of every Christian, and not something which can be restricted or delegated to a special class within the Church.

3. The third and most common word is *diakonos*, from which our term 'deacon' is derived. Like the others, it is applied to all and sundry in the Christian Church. Jesus and the apostles are given this title, and it is used of the humblest believer. It refers particularly to service to others, often menial service at that. The varieties of service included in the term are vast. In Acts 6, for instance, the apostles were administering the Word of God to the people; the Seven were administering food. Both are called *diakonia* (Acts 6: 1, 4). The New Testament does not make our false distinction between the sacred and the secular. The whole of life is seen as belonging to God. The Christian's service to others must be done in the light of his relationship to God. The Church was very conscious, in these early days, that it was commissioned to carry on the work of the Servant.

We find the word used in I Corinthians 16: 15 of what we would call specific church work. It is no less appropriate to the personal service rendered by Timothy and Erastus to Paul (Acts 19: 22) — including, no doubt, taking down his letters and cooking his meals! Prison visiting is given this honourable title in Philemon 13, and so is evangelistic preaching in Acts 20: 24. *Diakonia*, in short, belonged to the whole Church and to every member of it. No service was regarded as too menial or too exacting if only it would commend the Gospel of the grace of God. No one in the early Church would have quarrelled with Paul's statement: 'What we preach is not ourselves, but Jesus Christ as Lord, with ourselves your servants for Jesus' sake' (II Cor. 4: 5).

As Emil Brunner puts it: 'One thing is supremely important; that *all* minister, and that nowhere is to be perceived a separation or even merely a distinction between those who do and those who do not minister, between the active and the passive members of the body, between those who give and those who receive. There exists in the *Ecclesia* a universal duty and right of service, a universal readiness to serve, and at the same time the greatest possible differentiation of functions.'[1]

If then ministry of this sort, comprising devotion to Christ, worship of God, and service of others, must be the hallmark of every Christian, it must in greater measure characterize their leaders. This, as we have already seen, St. Peter is at pains to point out (I Pet. 5: 1–5). So is St. Paul: I Corinthians 4 is a case in point. He begins this chapter of rebuke to the proud, self-sufficient Corinthians by saying (v. 1): 'This is how one should regard us, as servants of Christ and stewards of the mysteries of God.' He goes on to contrast his own attitude with theirs (vv. 9–13); unlike them he gladly embraces the life of hardship, suffering and ignominy that goes with the loyal following of the Suffering Servant. He sees himself, to quote one of the pope's most noble (though not always most descriptive) titles, as *Servus Servorum Dei*, 'servant of the servants of God'.

B. THE SPECIALIZED MINISTRY

1. *Various Ministries within the Church*

The fact that service is to be the mark of all Christians, not merely of a ministerial *élite*, does not dispense with the need for specialization within the Christian community. St. Paul sees the Church as 'the Body of Christ'. That is to say, she is the agent of His purposes, the bearer of His life in the world. Christians are like members within the human body; they have different functions, offer different types of service to the whole Body, while they share the same life and belong together. Romans 12: 4–8 urges Christians to discover and make the most of their particular gift for the good of the whole. Paul mentions the *charismata* (God-given qualities) of prophecy, helpful service, teaching, encouragement, giving and leadership as examples of what he means, and love as the

[1] *The Misunderstanding of the Church*, p. 50.

21

bond which unites these diverse gifts into the harmonious unity of the Body. The function of leadership in the Church is just one among the other gifts of God to His Church.

I Corinthians 12 employs the same metaphor, and makes the added point that this differentiation of function within the Christian Body is the sovereign act of the Holy Trinity (vv. 4–6). God's purpose is that by mutual caring (v. 26) each member should use his proper gift for the edification and benefit of the whole Body. Paul concludes the chapter by showing them that different types of specialized ministry are God's gifts to His Church (v. 28). We may divide them, if we wish, into four rough groupings; ministry of the Word ('first apostles, second prophets, third teachers'); ministry of healing ('then workers of miracles, then healers'); ministry of administration and leadership ('helpers, administrators' – the word means literally governors or directors); and finally the ministry which the Corinthians – wrongly – prized most, that of ecstasy ('speakers in various kinds of tongues').

The Church is seen here as a living organism, in which there is this God-given differentiation of *function*. In fact, the contributions of various parts to the whole are described in this chapter by four interesting titles; they are *pneumatica*, functions assigned by the Holy Spirit; *charismata*, gracious opportunities of service together with a God-given ability to fulfil them; *energemata*, a word which draws attention to the active use of these opportunities or gifts; and *diakoniai*, a word which emphasizes that the purpose of it all is service to the Body as a whole.

Ephesians 4: 8–13 underlines this theme. Paul is speaking of the gifts of the ascended Christ to His Church: 'and His gifts were that some should be apostles, some prophets, some evangelists, some pastors and teachers, for the equipment of the saints for the work of ministry, for building up the body of Christ'. Once again we see a specialized ministry that is Christ's gift to His Church; the divine institution of the ministry could hardly be more strongly stated.

Furthermore, it can hardly be accidental that each of the ministries mentioned is a ministry of the Word. The apostles and prophets form Christ's foundation gift to the Church (Eph. 2: 20; 3: 5). The apostles, as we shall see later, occupied a unique and unrepeatable place in the history of the Church. They were chosen by Christ as witnesses of His saving work, who should proclaim it to the world (Acts 1: 8); men who could attest from personal experience the resurrection of Jesus (Acts 1: 22); eyewitnesses, in fact, whose testimony would enable those who had not been present to believe (Jn. 17: 20).

The prophets, too, belonged to the foundation layer of the Church. They were men, associated closely with the apostles, who spoke under the direct prompting of the Holy Spirit (for example Acts 11: 27 ff.; 21: 4, 9; Rev. 1: 3). They gradually died out after the end of the apostolic age. At all events, it became increasingly necessary to test their credentials (I Jn. 4: 1; Rev. 2: 20). In the *Didache* the genuine prophet is highly thought of, but men are well aware of counterfeits, and the shrewd advice is given that 'no prophet who orders a meal while "in the Spirit" shall eat of it; otherwise he is a false prophet' (11: 7)!

Evangelists and 'pastor-teachers', of course, have a continuing place in the Church for the spread and the deepening of Christian commitment. Very likely we should identify the latter with the teachers of I Corinthians 12: 28, and, indeed, with the presbyter/bishops of Acts 20 and the Pastoral Epistles; in both contexts great emphasis is placed upon their teaching the Word of God (Acts 20: 24–32; I Tim. 3: 2; Tit. 1: 9). This teaching function, we are told (Eph. 4: 11, 12), is the main purpose of the Christian ministry, which is that part within the Body expressly charged with the duty of equipping the 'saints' for their service in the world.

Now surely this is a very remarkable thing. We tend to assume, today, that the purpose of the ministry is primarily to do with the leading of public worship and the celebration of the sacraments. These functions are never once attributed to the ministry in the New Testament. The ministry there is concerned first and foremost with *didache*, the teaching of Christians so that they may the more effectively play their part in the world. That is to say that the ministry exists for the sake of the Church (and not *vice versa*, as is so often either taught or assumed), just as the Church in her turn exists for the sake of the world. The pattern of the Servant remains.

2. *Clergy and Laity?*

If we were to ask the New Testament writers, 'What is the difference between a clergyman and a layman?', they would not understand what we meant. For the Christianity of the New Testament does not know two classes of Christians, the professional and the amateur, so to speak. All Christians are the laity of God (I Pet. 2: 10 – Greek). All Christians, likewise, are ministers of God, and, as we have seen in these three Pauline passages, the tasks we consider perquisites of the clergy are mixed up quite naturally with others we would regard as lay. The New Testament knows nothing of a priestly caste. As Lightfoot put it in his celebrated Essay on *The Christian Ministry*,[2] 'the Christian ideal is a holy season extending the whole year round, a temple confined only by the limits of the habitable world, a priesthood coextensive with the human race' (p. 5).[3] He goes on to show how loyalty to this ideal did not, of course, preclude practical organization. Very soon we find Christian meetings for worship on the first day of the week (Acts 20: 7), fixed places for these meetings (for example Philem. 2), and various types of officers in the Church (for example Phil. 1: 1). This practical necessity did not however, prevent them from inveighing against those who 'observe days and months and seasons and years'. It did not stop them maintaining that 'God dwelleth not in temples made with hands.' 'It was,' Lightfoot continues, 'against the false principle that they waged war; the principle that ... gave absolute intrinsic value to subordinate aids and expedients ... (which) were no part of the essence of the Gospel; they must not be allowed to obscure the idea of Christian worship. So it was with the Christian priesthood. For communicating instruction and for preserving public order, for conducting public worship and dispensing social charities, it became necessary to appoint special officers. They are called stewards of God, servants or ministers of the Church, and the like; but the sacerdotal title is never once conferred upon them. The only priests under the Gospel, designated as such in the New Testament, are the saints, the members of the Christian brotherhood' (I Pet. 2: 5, 9; Rev. 1: 6, 5: 10, 20: 6).

That is why there is no hard and fast distinction between

[2] My quotations are from the edition published by Thynne & Jarvis (1927).
[3] He explains his meaning on p. 4, 'Every member of the human family was potentially a member of the Church, and, as such, a priest of God.'

24

clergy and laity in the New Testament. All alike are servants and ministers of God.

3. *Ordination?*

Nevertheless there is clear evidence of what we would call the ordained ministry in the New Testament period. We meet, as we shall see, bishops, presbyters, deacons, those that bear rule. There is evidence that in some cases at least they were set apart for this work with prayer and the laying on of hands. In Acts 14: 23 we read of Paul and Barnabas appointing elders in every church visited on the First Missionary Journey. The word used is *cheirotoneo*, which in later ecclesiastical usage means 'the laying on of hands'. However, in secular usage the word means simply 'to choose', 'select', 'appoint' (choice was originally made in the Greek city states by the people *raising their hand*), and this is the meaning of the word in its only other New Testament occurrence (II Cor. 8: 19), and in its three occurrences in Ignatius.[4] In the *Didache* (15: 1) the churches are told to select their own bishops and deacons, and *cheirotoneo* is the word used. This probably means that the congregation are to choose their leaders, though the possibility of their laying hands on them cannot be excluded. In Acts 6 it is uncertain whether the imposition of hands on the Seven is done by the multitude who selected them, or by the apostles before whom they were brought. In any case, Acts 6 looks not like an ordination but an *ad hoc* measure to relieve a particular situation, and must be regarded as of dubious relevance. The only other evidence on ordination in the New Testament concerns Timothy. Paul speaks (II Tim. 1: 6) of 'the gift of God which is within you through the laying on of my hands', which may, of course, refer to ordination; the context, however, does nothing to suggest it, and refers rather to the initial Christian experience of his mother and grandmother. It probably means, in Timothy's own case, the laying on of hands which accompanied baptism (Heb. 6: 1, 2; Acts 9: 17). In that case the only reference to Timothy's ordination, and the only certain reference to ordination in the New Testament would be in I Timothy 4: 14. This may be translated, with the R.S.V., as: 'Do not neglect the gift you have, which was given you by prophetic utterance when the elders laid their hands upon you.' Or it may mean, as Daube

[4] *Philad.* 10: 1; *Smyrn.* 11: 2; *Poly.* 7: 2.

and Jeremias[5] have suggested, 'when hands were laid upon you with the object of making you a presbyter'. In the former case we would have a corporate form of commissioning, as when the prophets and teachers at Antioch laid hands on Barnabas and Saul to separate them for the work of evangelism (Acts 13: 3). If, however, Daube's interpretation is right, it leaves open the question of who laid hands on Timothy—presumably the Apostle Paul, but we cannot say.

Despite the uncertainty about the imposition of hands, it seems reasonably clear that those who were seen to have the gift of leadership in the early Church were commissioned to perform this task in the congregation by some competent authority, either an apostle (as perhaps in the case of Timothy) or by an apostolic delegate (see Tit. 1: 5; ?I Tim. 5: 22), or by the elders already in office (?I Tim. 4: 14). There would thus be a public recognition by the Body of Christ of the gift of leadership imparted by God to a particular member, and a solemn commissioning of him, through their representatives, to exercise that gift for the benefit of the Body as a whole. In that sense, and that alone, is there any difference between 'clergy' and 'laity' in the New Testament. All too soon the 'double standard' (between the ordinary Christian and the particularly holy Christian), which has been so disastrous in the history of the Church, creeps in. Thus the *Didache* sees the 'ascetics' and those who can 'speak in the Spirit' as possessing *ipso facto*, a higher status than anyone else.[6] Already we are moving away from the primitive conviction that all Christians equally are called to serve.

C. THE RELATIONSHIP OF THE TWO

We have seen that in the New Testament *diakonia* is the prerogative of all. It is very interesting that this word should have been chosen to denote the particularly Christian conception of ministry. The term is scarcely used in the Greek Old Testament; it is not used of officers in pagan religious societies, and it is utterly incompatible with a hierarchical structure. This humble word, applied to all its ministries, reminds us that the Church of the New Testament renounces pomp and

[5] In *The New Testament and Rabbinic Judaism* (London, 1956), pp. 244 ff., and *Zeitschift für die neutestamentliche Wissenschaft* (1957), pp. 130 f.
[6] *Didache* 13: 3; 10: 7.

status for its officers, and acknowledges that the only greatness she knows is that of the Servant, the only specialized ministries those of special subordination. If we find ourselves thinking of the ministry in terms of office and status, of authority and validity, we go far astray from the thought of the Bible. Of course, ministry and authority are not mutually exclusive in the teaching of the apostles any more than we have seen them to be in that of Jesus. But the minister's authority does not demand obedience because of his position but because of his service. Thus Paul encourages the Christians at Thessalonica to 'respect those who labour among you and are over you in the Lord ... because of their *work*' (I Thess. 5: 12 f.). The proof that God has given a man the gift of ministry is seen when he exercises it for the benefit of the Church. The emphasis is less on office than on function. Thus leadership and teaching are the functions exercised by some within the Body (those whose *charisma* it is, I Cor. 12: 28), but nowhere do we meet the suggestion that clergy and laity (the very terms are not only anachronisms, but distortions of the New Testament position) have realms into which the other is not permitted to venture. Let us glance at three such realms normally reserved for the specialized ministry today.

Separate Spheres for 'Clergy' and 'Laity'?

1. Teaching is, as we have seen, an important function of the specialized ministry, and yet in the Corinthian church there was room for any member of the congregation to take part in the ministry of the Word if he had something to contribute (I Cor. 14: 26–29). Indeed, it is the fact that all take part in proclaiming the Word of God that convinces the unbeliever present that God is in their midst (24, 25).

2. Leading in worship may well have been a function of the specialized ministry, but there is no suggestion that it should be restricted to them. On the contrary, any member of the assembled congregation was free to contribute his piece of teaching, his piece of 'prophecy', his choice of a psalm, his speaking with tongues, provided all was done in an orderly and edifying manner (I Cor. 14: 26, 40). For centuries the element of *risk* in a vital, corporate worship of this kind has seemed too great; there is very little danger of disorder arising from excessive congregational participation in the older established churches of the world! There is an increasing

27

tendency, even among the Free Churches, towards a liturgical order of worship, and this was, of course, by no means entirely lacking in New Testament times.[7] But it is not these churches that are growing in a remarkable way today. Indeed, in most of them, as in the Church of England, these are days of retrenchment rather than advance. But when we turn to the Pentecostal churches, particularly in South America, we find a very different picture. They are growing at a spectacular rate, much faster than any other churches in the world today. The Elim Church, for instance, has only been in Brazil for nine years, but it has over 220 congregations – more than the Anglicans have built in 120 years. In São Paulo a vast church is under construction which will hold 25,000 – and it will be *filled*, probably nightly. The growth of the Pentecostal churches may be due to many causes, but not least is the fact that it is predominantly a *lay* church. They have, indeed, a ministry, but it is not a hierarchy. The ministers do a secular job, and they really seek to 'equip the saints for the work of service'. As a result every Christian bears constant witness to his faith in impromptu open-air meetings and in personal conversation with his friends. Every Christian is free to participate in the weekly – and nightly – meetings for worship. Doubtless these meetings are often somewhat disorderly, but they are *alive*, because the whole people of God take a real part. He would be a proud man who asserted that we have nothing to learn from them.

3. Or take the administration of the sacraments, which we tend to associate exclusively with the ordained ministry. It is significant that in the New Testament we are never told who should baptize and who should preside at the Lord's Supper. It apparently never occurred to the first generation of Christians that these actions hung together as a specific area into which no 'layman' might trespass. The word 'sacrament' is, of course, not found in the New Testament. It belongs to the heathen world of the Graeco-Roman Empire, and there is a good deal of truth in Brunner's contention that with Ignatius' emphasis on the eucharist as the *pharmakon athanasias*, 'the medicine for attaining immortality', and the bishop as the distributor of it,[8] we have passed from the New Testa-

[7] See Prof. C. F. D. Moule's *Worship in the New Testament*, Lutterworth Press, pp. 67 ff.
[8] *Eph.* 20: 2.

28

ment conception of the Church as a unity of persons redeemed by Christ, and united in the Holy Spirit, to a sub-personal conception of the Church as a collective whose unity flows from their common relationship to a thing, the sacrament.[9] Be that as it may, it seems reasonably clear that in the New Testament anyone may baptize. As E. Schweizer puts it most succinctly: 'The apostles do not as a rule baptize (Acts 10: 48; cf. 19: 5 beside 6a; I Cor. 1: 14-17); ordinary church members do (Acts 9: 18).'[10]

It seems likely, too, that anyone could preside at the Lord's Supper in the early days of the Church. Thus when there are abuses over the eucharist at Corinth, there is no one responsible person with whom Paul can expostulate. If in Acts 2: 46 the 'breaking of bread from house to house' refers to the holy communion, as most commentators think it does, then that settles the matter; for it is expressly stated that this is what the *converts* did. It was a 'lay' celebration. In the Pastoral Epistles Paul expresses great concern over church order, but he never suggests that the celebration of the eucharist or baptism is a function peculiar either to the presbyter-bishops whom Timothy and Titus are to ordain, or to the apostolic delegates themselves. Even as late as Justin (*Apology*, 1:65), in the middle of the second century, we find the celebrant referred to simply as *ho proestōs*, 'the president', presumably because, as in the *Didache*, it is not yet invariably the task of one particular official.

I am not in the least advocating indiscriminate celebrations of holy communion, but I believe the principle to be important; the New Testament knows of no special body to whom is entrusted the celebration of the sacraments, no priestly caste within the Christian Church. There may be something to be said for the practice of the Congregational Church in having a layman to preside at the eucharist once a year in order to make plain that the restriction of this function to the ordained ministry is a matter of order, not of doctrine. There is certainly a great deal to be said for celebration by a godly layman in areas such as isolated mission stations which would otherwise be deprived of the holy communion except for once or twice a year when a priest is available. In many places in the Far East pioneer missionary work is carried out

[9] *Op. cit.* chapters 7–10.
[10] *Church Order in the New Testament*, p. 186.

29

solely by women missionaries, while Christian men hold back from offering themselves for such arduous service.[11] The evangelization of primitive tribes is carried on by these dedicated women; the first baptisms are administered by them, the second by the missionary and the first believers jointly, and thereafter by the nationals themselves; the first eucharists are celebrated, probably in milk and rice, by the woman missionary, and are transferred as soon as possible to the local believers. Are we to stay in the shelter and comfort of our Western ivory-towers and proclaim such ministries invalid, irregular and the like? We may do so if we wish; but we shall find no warrant in the New Testament for our position. The New Testament presents to us not a hierarchy of ministers but a body of co-operating members, each exercising their God-given gifts and functions for the good of the whole and the carrying out of the work of the Servant in the world. 'It is not only the attitude of the earthly Jesus that determines this nature of all ministry in the New Testament; it is also the fact that the call to service can be understood only as an unmerited gift of grace. This is true of the calling of the disciples, according to the Synoptic testimony (Lk. 5: 8–10; Mk. 2: 14–17; Mt. 10: 8), as well as of the missions in Acts (14: 26; 15: 40; 3: 12; 14: 15), but especially in the Pauline writings. Paul knows, not only that all service is the act of God Himself (I Cor. 3: 7; 15: 9 f.), but that an essential part of the New Testament ministry is that an unqualified person is called to it 'to show that the transcendent power belongs to God and not to us' (II Cor. 4: 7).[12]

Very soon after New Testament days, however, a development set in which changed the Christian organism with its dynamic ministries into an organization with institutionalized offices. When Paul wrote to the Corinthians he urged them to submit to Christian leaders in recognition of the quality of their service (I Cor. 16: 16). When Clement wrote to the Corinthians, hardly half a century later, he urged them to reinstate their deposed presbyters because they had been properly appointed (I Clem. 44). The Christian fellowship had begun to give way to the ecclesiastical institution. The dynamic view of ministry had begun to give way to the

[11] Since the Second World War eight women to every one man have offered themselves for overseas missionary service.
[12] E. Schweizer: op. cit., p. 179.

static view of 'office'. The servant had begun to savour of the master.

Two Current Dangers

If we today are to preserve the New Testament conception of a servant ministry authorized by Jesus Himself, modelled on His example, and indeed in a measure continuing His work among men,[13] we must be careful to avoid twin and opposite dangers. Both clericalism and anti-clericalism, both prelacy and anarchy, stand condemned in the light of the New Testament.

There is a tendency in some circles, and by no means only in 'Catholic' ones, for the ordained minister to lord it over the flock committed to him. Nothing can be done of any importance in the Church if he is not there. The wishes of the people in matters as widely different as ritual or policy are subordinated to his own. I know of a parish where the parochial church council does not even have its statutory say in the finances of the church; they are administered entirely by the rector. I know of another where no meeting for prayer or Bible study even in private homes is allowed by the vicar, unless he is present. These are extreme but by no means isolated examples of the danger of overvaluing the office of the ordained minister. It is, of course, bad both for the clergy and for the laity involved in such a situation. The former have an exaggerated estimate of their own importance in the Christian Body, and the latter have initiative quashed and are given little sphere in which to exercise their Christian ministry, and even less direction on how to discover it. Wherever the principle of Romans 12, of diversity in unity, is forgotten, the Church suffers. The Christian Church consists of interdependent members, and it is of the utmost importance to preserve the exercise of the different gifts the Holy Spirit has given to His people for the enrichment of the whole. When one member exceeds his place, he impoverishes the whole.

Equally dangerous, and scarcely less widespread, is a tendency to disparage the ordained ministry, which has sprung up as a reaction against clerical domination. Some Christians,

[13] So Paul, 'I will not venture to speak of anything except what Christ has wrought through me' (Rom. 15: 18). There is, in a sense, only one ministry in the Church, the ministry of Jesus carried on through the members of His Body.

notably the Brethren, have no ordained ministry at all. Others interpret the priesthood of all believers as though it meant the priesthood of no believers; while others, as B. L. Manning warned the Congregationalists, fall into the mistake of regarding the sacred ministry as a 'secretaryship, a sort of general manager's job, a device to save trouble for the majority of the church members by concentrating nearly all their duties upon one or two'.[14] This is to forget that the minister is not merely servant of the Church, but servant of Christ from whom he derives his authority, and to whom he owes supreme allegiance. In His earthly life Jesus took immense pains to train those whom He later commissioned to be apostles in His Church; after His resurrection He continued to 'give' ministers to His people (Eph. 4: 11). There are those who bear rule in the Christian churches (Heb. 13: 7; I Thes. 5: 12; I Tim. 5: 17), and consequently there are those who are ruled. The ordained ministry combines both the dignity and the lowliness of Jesus who commissions it.

Difficult though it is to reconcile these two elements in practice, it is clear that neither the complaisant nor the autocratic clergyman represents anything but a travesty of New Testament ministry. The minister must first and foremost be the servant of the Lord; and this will inevitably mean that he sets himself to be the servant of his people, dedicated to bringing them to Christian maturity and equipping them for Christian service in the world. Only in such an extension of the work of the Servant can the true balance between the authority and the lowliness of the ordained ministry be preserved.

Distortion, and often disaster, comes when the people forget that the minister is the representative of Christ to them, and when he forgets that he is called to serve.

[14] B. L. Manning: *A Layman in the Ministry*, Independent Press (1943), p. 152.

CHAPTER THREE

PRIESTS OR PRESBYTERS

A. THE THREEFOLD MINISTRY

THE Preface to the Anglican Ordinal asserts roundly, 'It is evident unto all men diligently reading the Holy Scriptures and Ancient Authors, that from the Apostles' time there have been these Orders of Ministers in Christ's Church: Bishops, Priests and Deacons.' This statement is widely misquoted as if it said, 'there have been *three* Orders' — that is, three only. The purpose of this Preface, however, is not in the least polemical. It does not set out, and the Reformers who framed it did not set out, to stigmatize, much less to unchurch, those with, for example, a presbyterian form of church government. The views of the Reformers are well known on this matter; they were agreed that all necessary doctrine was plainly set forth in Scripture, and the importance of episcopal ordination was not plainly set forth there. Thus Cranmer can say: 'I do not set more by any title, name or style than I do by the paring of an apple, further than it shall be to the setting forth of God's word and will',[1] and Bishop Hooper can write: 'I believe the Church is bound to no sort of ministers or any ordinary succession of bishops . . . but unto the only Word of God.'[2] It is significant that when the marks of the Church are given us in Article XIX there is no suggestion that any particular form of church government is essential. They are, on the contrary, precisely the same marks of the visible Church that are laid down in the Reformed Continental Confessions of Augsburg, Saxony and Switzerland. Again, Article XXIII *Of Ministering in the Congregation* reproduces a form of words from Article X (of the XLII Articles of 1553) which was deliberately designed not to exclude the Lutherans.[3]

What the Preface is concerned to maintain is that the Church of England in retaining at the Reformation the catholic orders

[1] *Remains and Letters*, p. 305.
[2] *Later Writings*, p. 90.
[3] See J. W. Hunkin: *Episcopal Ordination and Confirmation*, p. 4.

of bishop, priest and deacon, did so because they saw these orders to be agreeable both to Scripture and to history. Cranmer constantly showed his desire to abolish only what he must, and to retain, as he puts it in his Preface to the Prayer Book, what of 'the old may be well used'. Nor can his judgment be opposed on biblical or historical grounds. All three titles, though not necessarily corresponding to our conception of the offices involved, are scriptural. Moreover, not only are the names scriptural; there is a threefold division of function to be found at any rate in the later writings of the New Testament. In the Pastoral Epistles we see it most clearly. There are the presbyters or bishops; there is the subordinate ministry of deacons to assist them; and there is a superior or ordaining ministry which is exercised by Timothy and Titus (Tit. 1: 5).

If we look at the matter historically, precisely the same conclusion is reached. Nowhere do we find a 'parity of ministers'. Everywhere we find a gradation of offices in Christ's Church. The threefold ministry meets us as an established fact in the Asiatic churches at the end of the apostolic age, as the writings of Ignatius and Polycarp make plain. By the middle of the second century the threefold ministry of bishop, priest and deacon is the normal, almost universal pattern for Christian ministry the world over.

On the other hand, we must remember that other orders of ministry continue. 'Apostles', in the sense of wandering evangelists, are highly regarded in the *Didache* (11:3). There are still prophets and prophetesses,[4] still exorcists and miraculous healers towards the end of the second century. Witnesses as far apart as Justin in Rome,[5] Irenaeus in Gaul,[6] and Tertullian in North Africa[7] not only attest the fact but regard them as part of Christ's gift to His Church. Irenaeus is quite prepared to recognize some of his contemporaries as possessing the 'divinely bestowed power of prophesying'; in this case they 'speak when and where God pleases'.[8] Ignatius is aware that, when preaching to the Philadelphians the spirit of prophecy came upon him, and he cried out 'with the voice of God.'[9]

[4] See A. Ehrhardt: *The Apostolic Succession*, chapter 4.
[5] *Dial.* 38, 82.
[6] *Adv. Haer.* 2.32.4, 5.
[7] *De Anima* 9.
[8] *Adv. Haer.* 1.13.4.
[9] *Philad.* 7.

The four prophesying daughters of Philip (Acts 21: 9) made a great impression on the second-century Church, a Church which could not deny the possibility of a resurgence of prophecy in the Montanist movement, and therefore concentrated on launching personal attacks on the principal Montanists! It is interesting, furthermore, as a corrective to the common view which sees the prophetic and settled ministries as essentially incompatible with one another, to remember that the Montanists combined their emphasis on the prophetic office with a retention of the threefold orders of the catholic Church; the two remain side by side, of course, in the *Didache* as well.

Furthermore, even the Roman Catholic Church does not recognize only three orders, but rather divides ministries into major and minor. The major orders include a fourth office, that of sub-deacon, in addition to those of bishop, priest and deacon.[10] Indeed, many eminent Catholic theologians, including Thomas Aquinas, have refused to regard the episcopate as a separate order distinct from the priesthood. Jerome took this position with truly Presbyterian fervour, and the Council of Trent defined that bishops and presbyters differ in *gradus* but not in *ordo*.[11] It would be precarious, therefore, to interpret the Anglican Ordinal in any exclusive sense. This can easily be proved, if proof be needed, by the fact that the Church of England in the sixteenth and seventeenth centuries enjoyed the closest of relationships, including intercommunion and occasional exchange of ministers (without reordination), with Reformed churches on the Continent who had not retained the threefold ministry. What we may maintain with confidence, however, is that the threefold ministry is securely grounded both in Scripture and history; and so, without prejudice to other ministries, we shall proceed to examine those of bishop, priest and deacon.

B. THE PRIEST OR PRESBYTER

We shall take first the priest or presbyter, for he is the minister who meets us most frequently in the pages of the New Testament. As we shall see later, the Christian priest has nothing

---

[10] In the Roman Church of the mid-third century we find a fascinating catalogue of ministries: 46 presbyters, 7 deacons, 7 sub-deacons, 42 acolytes, and 52 exorcists, readers and doorkeepers (Eusebius, *H.E.* 6: 43).

[11] *Session* 23, esp. chapter 2.

to do with the sacrificing priesthood of the Old Testament. The word is derived both historically and linguistically from the 'presbyter' or 'elder' of the New Testament.

1. *Presbyters in Judaism*

There is general agreement that the Church took over this office of presbyter from the organization of the Jewish synagogue. In the early days, Christians must have been regarded as simply another of the many groups within Judaism, distinguished by their peculiar belief that Jesus was the long awaited Messiah. Any ten Jewish men could band together to form a synagogue—we find a varied list of some of the Jerusalem synagogues in Acts 6: 9—so it is hardly surprising that in Jewish areas Christian congregations were long called synagogues (Jas. 2: 2). Now the civil and administrative duties of the synagogue devolved upon a board of presbyters. They saw that the Law was observed, administered taxes, represented the synagogue in relations with pagan authorities, and in their hands lay the right of excommunication. It is not clear, however, that they had any liturgical function. The responsibility for public worship and the task of presiding at it fell to a quite different official, the 'ruler of the synagogue' (cf. Lk. 8: 41). He was not a priest of the Aaronic line; he was another layman who was elected for the office.

2. *Presbyters in the Early Church*

It seems clear, then, that the Jewish presbyterate was the model taken over by the early Christians and adapted for their own purposes. This probably happened first in Jerusalem, as Luke suggests (in Acts 11: 30 the presbyters of the Jerusalem church are mentioned without any introduction or explanation). The system proved satisfactory, and was widely used in Christian congregations as they spread throughout the Mediterranean basin. We find presbyters in Ephesus (Acts 20: 17), presbyters throughout Asia Minor (I Pet. 5: 1 cf. 1: 1), presbyters among the Jewish Dispersion (Jas. 5: 14 cf. 1: 1). We find Paul and Barnabas 'appointing elders in every church' on the First Missionary Journey (Acts 14: 23). So universal is the pattern that we find them figuring prominently in John's vision of heaven, where the four and twenty elders (the representative numbers of the Old and New Covenants) worship God continually (Rev. 4: 4, etc.).

If this is so, why do we find no mention of presbyters in Paul's letters (apart from the Pastoral Epistles)? A number of considerations may help to answer this at first rather surprising fact. Chance may have something to do with it. We would have no mention of 'bishops' either, if Philippians had not been preserved. But, more important, it seems probable that the presbyters (or elders) were called bishops (or overseers) in Gentile churches, for that word was commonly used to denote any sort of supervision in the Graeco-Roman world. It is certainly interesting that at Philippi (Phil. 1: 1), in Asia Minor (Acts 20: 28; I Pet. 2: 25, 5: 2), and in Crete (Tit. 1: 7) the presbyter is called bishop. As we shall see later, the two offices were the same, and it was merely a difference of nomenclature in Jewish and Gentile churches. However, 'bishop' never completely replaced 'presbyter' even among Gentile congregations (I Tim. 5: 17; I Clem. 21: 44).

Furthermore, there is a variety of expression in the New Testament, and particularly among the Pauline circle, to denote the ministerial office. The function is so much more important than the name. We are probably right in seeing the presbyter in the 'leader' of Hebrews 13: 7, 17, the 'man who bears rule' of I Thessalonians 5: 12, 13, and Romans 12: 8, while the 'pastors and teachers' of Ephesians 4: 11 is almost certainly a hendiadys for the same office.[12] Again, we should probably regard the 'helps and leaderships' of I Corinthians 12: 28 as two sorts of divine gifts which soon crystallized in the diaconate and presbyterate respectively.

Of these names the most interesting is 'those who bear rule'. The *proistamenos* (and its cognate form *prostates*) originally denoted the powerful Roman 'patron' who had his 'clients', and the word then came to be used widely of any person of wealth and influence, who exerted himself on behalf of poorer, weaker friends. Once Clement applies it to Jesus, whom he calls 'the patron of our weakness' (36: 1). The word sheds a fine light on the nature of Christian leadership. It is no doubt because of her championing the cause of her poorer and less influential Christian friends that Phoebe, the deaconess of the church at Cenchreae, is given this lovely title (Rom. 16: 2).

[12] Thus the task of acting as 'pastor' is assigned to presbyter/bishops in Acts 20: 28, I Pet. 5: 2, while teaching is always regarded as a prime function of a presbyter/bishop (I Tim. 3: 2; 5: 17).

3. *The Task of the Presbyters*

These different titles give us some idea of the job of the minister. He is, first and foremost, a *presbyter*, and the word meant primarily a senior, an elderly man. Indeed, it is notoriously difficult to know whether age or office is meant in some of the New Testament references to presbyters. Thus in I Timothy 5: 1–3 it is clearly an older man that is in view, but v. 17 of the same chapter equally clearly points to a specific office. The same ambiguity is present in I Peter 5: 1–5, and this suggests that the elders were normally drawn from among the senior men in the congregation. One was considered a young man in both Greek and Hebrew culture until past the age of forty.

Then the title *bishop* describes the main function of these elders (Acts 20: 28; I Pet. 5: 2, see p. 42 f.). They are to superintend and oversee the Christian congregations committed to them. It has often been remarked that presbyter more properly describes the *office*, and bishop the *function* of the early Christian minister. This oversight will mean that they are *pastors* (I Pet. 5: 2; Acts 20: 28) who feed the flock with the Word of God, and *leaders* in every Christian enterprise, not least, no doubt, in public worship. They are to act like *patron* to client, and this will involve both material assistance when needed, and the ministry of admonition to the unruly (I Thess. 5: 12) and support for the weak (Acts 20: 35). Theirs is supremely a teaching office (I Tim. 3: 2; Tit. 1: 9), and this grows more important as the Church spreads and the apostles die out. Thus their work is in some ways parallel to, and in some ways much wider than that of the Jewish elder. Both bear rule, both have administrative functions, both excommunicate (this is hinted at, perhaps, in I Cor. 5: 4, 5); both, no doubt, have the task of representing their communities to pagans. But unlike the Jewish presbyters the Christian minister has a pastoral and probably a liturgical function as well. Unlike them he is supremely a teacher; unlike them he is entrusted with a specific ministry of prayer (Jas. 5: 14). Perhaps the greatest difference was this: all Christian rule was marked with the imprint of Jesus the Servant. Had He not both told them and demonstrated to them (Lk. 22: 26) that the leader (*hegoumenos*) among them was to adopt the role of the servant (*diakonos*)? How could they ever forget, when they used this

38

title *hegoumenos* of Christian presbyters, that its supremacy was one of service? How could they ever be domineering over the flock in their work as bishops (I Pet. 5: 3) whilst they kept in mind the type of oversight exercised by Jesus, the Bishop of their souls (I Pet. 2: 25)?

4. *Presbyters—a Corporate and Settled Ministry*

Two further points emerge clearly from the New Testament evidence we are considering. The first is that the presbyters are the settled ministry of the Church, as opposed to the itinerant apostles, evangelists and prophets. This holds good of every place where they are mentioned in the New Testament. It is particularly noticeable in the Jerusalem church, where, in the absence of the apostles on missionary journeys we read simply of the presbyters (Acts 11: 30) or James and the presbyters (Acts 21: 17).

The second point, too, is noteworthy; these Christian ministers always appear in the plural. The Jewish presbyteral system is maintained by the Church throughout all the variety of nomenclature. There are two apparent exceptions, which prove to have no substance upon examination. In I Timothy 3: 2 and in Titus 1: 7 the 'bishop' appears in the singular, and from this some have assumed that here we have an officer different from (and superior to) the presbyters. It is clear, however, when the context is examined, that this is not the case. For in Titus 1: 5–7 Titus is ordered to ordain 'presbyters in every city . . . if any be blameless . . . for a bishop must be blameless . . .' In other words, the singular is a generalizing singular, and the presbyters and the bishop are one and the same here as they are in the rest of the New Testament. The other rather strange use of elder in the singular comes in II John 1 and III John 1. The author is apparently so well known that he can simply call himself *the* Elder without fear of being misunderstood. How can this be? Archbishop Carrington has shewn, in the last chapter of his *Primitive Christian Catechism*, that the Church took over the Jewish system of teaching or *tannaite* elders. A famous rabbi like Hillel is often called in an absolute sense '*the* elder'. It seems likely that the John who wrote these letters acquired in Asia a teaching authority equal to that of Hillel among the Jews, and was simply known as *The Elder*. Indeed, this honorific title did not soon die out. Irenaeus calls the bishops of Rome by it, and Hippolytus' favourite name for his master Irenaeus is 'the elder'. It is the affectionate title of respect accorded to the most influential teacher of his age and is used irrespective of whether the recipient be apostle, bishop or presbyter.

5. Two Types of Presbyter?

One question remains. Does the New Testament teach that there were originally two types of elder, corresponding to the lay or ruling elders and the ministerial or teaching elders of Calvin (*Institutes*, Book IV), and some of the Presbyterian churches? The question largely turns on the interpretation of I Timothy 5: 17, 'Let the elders who rule well be considered worthy of double honour [or *pay*], especially those who labour in preaching and teaching.' There can be little doubt that it is the function of all elders to 'rule'. It seems, however, to be strongly implied that not all elders 'labour' (a technical term for ministerial activity—I Thess. 5: 12; Gal. 4: 11, etc.) at preaching and teaching. Does this mean that there is an *élite* within the presbyteral board which *does* spend itself in preaching and teaching? Lightfoot regards this view as untenable,[13] and there is certainly little enough in the rest of the New Testament to support it; many modern Presbyterian writers are also included to abandon it.[14] Nevertheless, it cannot be denied that Cyprian knows of *presbyteri doctores*, teaching elders, as opposed to other presbyters,[15] and this may well have come down from early times. Certainly it makes clear that even in his day there were some presbyters who did not belong to the class of teachers. This becomes all the more plausible when we recall the distinction between tannaite and nontannaite elders within Judiasm which Carrington argues was carried into Christianity. Whether, therefore, we believe there were two classes of elders in the early Church, or whether, with Lightfoot, we interpret this verse as meaning 'as each had his special gift, so would he devote himself more or less exclusively to the one or the other of these sacred functions', does not make a great deal of difference in the last analysis. On any showing the presbyterate of the early Church exercised a far more corporate oversight than that of most Anglican

[13] *Op. cit.*, pp. 22 f.
[14] See *A Manual of Church Doctrine according to the Church of Scotland*, ed. Torrance and Wright (1960), p. 100.
[15] *Ep.* 29.

incumbents and their church councils. The virtual autocracy of many a parish priest today is good neither for him nor for the parish; it is clearly at variance with the pattern of the priesthood in the New Testament; and it obscures the fact that he is called to serve.

CHAPTER FOUR

BISHOPS

1. *Presbyter-Bishops in the New Testament*

In the New Testament bishops and presbyters are the same. This, as Lightfoot has shewn, is the plain meaning of Scripture. His conclusions are accepted even by representative Roman Catholic authorities like the *Catholic Dictionary*, and the attempt of Dr. Austin Farrer in *The Apostolic Ministry* to overthrow it can only be described as an ingenious *tour de force* which has failed to convince anybody. Even he admits (p. 168) that he has not proved his case!

The evidence upon which the identification of presbyter and bishop is based is as follows. In Acts 20 the elders of v. 17 (*presbyteroi*) are called to exercise the function of bishops in v. 28 (*episkopountes*). In I Peter 5: 1, 2 the presbyters are again, in most manuscripts, told to act as bishops of the flock, though some important manuscripts omit the word *episkopountes*.[1] In I Timothy 3: 1-7 we have a description of a bishop, followed immediately by the requirements for a deacon, while in 5: 17-19 the former ministers are referred to and given the name of presbyters. Titus, as we have seen, is told to 'appoint elders in every town . . . for a bishop must be blameless' (Tit. 1: 5-7). It is interesting that Jerome in his commentary on this passage, says plainly, '*Idem est ergo presbyter qui episcopus*'–'the bishop, therefore, is the same as the presbyter', and his view was widely shared in the Church. The identity of presbyters and bishops is the obvious conclusion to be drawn from Philippians 1: 1: 'to all the saints in Christ Jesus who are at Philippi, with the bishops and deacons'. We can hardly imagine the apostle singling out the first and third orders of the ministry with a plurality of bishops thrown in as an extra anomaly! Clement of Rome at the end of the first century knows no difference between the orders. Three times

[1] If the word is not part of the original text, its later inclusion is all the more impressive, because so soon the office of bishop became separate from that of presbyter.

he mentions bishops and deacons together as in Philippians, which is all the more striking because the whole object of his letter is to secure the reinstatement of the deposed presbyters (chapters 42–44). In the *Didache*, too, we meet just two orders, bishops and deacons. As late as the fourth century some memories of this early use survive. The *Apostolic Constitutions* (2: 26, 28) state that it is the presbyters who stand in the place of the apostles. This is not an anti-episcopal claim, but rather a recognition that presbyters and bishops were, in New Testament times, a single order.

2. *Monepiscopacy from the Second Century*

Nevertheless, it must be recognized that by the very beginning of the second century a new phraseology begins. The letters of Ignatius, whose lifetime certainly overlapped considerably with that of St. John, make it certain that monepiscopacy, rule by a single bishop, was a regular feature in the churches of Asia Minor in his own day. As bishop he writes to the bishops of Ephesus, Philadelphia, and so forth. He is almost obsessed with the importance of the episcopate, and he often speaks with great clarity about the threefold ministry. Thus in *Magn.* 6 he urges his readers to 'do all things in unity, under the bishop presiding in the place of God, the presbyters in the place of the Council of the Apostles, and the deacons . . . who are entrusted with the service (*diakonia*) of Jesus Christ'. Though he himself has nothing to say about apostolic succession, we learn from Tertullian (*Adv. Marc.* 4: 5) and Clement of Alexandria (in Eusebius *H.E.* 3: 23) that the Apostle John went round in his old age appointing bishops in Asia Minor. If this were not the case, it seems almost incredible that they should have become so marked a feature of Roman Asia within such a few years of the death of the apostle, although Streeter is probably right in suspecting that the very stress laid by Ignatius upon the indispensability of the bishop is an indication that monepiscopacy is not yet really as firmly established as he would wish (*The Primitive Church*, p. 173 ff.). Indeed, early as its appearance is in the East, it may well have come to the West considerably later. The Roman church was governed by a board of presbyters in the closing years of the first century, as we have seen in I Clement. The same holds good thirty or forty years later when Hermas wrote. He twice refers to bishops, each time in the plural (*Vis.* 3.5.1; *Sim.*

43

9.27.2), and otherwise refers either to the 'elders who preside over the Church' (*Vis.* 2.4) or to 'the rulers of the Church that occupy the chief seats' (*Vis.* 3.9.7). Dr. Telfer, after a careful examination of the evidence, concludes that monarchical episcopacy came to the West almost a generation after Ignatius, and owed a good deal to his teaching on episcopacy which he sealed with his martyrdom (*The Office of a Bishop*, p. 88 ff.). It is interesting that whereas Ignatius could write to the bishop in the Eastern churches, he could not do so—and does not do so—in his letter to the Romans. The same holds good of his contemporary Polycarp. Though himself a bishop in the Ignatian sense (Ignatius, *Polyc.* 1: 1), he knows that this form of polity does not pertain at Philippi. And so, with gracious Christian tact, he begins his letter: 'Polycarp and the presbyters with him, to the Church of God sojourning at Philippi'; he makes no mention of the bishop anywhere in his letter, but refers to the Philippians' own ministers as presbyters (6: 1) and deacons (5: 2). That was in A.D. 115. It is plain that monepiscopacy was unevenly distributed in the first half of the second century.

3. *The Background of Monepiscopacy*

What is the background of this office that springs immediately to full flower in the pages of Ignatius ? The problem is notoriously difficult. There is no obvious parallel in Judaism. Attempts have certainly been made to seek a model in the ruler of the Jewish synagogue who presided over worship and acted as arbiter in synagogue affairs; furthermore, he had an assistant, the *hazzan* who would, on this showing, prove an admirable prototype for the deacon. However, the work of the Christian bishop could no more be derived from that of the ruler of the synagogue than the title *episkopos* from that of *archisynagogos*. A more hopeful source is suggested by the 'overseer' of the Qumran community, particularly since there is increasing evidence of connections between the men of Qumran and the early Christians. At the head of each group of Covenanters, as they were called, was a *mebhakkēr* (overseer or bishop) who presided at meetings and was probably concerned with admission of new members.[2] The Church may possibly have derived the title from this source, but the corporate nature of

[2] See H. H. Rowley: *From Moses to Qumran*, Lutterworth (1963), p. 256.

the New Testament episcopate shows that this solution is no more probable than the last. Monepiscopacy owes more to the precedent set by James of Jerusalem.

4. *The Position of James, the Lord's Brother*

Eusebius,[3] Epiphanius,[4] Chrysostom[5] and Jerome[6] all agree in seeing James as the first bishop of Jerusalem; their accounts differ as to whether he was instituted by the apostles or by the Lord Himself. The evidence is complex, and recent treatments of it have produced radically different results, as may be seen by consulting Telfer's *The Office of a Bishop*, Ehrhardt's *The Apostolic Succession*, Cullmann's *Peter* and Karrer's *Peter and the Church*. What does seem to be clear is this: We know from John 7: 5 that James, along with the other brothers of the Lord, did not believe in Him during His ministry. We know from I Corinthians 15: 7 that the risen Christ appeared to him. From then on he meets us as a Christian. Indeed, in a remarkably short time he rose to a position of extraordinary eminence in the Church. Paul mentions him before Peter and John when he speaks of the 'pillars' of the Jerusalem Church (Gal. 2: 9). Luke (Acts 15: 13–21) records his presidency at the Apostolic Council of apostles and elders at Jerusalem in the late 40's. He is in undisputed leadership of the Jerusalem Church, in fact, after the departure of Peter from Jerusalem (Acts 12: 17). Acts 21: 18 ff. make this particularly obvious. He had, we learn from our scanty extra-biblical sources, a remarkable reputation for piety among non-Christian Jewry; he was so distinguished that he could write a general letter headed 'James, a servant of God and of the Lord Jesus Christ', and everyone would know who was meant; and he left an unparalleled impression on Jewish Christians as the Pseudo-Clementines make plain; to them he is the 'bishop of bishops'.

When we ask what was the reason for this remarkable ascendancy, we shall not find the answer in his undoubted holiness, nor yet in his possible membership of the apostolic band (the meaning of Gal. 1: 19 is ambiguous). He was the nearest male relation to the Saviour. Herein lay his great influence, particularly in a society as dedicated to family

[3] *H.E.* 7: 19.
[4] *Panarion* 78: 7.
[5] *Hom.* 38: 4.
[6] *De Vir. Ill.* 2.

solidarity as were the Jews. It is not without significance that Paul calls him 'the Lord's brother'. If confirmation were wanted that his physical relationship to Jesus was of supreme importance, it is provided by the fact that after his martyrdom 'Symeon, the son of Cleophas, our Lord's uncle, was appointed the second bishop, whom all proposed, as the cousin of the Lord'.[7] Clearly the Jewish Church adopted what Streeter has aptly called a 'caliphate', and if we take the hints given in other parts of the New Testament (for example Mk. 3: 31 ff.; II Cor. 5: 16; Gal. 2: 5-9), we may believe that this was strongly resented in some parts, at least, of the Gentile church. To the claim of the Pseudo-Clementines that James is the bishop of bishops, the Gentile reaction is reflected in the question discussed by Origen, whether a Jewish believer could possibly be a Christian at all. Origen thought he could, but was aware that he was presenting a minority report![8] Jerome is, characteristically, less charitable.[9] While, therefore, there is little doubt that James furnished an obvious precedent for second-century bishops, with his settled abode at Jerusalem, his wide supervision, and his constitutional rule together with the elders (Acts 21: 18), nevertheless, in fact, by his physical connection with the Lord, and because of the destruction of his line in the early years of the second century, he represented the very antithesis of the emerging monepiscopacy of the Catholic Church.

5. The Growth of Monepiscopacy

If the precedents for this office are obscure, so are the stages by which it became separated from the presbyterate. How did *episkope*, the oversight originally vested in all the presbyters, become concentrated in the hands of one? The question has been endlessly debated; the almost complete lack of evidence leaves us very much in the dark, and we can at best deal with probabilities. Certain things, however, are self-evident. If you have a board of elders, one man must obviously preside; otherwise nothing gets done. It is therefore, as Lightfoot saw, most probable that the monarchical bishop arose out of the board of presbyters by virtue of his chairmanship. When we

[7] Eusebius: *H.E.* 4: 22.
[8] See his *Contra Celsum* 2: 1; 5: 61, 65.
[9] *Ep. ad August.* 89. 'They want to be both Christians and Jews. In fact they are neither.'

come to the second century, we find that the bishop is constantly associated with certain activities which would tend to emphasize his supremacy. First and foremost, the bishop is always the president at the eucharist which, from the nature of the case, requires a single celebrant. Secondly, the bishop is always in charge of the property of the church. This remained very little until the very end of the second century, when permanent buildings for worship began to be built. It consisted in the early days almost entirely of the gifts of the Christians in money and kind at the holy communion, and these, naturally, were administered by the bishop as the celebrant. Thirdly, we find the bishop acting as the focus of unity amid the varying sectional interests and, in the early days, house churches of a large town. 'Do nothing without the bishop,' cries Ignatius; 'cherish union; shun divisions' (*Philad.* 7). Fourthly, he appears as the bastion of orthodoxy, the guardian of the apostolic message, particularly in the centuries before an authoritative canon of Scripture was universally recognized. The succession of bishops in a see was regarded, particularly by Irenaeus, as a safeguard against the heretical intrusions of the Gnostics, and a guarantee of continuity with the teachings of the apostolic age. Fifthly, the bishop always appears as, so to speak, the foreign secretary of his church;[10] through him it communicates with others, and through him visitors from other churches are welcomed, and hospitality found for them. In some such ways as these, we may believe, the chairman of the presbyters became the bishop of Catholic Christendom.

6. *The Theory of Monepiscopacy*

But what was the theory behind it? I believe that, quite simply, the idea of sole episcopacy originated in the sole oversight of God Himself. In the New Testament, *episkope* and its cognates are more than once referred to the Holy Trinity. Almighty God oversees the world, and will judge it (Lk. 19: 44; I Pet. 2: 12). Jesus Christ exercises a shepherd's loving oversight over His people (I Pet. 2: 25), while the Holy Spirit sets apart men to exercise this oversight in the Church (Acts 20: 28) as the undershepherds of Christ (I Pet. 5: 4). *Episkope*, therefore, is an attribute of God Himself which in

[10] So Hermas *Vis.* 2: 4: 'Clement will send his [copy] to the foreign countries, for commission has been given to him to do so . . .'

His grace He delegates to some members of His Church. Indeed, it may well be argued that *episkope* belongs to *all* Christians;[11] such seems to be the plain inference from the use of the verb in Matthew 25: 36, 43, James 1: 27 and Hebrews 12: 15. Moulton and Milligan quote papyrus examples of the use of the verb as a common closing salutation meaning to 'look after so and so'. This seems to be the force of Hebrews 12: 15, 'See to it that there is none of your number who . . .' It would seem that, like servanthood and priesthood, oversight belongs to the whole Church. If this is the case, then the supreme oversight is indeed God's, Father, Son and Holy Spirit. He delegates it to the Church, without surrendering His responsibility, and the Church delegates it to the ministry, again without surrendering its own responsibility. No wonder, then, that Paul wrote: 'If anyone aspires to *episkope*, he desires a noble task' (I Tim. 3: 1). No wonder Ignatius exclaims that the bishop is the type, the representative, of God the Father (*Magn.* 6: 1; *Trall.* 3: 1).[12]

7. The Value of Monepiscopacy

Therefore, although the Ignatian type of episcopacy can neither be found in the New Testament nor in many parts of the early Church for a long time to come, nevertheless it remains true that the New Testament does know of pastoral oversight exercised by the apostles and their delegates over local ministers. The need for this sort of oversight increased with the death of the last apostles. With the spread of the Church throughout the world there is more than ever a need for a focus of unity within the churches of a given area. There is still the need to defend the apostolic faith against attenuation or perversion, though whether the episcopate has been particularly successful in this respect down the centuries, and particularly at the present day, may be doubted.[13] Most important of all is the crying need for a ministry to ministers, an oversight of overseers, as none know better than the clergy.

[11] I owe this suggestion to the Rev. J. R. W. Stott.
[12] Ignatius is expressing this same conviction in another way when he says that after his martyrdom the church in Syria will have God for its Shepherd and Christ for its Bishop *in his place*! (Rom. 9: 1).
[13] As the Minority Report in the Anglican-Methodist Conversations puts it (*Report*, p. 58), historic episcopacy 'has notoriously failed to act as the safeguard it is claimed to be. This is sufficiently illustrated by the history of the medieval and renaissance papacy'.

On these grounds it can be urged that not merely the name but the office of bishop is scriptural, primitive, and of abiding value in the Church.

This is becoming increasingly recognized among Free Churchmen. There *is* value in monepiscopacy, and clearly it is the only form of church government that can possibly command universal consent in the reunion of Christendom. But that is not to say that episcopacy as we know it in England is commendable. The larger the diocese, the less justification there is for monepiscopacy. Sole leadership of a million or more people cannot possibly be pastoral, and runs great danger of becoming prelatical. This has been a weakness in English episcopacy for years. Very often counsel is darkened because the Ignatian arguments are applied to the present scheme of things in England, and it is forgotten that episcopacy to Ignatius is more like a vicar's presidency over half a dozen curates than diocesan episcopacy where the bishop presides (if the word is meaningful in such a context) over hundreds of local churches. Ignatius does not speak to our condition, for he does not speak of our sort of bishops. The collegiate nature of Ignatian episcopacy is in sore need of being recovered in England. Twelve times in his epistles does he mention the three orders of ministry, and in ten of them they form an inseparable unity—the other two references are indecisive. We could not realize this today without far smaller bishoprics—the size, perhaps, of an archdeaconry, coupled with some form of synodical government.

The present drift (particularly evident in current ecclesiastical legislation) away from this collegiate conception of oversight in the Church, and the tendency to remove power from the hands of the parish clergy and concentrate it in the hands of the episcopate (with all the growth of ecclesiastical bureaucracy that inevitably accompanies it) is most unhealthy. The Free Churchman regards it with suspicion, and feels that the growing transformation of the bishop from the 'under-shepherd' into the 'lord' of the flock is derogatory to the supreme headship of Christ over His Church. The Eastern Orthodox would be equally dissatisfied with our system. For although they retain a hierarchy of ministries, they recognize that it is the Church as a whole, and not the clergy, let alone the episcopate, who are the inheritors of the truth of God. The bishop is nothing without the laity, nor the laity without the bishop, through whom they are linked to the world-wide Church. The bishops in ecumenical council may seek to define more clearly some aspect of the truth of God, but these definitions must then be acclaimed and lived by the whole people of God before they are recognized as the voice of the Church. This solidarity between bishop and people has nothing quite like it in the West, and their Consecration Prayer that the new bishop may, like the Good Shepherd, lay down his life for the sheep, instruct them faithfully, and in the Day of Judgment be able to hold up his head among those 'who have suffered for the preaching of Thy Gospel' shows that the Eastern Church has come very near the New Testament pattern of the bishop as a leader who is called to serve his people; a pastor who knows, loves, teaches and suffers with his flock.

CHAPTER FIVE

DEACONS

OUR knowledge of the deacon in the primitive Church is as scanty as it is of the bishop, but for a different reason. As we have seen, service (*diakonia*) was the ideal and the task of every member of the Church, and there was no immediate tendency to restrict the title to any particular group within it.

The word 'deacon' is used of Jesus Himself (Rom. 15: 8; Gal. 2: 17), and in consequence is applied very naturally in the New Testament to any kind of service done for His sake. To be sure, in Philippians 1: 1 it does appear to denote a special order of ministry, and in I Timothy 3: 8–13 this is even more obvious. Nevertheless, as if to warn us that the word is still used only in a semi-technical sense, we find Timothy, only a few verses later, being called a deacon (I Tim. 4: 6), while in 1: 12 Paul has used the word to describe his own ministry! Nothing could demonstrate more clearly that the pattern of the Servant was normative for *all* Christian ministry.

1. *An Auxiliary Ministry*

Nevertheless, despite these ambiguities, it is plain from the New Testament that there are ministries of leadership and ministries of assistance, superior and subordinate functions within the Body. The differentiation is first emphasized in Acts 6: 1 ff., where the apostles find the administration of the infant Church too time-consuming and seek out men full of the Spirit to whom they can delegate the financial and administrative tasks arising from the communism of goods practised for a while by the Jerusalem church. Leaving aside the question whether these Seven are to be regarded as deacons in the technical sense, we have here a prime example of the institution of a subordinate and auxiliary ministry, for the Seven are set aside to '*deacon*' tables, thus releasing the apostles for the task of '*deaconing*' the Word (Acts 6: 4).

We find the same differentiation in I Corinthians 12: 28.

Some are given by the Lord the task of being 'rulers' among His people, others are 'helps'. It is possible that in Romans 12: 7 the diaconate is contrasted with the ministry of teaching and exhortation, and the vagueness of St. Paul's language may be due to the fact that he was unaware of the titles given in the Roman church to those who performed these two functions. In Philippians 1: 1, written at much the same time, Paul knows whom he is addressing; they are bishops and deacons. But the same distinction between those who lead and those who assist is present. So, too, in I Timothy 3, we find the diaconate ranged alongside the episcopate as an auxiliary office, though, rather curiously, in the letter to Titus it is not mentioned.

2. *Its Origin*

Some liturgiologists have sought the origin of the deacon in the *ḥazzan* or attendant of the synagogue. This would be suitable enough precedent as far as the liturgical functions of the deacon are concerned, were it not for the fact that where the synagogue attendant is actually mentioned in the New Testament, *ḥazzan* is translated not by *diakonos*, but by a quite different word, *huperetes* (Lk. 4: 20)! In any case it would provide no precedent at all for the administrative and pastoral duties of the Christian deacon. It seems evident that precise analogies are not to be sought outside Christianity; otherwise it would be hard to explain why Clement of Rome (chapter 42) finds it necessary to introduce deacons by force into the text of Isaiah 60: 17!

It is difficult to decide whether Luke thinks of the Seven of Acts 6 as the first Christian deacons. It would be very helpful if so; for it would tell us that deacons were ordained by prayer and the imposition of hands; that they had to be wise men full of the Holy Spirit; and that their functions besides being financial and administrative, involved preaching and disputing with the Jews, evangelism and the performance of wonders and miracles (Acts 6: 7–10; 21: 8). The later Church from Irenaeus onwards certainly saw these Seven as deacons, so much so that there was a tendency in more than one great church of the Roman empire to restrict the number of deacons to seven.[1] Furthermore, there is substance in Lightfoot's contention that

---

[1] The Council of Neo-Caesarea in A.D. 315 passed as one of its canons: 'The deacons ought to be seven, even if the city be great.'

the prominent position given by Luke to this incident is designed to draw attention to the creation of a new office, while the incidental mention of the presbyters in Acts 11: 30 is casual and allusive simply because they do *not* represent a new departure, but are modelled on the presbyters so familiar to Judaism.

Nevertheless, it is a plain fact that the Seven are not called deacons in Acts 6; their functions of preaching and evangelism hardly correspond with the duties assigned to the later diaconate; and when Philip, 'one of the Seven', is mentioned later in the narrative, he is described not as 'the deacon' but as 'the evangelist' (21: 8). No confident conclusion can be drawn on this point, but if the appointment of the Seven is dissociated from the institution of the diaconate, we have no knowledge whatever of the origin of the office, and can only assume from Philippians 1: 1 that this was the name given to a subsidiary office which assisted the presbyter-bishops particularly in financial matters.[2]

3. *Its Function*

The Seven were appointed in the first instance to supervise and administer poor relief. Men like Stephen and Philip would turn to good account the opportunities that came their way as they moved in and out among the poor believers, and so, as Lightfoot has it, 'without ceasing to be dispensers of alms, they became also ministers of the Word'. Whether or not the Seven were deacons, this task of a subsidiary ministry engaged primarily on poor relief fits in well with such scanty references to their function as we find elsewhere in the New Testament. As we have seen, it accords well enough with Philippians 1: 1, and is no less appropriate in I Timothy 3: 8–13. Here it is required that a deacon should be consistent in what he says, and not greedy for money, both important qualities in a man who was constantly moving from house to house and distributing financial help. We are not told that he must be talented at preaching or teaching, but we are told that his life must be exemplary, and that his grasp of the Christian faith must be sound and comprehensive. Because of the pastoral nature of

[2] Paul's letter to the Philippians is a thank-you letter for a contribution given him by the church; and it is reasonable to see the 'bishops and deacons' as the organizers of that collection; hence their separate mention in 1: 1.

their work it is important that deacons be sober, balanced men, aware of the dangers of drink and gossip, cherishing a pure conscience before God, and of unimpeachable character before men. That is why they must be subjected to careful scrutiny before they are accepted for the office.

In subsequent generations we find the deacons closely associated with the bishop whose assistants they are in both administrative and liturgical functions. Indeed, this close association with the bishop led not infrequently to a deacon succeeding to the bishopric without ever being ordained priest. Two things are never forgotten about them; they represent the ministry of the Servant Jesus in His Church,[3] and their supposed origin in 'serving tables' is remembered both in the part they play in administering the holy communion, and in the task which Justin[4] tells us fell to them afterwards, of taking the consecrated elements to any who were unable through sickness to be present at communion.

In the early Church a man would often remain a deacon for life, and so it remains in the Eastern church, where the deacon does a 'lay' job. However, in Western Christendom the office merely became a stepping stone to the priesthood, as, indeed, it still remains in the Roman and Anglican churches.[5] At the Reformation some attempt was made to recover the primitive diaconate, and in Congregational and Baptist churches today the word 'deacon' is used to denote what the Presbyterian churches prefer to call 'elder'. This is a 'lay' office, and does not normally lead into the ordained ministry. Such a man is a representative of the congregation who takes part with the ordained ministry in three ways in particular: by assisting in exercising discipline, by undertaking administrative work, and by distributing the elements at holy communion. The diaconate of the New Testament is awaiting rediscovery within our Church, and should become subject for serious

[3] Ignatius is at pains to emphasize the parallel between the deacons and Jesus. They are 'entrusted with the *diakonia* of Jesus Christ' (*Magn.* 6: 1).

[4] *I Apology*, 65.

[5] One widely accepted explanation of I Timothy 3: 13 would suggest that Paul saw the diaconate as a stepping stone to full oversight. This appears to be an anachronism, and the verse probably means that those who have served well as deacons will gain a good standing for themselves; they will find it, like oversight (3: 1), a thoroughly rewarding task.

study and research in a communion that professes such respect for the threefold historic ministry.

4. *Deaconesses*

There is evidence to suggest that the primitive diaconate included women. In Romans 16: 1 Paul speaks of Phoebe as a woman who clearly held some official position, and was about to be sent by him on definite Church work (traditionally to deliver his letter to the Romans). He describes her as *diakonos* of the church at Cenchreae, and most commentators agree in seeing this as the title of her office. Furthermore, the context of I Timothy 3: 11 and the way in which it is phrased makes it likely that Paul is speaking not of the wives of deacons (to whom he alludes in v. 12), but to woman deacons. Certainly the Greek fathers took this verse to refer to deaconesses; the absence of the definite article would make the translation 'their wives' very harsh, and no one has explained why, if the wives of deacons are meant here, the apostle omits to mention the wives of bishops who would, presumably, have an even more important role. No, we must see this as a reference to deaconesses, and we know from Pliny's letter (10: 96), written about A.D. 112, that there was such an order of ministry in the early Church. He tells us that he examined under torture two deaconesses (*ministrae*). Their value was, of course, immense in an oriental culture which kept women in considerable seclusion. In later times they visited, instructed and assisted at the baptism of woman adherents to the faith. Doubtless, they did the same in the early days as well.

The pattern for such ministry of women is afforded by Luke 8:3. It was not forgotten that dedicated women had followed Jesus about and '*deaconed*' for Him. Indeed, the place of women in early Christianity is in striking contrast to anything to be found in other religions. Christians not only proclaimed that in Christ 'there is neither male nor female' (Gal. 3: 28); they acted upon it. It was to women that Jesus entrusted the first tidings of His Resurrection (Mt. 28: 7). The women are next seen at prayer with the apostles (Acts 1: 14), waiting for the promised outpouring of the Spirit on sons and daughters alike (Acts 2: 17). We find them owning houses which they use for Christian worship (Acts 12: 12); we find them, with their husbands, selling property (Acts 5: 1). We find them engaged in Christian work, women like Mary, Tryphaena and

Tryphosa who 'labour in the Lord' (Rom. 16: 6, 12). We find them associated with Paul in spreading the Gospel (Phil. 4: 3), and it is hard to imagine that this did not sometimes include preaching. Certainly Priscilla seems to have been a women of remarkable gifts who so eclipsed her husband that four times out of the six that they are jointly mentioned her name stands first! It was she, as well as her husband Aquila, who gave Apollos his early instruction in the Christian faith (Acts 18: 26). No doubt preaching, at all events to a mixed congregation, was not usually one of their tasks, though despite Paul's disapproval (I Tim. 2: 11–13) it must on occasion have happened. What are we to make, otherwise, of the four prophesying daughters of Philip? In the Corinthian church women were abusing the new freedom that they found in the Gospel, and not only prayed and prophesied at the meetings for worship (I Cor. 11: 5), but also spoke in tongues (I Cor. 14: 34 in context). Speaking in tongues can be controlled (14: 27), and so women are forbidden to use this gift in public, for if male glossolalia leads to disorder, female glossolalia leads to chaos, as the Irvingite movement discovered. But prophecy is a different matter, so is prayer. So Paul merely insists that when a woman is exercising these gifts in the assembly she should be properly veiled, as the decencies of the time dictated (11: 1–15). She is certainly not relegated to a merely passive role in the conduct of public worship. This is a point of some consequence in these days when the ministry of women is being considered anew. Scripture makes it plain, however, that theirs is, like the male diaconate, an auxiliary ministry. The woman shares a community of life with the man, but has a different and subordinate function; precisely the same holds good of man's relationship with God (I Cor. 11:3). The man is head of the family unit; it is his responsibility to lead, not hers (I Cor. 11:3; Eph. 5:22 ff.). The woman's normal place is not in the pulpit but in the home (I Tim. 2:11–15). And through woman's gossiping of the Gospel in the home, at the laundry, and to her friends, quite as much as through formal preaching by the man, the Christian message pervaded the ancient world.

The diaconate of women has indeed been restored in the Anglican Communion for over half a century now, but its possibilities have not yet been fully explored, nor its challenge laid before girls in the same way as ordination has been held up before boys. It is only on the mission field that the woman worker really comes into her own, and even there it is largely because of the lack of men. The New Testament lays before us an ideal of *diakonia* in which women engage as fully as men. The Church of the Servant must not neglect this pattern; it cannot afford to.

CHAPTER SIX

BARRIERS TO REUNION–
APOSTOLIC SUCCESSION

THE Ecumenical Movement is the most remarkable development in the Church of the twentieth century. Everywhere
churches are looking towards reunion. There are, however,
two elements in the doctrine of the ministry which are proving
serious barriers to reunion. They have been spotlighted in the
Anglican-Methodist Report; they lurk like submerged ice-
bergs in the Anglican-Presbyterian Conversations at present in
progress. They are, of course, apostolic succession and sacrificial priesthood. We shall examine apostolic succession in this
chapter, and priesthood in the next.

A. THE PLACE OF THE APOSTLES IN THE CHURCH

The word 'apostle' is so loosely used in current talk about
'apostolic orders', 'apostolic delegates', 'the apostolate of the
laity', and the like, that it may be profitable to glance briefly
at the place the apostles occupied in the early Church. This is
not at all easy, for there are many questions to which we do not
know the answer. We do not know how many they were; we
have almost no hint as to what they did after the early chapters
of Acts, where, in any case, only Peter and John are prominent.
We do not know for certain that a woman might not have
been an apostle! Romans 16: 7 may be translated 'Andronicus
and *Junia* . . . who are of note among the apostles'. C. H. Dodd
in his *Moffatt Commentary* refers to Chrysostom's homily on
the subject and says drily: 'Chrysostom, preaching on this
passage, saw no difficulty in a woman-apostle; nor need we.'[1]
Most important of all, we do not know for certain that the
apostles had much to do with ordination and the administration of the sacraments. As far as the latter goes, we know that

[1] P. 239. There are, of course, other ways of explaining this
verse!

Paul was not in the habit of baptizing (I Cor. 1: 14), and there is no actual evidence that they normally presided at celebrations of the holy communion. Certainly there is not a hint that a 'valid' communion could not be had without the imposition of their hands upon the celebrant. As a matter of fact, the New Testament evidence that the apostles made a habit of ordaining is far from conclusive. Thus Eduard Schweizer says: 'We have seen Paul does not know ordination ... there is in the churches of which he has the care no rite by which people are either installed or ordained for particular ministries, and that it would be impossible for him to regard any such rite otherwise than as a subsequent recognition of a ministry which had been bestowed previously. The same is true of John's Gospel and Letters. Thus in the New Testament there were large sections of the Church where no special action was performed to assign a special ministry.'[2] W. Telfer finds in the New Testament 'no evidence that presbyter-bishops could only become such by apostolic appointment, or that, when appointed, they received a laying on of apostolic hands';[3] and A. T. Hanson, in commenting on the view that the apostles took steps for the preservation of the ministry, asks: 'What steps did they take? Except for Paul, the only possible way in which the ministry could have been described as being perpetuated was in the presbyters of the Jerusalem church in Acts. But to describe these presbyters as successors of the apostles is absolutely fatal to the "Catholic" theory of the ministry. That is why everyone who tries to find evidence for the "Catholic" theory has to invent or discover a set of bishops (who were also called presbyters) to carry on the essential succession from the apostles to the bishops of the second century'.[4]

One final difficulty is that the word 'apostle' appears to have been used to denote two different categories of people in the early Church. The word means 'sent', and was so applied to special delegates sent out from a church (II Cor. 8: 23; Phil. 2: 25; Acts 14: 4, 14; and often in the *Didache*). But it was, of course, used, *par excellence*, of the apostles of Jesus Christ, and it is with them that we are concerned.

The title is conferred only sparingly on the Twelve during

[2] *Op. cit.*, p. 207.
[3] *The Office of a Bishop*, p. 41.
[4] *The Pioneer Ministry*, p. 144.

the ministry of Jesus. They were called primarily that they might be with Him, and secondarily that He might send them forth to preach, heal and exorcize (Mk. 3: 14, 15). They are represented throughout the ministry as learners, 'disciples'. They will be 'apostles' later, when their Master is no longer with them. This, indeed, happens in the Book of Acts, where 'apostles' is their constant title, and that of 'disciples' disappears. In just one place in his Gospel Mark gives them the title 'apostles', and it is, significantly, when they return from the mission of preaching and healing on which Jesus has sent them (Mk. 6: 30). Matthew also only uses the word of the disciples on this mission (10: 2 ff.), and gives us a very clear idea of what apostleship meant. For they go forth clothed with His authority to do His work. Their message is His message, to preach that the kingdom of heaven is at hand (v. 7). Their function is His function, to be the Servant of the Lord and heal the sick, cleanse the lepers, raise the dead, cast out devils (v. 8). It is precisely the same programme that He Himself fulfils in His message to John the Baptist (11: 5): 'The blind receive their sight and the lame walk, lepers are cleansed and the deaf hear, and the dead are raised up, and the poor have good news preached to them.' They are to be His representatives plenipotentiary—'whosoever receiveth you receiveth me' (10: 40); and here we are given a miniature of the apostolic mission as it would develop after the resurrection. Meanwhile their task is to be with Him, and to get to know Him whom later they would represent. So as soon as they return from this mission they become 'disciples' again, and so they remain until the end of the book.

After the resurrection the apostolic band takes the place of Jesus (Mt. 28: 18–20; Acts 1: 8). They are to become witnesses to Jesus, as He was to the Father, and the Spirit will bear witness, too (Jn. 15: 26, 27). They will be led by that same Spirit into all the truth about Jesus, and become the authoritative interpreters of the person and work of Jesus (Jn. 14: 26; 16: 13–15). Thus the apostles become the norm of doctrine in the early Church (Acts 2: 42). 'That is why,' writes Cullmann, 'the New Testament attributes the same images to Jesus as to the apostles: "rocks" and the corresponding images of "foundation", "pillars". Never are these images used to designate the bishop.'[5] So closely are they integrated with the

[5] *Christianity Divided*, Sheen & Ward (1961), p. 10.

person of their Master that Cullmann can say with truth: 'The Apostolate does not belong to the period of the Church, but to that of the Incarnation of Christ.'[6] Indeed, so close is the identity between the Sender and the sent that the New Testament can regard the apostolic tradition and teaching about Jesus as from the Lord Himself.[7] The exalted Lord proclaims through His apostles His own teaching and the extension of what He had said while He was on earth. Then it was a case of having many things to say to them which, at the time, they were not able to assimilate.

Since Pentecost, however, the Holy Spirit has actualized for the apostles the mind of the Lord Jesus (I Cor. 2:16), as He Himself promised: 'When the Spirit of truth comes, He will guide you into all the truth, for He will not speak on His own authority . . . He will glorify me, for He will take what is mine and declare it to you' (Jn. 16: 13, 14); and again: 'The Holy Spirit whom the Father will send in my name, He will teach you [that is, you apostles] all things, and bring to your remembrance all that I have said to you' (Jn. 14: 26). As A. F. Walls succinctly puts it: 'This witness, being grounded in a unique experience of the incarnate Christ, and directed by a special dispensation of the Holy Spirit, provides the authentic interpretation of Christ, and has ever since been determinative for the universal Church. In the nature of things the office could not be repeated or transmitted; any more than the underlying historic experiences could be transmitted to those who had never known the incarnate Lord or received a resurrection appearance.'[8]

This unique teaching office, springing from the fact that their witness to Jesus was *direct*, while all other witness is *derived* (or, as Paul puts it in Gal. 1: 1-12, their reception of the Gospel was *di'apokalypseos*, by revelation, not *di'anthropou*, through human intermediaries), sets the apostles apart, and this fact was recognized by the second-century Church when they took care to admit to the canon only those writings which they knew emanated from the apostolic circle. Through the

[6] *Op. cit.*, p. 10.
[7] See Cullmann's essay 'The Tradition' in his book *The Early Church*, S.C.M. (1956), and on the supreme teaching office of the apostles, N. Geldenhuys' *Supreme Authority*, M.M.S. (1953).
[8] Article 'Apostle' in the *New Bible Dictionary*, I.V.F. (1962).

witness of the apostolic band[9] the first-century world was enabled to encounter Jesus; through their witness, recorded in the Scriptures of the New Testament, twentieth-century men can still meet their Lord. And just as the early Church was bound by the apostolic witness both for doctrine and behaviour,[10] so is the Church of subsequent ages. We are bound to the apostles and their testimony; we cannot get behind them. We believe because of their word (Jn. 17: 20). This is the apostolic succession that was envisaged by Jesus. The apostles are, in fact, historically unique and doctrinally normative.

But in other respects, of course, the apostles do have successors. As missionaries, as preachers, as servants of the Lord, as ministers of the Gospel and the sacraments, as leaders of the Christian community, they have successors. The question is, wherein does this succession lie?

B. THE SUCCESSION TO THE APOSTLES IN THE CHURCH

Apostolic succession is a phrase with several meanings. It can refer to doctrinal succession whereby later generations recognize that they are bound by the teachings of the founder-members of the Church, the apostles who were themselves taught by Jesus.

The phrase is also applied to a succession of function and authority. It was used in this sense by Irenaeus and Hippolytus at the end of the second century to describe the succession of one bishop to another in a see. This succession was a valuable guardian of the apostolic faith, especially in the days when Gnostic error was encroaching on the Church, and when the canon of apostolic writings was not yet clearly defined. Indeed, through such a succession of bishops in their sees the Church at large learnt to express its conviction that the ministry is one

[9] It was a corporate witness, not the perquisite of any one individual. The homogeneity of this witness, and the extent to which it underlies every stratum of the New Testament, have been shewn in C. H. Dodd's books *The Apostolic Preaching and its Development*, Hodder and Stoughton (1936) and *According to the Scriptures*, Nisbet (1952).

[10] I Tim. 6: 3–5; II Thess. 3: 14; II Jn. 10; and supremely I Cor. 14: 37 f.: 'If any one does not recognize this (that what I am writing to you is a commandment of the Lord), he is not recognized.'

throughout the world and down the ages. It is, therefore, reasonable to expect that in the future reunited Church of God episcopacy will have an important and expressive part to play.

It is with the third interpretation of 'apostolic succession' that violent disagreement sets in. This view claims that the apostles ordained the bishops to succeed them, and that the historic episcopate, stretching in unbroken succession back to the apostles, is essential to the Church. Without such ordination it is impossible to exercise a 'valid' ministry or celebrate a 'valid' sacrament.

This view has occasionally been found in individual Anglican writers since the Reformation, but it came to the fore only last century with Newman's first *Tract for the Times* at the beginning of the Oxford Movement. The traditional exposition of the doctrine from then on has been that the threefold ministry is a divine institution stemming from the apostles and secured by an unbroken line of ordinations. The publication of *The Apostolic Ministry* in 1946, however, gave a new turn to the argument. It divided ministries into *essential* (that is, that possessed by the episcopate, in succession to the apostles) and *dependent* (that is, all other ministries). Such a doctrine was flattering to the bishops, and seems to have strengthened the current ecclesiastical tendency towards the separation of the bishops from the presbyters, but it was very damaging to the old 'catholic' dogma of the threefold ministry.

Dix goes so far as to say that all this talk about the historic episcopate is beside the point. He recognizes that the non-conformist ministries should not be offered *episkope*, for they already possess it. Indeed, in one respect they are more entitled than the Anglicans to the title of *episkopoi*, for their ministers are freely chosen by their own churches, in contrast to Anglican bishops who are nominees of the state (p. 295 f.). 'What is really in question in our present discussions about "episcopacy" is not the "episcopate" at all. It is the "apostolate".' Dix is not interested in the pros and cons of the concentration of *episkope* in the hands of a single individual; this is unimportant and could be disastrous, as the New Testament precedent of Diotrephes shows. (He, of course, of all figures in the New Testament acts most like a later monarchical bishop, and is condemned in the most uncompromising terms in III John.) No, Dix, together with Kirk in the introductory essay, argues that the essence of apostolic authority is its derivation from the Lord. The principle is plain, 'as the Father has sent me, even so send I you'. This commission from Jesus the apostles passed on to the bishops who are the custodians of it today.

That is the theory in its essentials; and in order to bolster it up, Dix propounds, and Kirk accepts, the doctrine of the Jewish *shaliach*. This officer figures a good deal in rabbinic writings. He is a delegate with plenipotentiary powers; thus 'he that is sent is as he that sent him.' There is indeed some evidence to suggest that such a view as this underlay the idea of apostle, as Rengstorf has shewn.[11] It would account very well, for one thing, for the unique authority of the apostles to which the second-century Church wistfully looked back. It is not conclusive evidence, however. For one thing, the *shaliach* always acted within Judaism and had no missionary function, which was the main *raison d'être* of the apostles. More serious still, there is little evidence to suggest that the idea of *shaliach* had arisen in Judaism by the first century A.D. But what is so damaging for the whole theory, as T. W. Manson, L. Morris and A. Ehrhardt[12] have pointed out with devastating clarity, is that the *shaliach* could *not transmit his authority*. 'We are therefore forced to conclude', writes Dr. Ehrhardt, 'that unless Dr. Kirk abandons Rengstorf's theory that the apostle was the *shaliach* of Christ, he cannot very well maintain the doctrine of apostolic succession' (p. 20). It should be noted that this criticism comes from one who is sympathetic to the doctrine in some form, and so unsatisfactory does he find the attempt of the *Apostolic Ministry* to demonstrate this succession in the early period, that he writes his book to try and prove it another way, by means of a priestly succession through James of Jerusalem—an attempt which must be adjudged no more successful.

There is, therefore, considerable confusion in the arguments with which the Anglo-Catholic position has been supported

---

[11] See his article 'Apostleship' in Kittel's *Theol. Wörterbuch zum Neuen Testament*, translated in A. and C. Black's *Kittel Bible Key Words* (1952).

[12] T. W. Manson: *The Church's Ministry*, pp. 35–52; A. Ehrhardt: *The Apostolic Succession*, chapter 1, and L. Morris: *Ministers of God*, pp. 114–118.

in recent years,[13] and it is probably true to say that only a small minority in the Church of England accept it. Nevertheless, it is a vociferous and influential minority, and so it may be as well to ask four questions of this theory. Is it the biblical teaching? Is it sound theology? Is it historically demonstrable? Is it Anglican doctrine?

1. *Is it the biblical teaching?*

The Church of England takes its stand fairly and squarely on the supremacy and sufficiency of Scripture. Article VI declares explicitly that 'Holy Scripture containeth all things necessary to salvation, so that whatsoever is not read therein, nor may be proved thereby, is not to be required of any man, that it should be believed as an article of the Faith, or be thought requisite or necessary to salvation'.

Nobody has yet succeeded in demonstrating that apostolic succession is taught in Scripture, certainly not the authors of *The Apostolic Ministry*, where a great deal of special pleading is supported by such expedients as typology and rabbinic

[13] Indeed, an example of even greater confusion—or is it the beginning of a new attitude among Anglo-Catholics?—is to be found in an article in the Kelham magazine, *S.S.M.* for March 1964 by Gilbert Sinden. He abandons the identification of apostle and *shaliach* because of the fatal objection that 'a *shaliach* cannot pass on his authority to someone else (cf. *Gittin* 3: 6)', and recognizes that 'the Twelve were regarded as a once-for-all body within the Church; the "apostles of the churches" were occasional officials and in no sense "successors" of the Twelve'. Earlier in his article he had already rejected Dix's notion that the episcopate was regarded as the same office as the apostolate in the New Testament and the early Church. His conclusion is that 'the Church herself was apostolic, "sent" by the Father as Jesus had been "sent" by the Father . . . So far as the New Testament is concerned, there is no suggestion that Jesus, or the Twelve, had instituted a ministry of bishops, priests and deacons, but the New Testament is very clear that the Church's very nature is to exercise pastoral care (*episkope*), priesthood—and especially an evangelistic priesthood of the Gospel (*hierosyne*), and service of all kinds (*diakonia*) both to its own members and to the world at large for whom Christ had died. These are the marks of the Church, and it was only natural and proper that its organization should reflect its nature.' If this really is the latest Anglo-Catholic position, it is precisely that advocated by the Free Churchman, Professor T. W. Manson, in chapters 2 and 3 of his book *The Church's Ministry*, and while boding well for future inter-church relations, makes current Anglican intransigence over the necessity of episcopal ordination look particularly dated.

precedents. It is true that the 'apostles'[14] Paul and Barnabas are once represented as appointing presbyters in every town. Very likely it was their regular practice, doubtless with the laying on of hands with prayer. But we are never told that the apostles had hands laid on them by our Lord. We are never told that the ministry in all Christian communities had to wait for an apostle to come and authorize it. Indeed, the New Testament indications, quite as much as the probabilities of the case, suggest that the first ministers in any congregation were appointed by the missionaries (often relatively unknown folk, see Acts 8: 1–4; 11: 19–26), and then became self-recruiting. There was certainly a ministry in Rome and Antioch before these cities were visited by any apostle, and it is interesting to note that when Paul left Philippi after his first visit there was only a tiny group of believers and no hint of any regular ministry (Acts 16), whilst when he came to write to the Philippians a few years later (without having visited them in the meantime), there is a flourishing ministry of bishops and deacons (1: 1). There is, in fact, no suggestion that apostolic commissioning was indispensable for the ministry; to think in these terms is an anachronism. Not until early in the third century did the doctrine of manual transmission of the grace of orders begin to arise.[15]

Furthermore, the holders of this view fail consistently to recognize the fact that there was a diversity of practice in New Testament times, and that 'primitive catholic uniformity' is nothing but a romantic myth. Karl Holl and Eduard Schweizer[16] in influential books (entirely neglected by the authors of *The Apostolic Ministry*) have shewn that there is a diversity of practice in the New Testament itself. The prototype of 'catholic order' is represented by James and the Jewish church; the second-century episcopal lists mostly claimed to reach back to him.

The Pauline churches, on the other hand, are interested in

---

[14] Paul and Barnabas are only called 'apostles' in the Acts in chapter 14, when they are delegates of the Antioch church (13: 1–5 cf. 14: 26–28). We do not know whether Barnabas was an 'Apostle of Jesus Christ'.

[15] This is recognized by Dix, *op. cit.*, pp. 200 f.

[16] K. Holl: *Gesammelte Werke* II, pp. 44 f., and E. Schweizer: *Das Leben des Herrn in der Gemeinde und ihren Diensten*, Zurich, 1946.

order but not in succession.[17] Paul himself was called in no succession; no one laid ordaining hands on him, and he is clear that anyone, however impeccable his ministerial pedigree, must be judged by his faithfulness to the Gospel message (Gal. 1: 8). After all, Judas was an apostle. He too has had a succession in the history of the Church!

There is discernible a third attitude to church order in the New Testament, that of the Johannine writings, where there are no offices as such, no special ministries, even the word 'apostle' has disappeared; the gift of the Spirit, and the believer's direct union with God and love for the brethren take their place.[18]

Even if there were not this variety within the church order of the New Testament itself, the silence of Scripture would be decisive. If episcopacy were essential to the Church, God would have made it quite clear to us. Would the God who attested the certainty of our forgiveness by the resurrection leave us with no clear direction as to church order, had it been necessary for man's salvation, as this theory asserts?

2. *Is it sound theology?*

The strength of the view we are considering is that it takes very seriously the visible Church of God as the society which, for all its faults, Jesus left to carry on His work in the world. But such an approach is exposed to several dangers.

It tends to limit the grace of God to episcopal communions, and regards with grudging reluctance the evidence, which is plain for all to see, that He works just as effectively in non-episcopal churches. It simply will not do to dismiss this evidence with talk of 'uncovenanted mercies' and the like.

Secondly, such a view is in great danger of depersonalizing the grace of God; instead of the loving relation of the Father to His child, grace becomes a commodity which may only be obtained through the proper channels. This is a serious declension from the New Testament concept of the grace of God.[19]

Thirdly, this view tends to regard the grace of God and the

[17] No later churches drew succession lists from a ministry ordained by Paul or his lieutenants Timothy and Titus.
[18] See Schweizer: *Church Order in the New Testament*, pp. 117–130.
[19] See Brunner's passionate protest against such depersonalization in his *Misunderstanding of the Church*.

working of His Spirit as something that can be organized and controlled. Once you start thinking, as the authors of *The Apostolic Ministry* avowedly think, of those in the apostolic succession as 'plenipotentiaries' of Christ, you fall little short of blasphemy against the Holy Spirit, Christ's true 'plenipotentiary'.[20] It is, no doubt, very comfortable, but entirely false, to think that the external form inevitably carries with it the internal grace. God remains sovereign in His working. No system of dogmatics, no method of church order can get Him 'taped'. Catholicism runs the same danger as did Judaism, of forgetting that the Church stands or falls by the response of faith to grace — and not by a succession. The Jews felt they had something (the Law), by keeping which they could exert a claim on God. The whole New Testament gives the lie to any such claim on the part of men, and yet the doctrine of apostolic succession comes perilously near to reasserting it. As Bishop Robinson emphasizes in his essay on the subject, the Church is not the Kingdom; it always remains subject both to the kingly rule and the judgment of God: 'To claim that the Church now has "the plenitude" is to forget that. Ecclesiasticism is always in danger of subordinating both the spiritual and the eschatological to the historical.'[21]

One other point is important. This doctrine of apostolic succession reverses the New Testament picture of a ministry dependent upon the Church. Instead we are presented with a Church so dependent upon the ministry that if, as could well have happened at some periods of church history, such as the Diocletian persecution, all Christian ministers standing in the supposed succession had been rounded up and killed, that would have been the end of the Church. Such a view, of course, borders on fantasy, but what else can Bishop Kirk mean when he says, 'should such a ministry (that is, the "essential ministry" of bishops in the succession) fail, the apostolic Church, which is the Body of Christ in space and

[20] Indeed, both those who accept and those who reject this doctrine of apostolic succession recognize that in the last analysis they have a different conception of *God*. Thus Bishop Stephen Neill 'cannot recognize as Christian the doctrine of God' underlying *The Apostolic Ministry* (*The Ministry of the Church*, p. 28), while Bishop Kirk (*The Apostolic Ministry*, p. 32) admits: 'In the end these [different doctrines of the ministry] will be discovered to involve divergent beliefs about the nature of God Himself.'

[21] *The Historic Episcopate*, pp. 18 f.

time, would disappear with it (for the two are inextricably bound together)'[22] ? But according to the New Testament, the fullness of the Godhead, which indwelt the incarnate Christ, now dwells in all Christians corporately (Col. 2: 9, 10; Eph. 1: 23), not in any ministerial *élite*. The ministry, like all the other members in Christ's Body, exists for the sake of the Body (Eph. 4: 11–14; Col. 1: 24, 25). It exists to build up the saints for the work of ministry (Eph. 4: 12). For it is not merely the ordained ministry but the whole Church which has inherited the apostolic commission, 'Go and make disciples of all nations, baptizing them . . . teaching them to observe all that I have commanded you; and lo, I am with you always, to the close of the age' (Mt. 28: 19 f.). The whole Church succeeds to the apostolic charge because she is called, empowered, instructed and sent by Christ to go and make disciples of the nations.

3. *Is it historically demonstrable?*

Once again the answer must be 'No'. Ignatius holds an immensely high doctrine of episcopacy, but he has not a word to say about any supposed succession from the apostles. Indeed, he goes to some lengths to dissociate himself from them; thus: 'I do not command you, as Peter and Paul did. They were apostles, I am a convict' (*Rom.* 4, cf. *Trall.* 1). The *Didache*, furthermore, which enjoyed vast prestige in the early Church, enjoins on the congregations to which it writes the necessity of their *appointing their own bishops and deacons* (15: 1)! Clement of Rome knows that—at Corinth—the apostles appointed bishops (44: 1) or presbyters (44: 5) 'with a further enactment that if they should fall asleep other approved men should succeed to their ministry'. It is perverse to make the 'their' refer to the apostles; it clearly refers to the deceased bishops, and we have, therefore, in Clement a corporate succession in office which is the precursor of the monarchical succession to be found first in Irenaeus and Hegesippus at the end of the second century. These writers still have not any doctrine of manual transmission of grace. Irenaeus, it now seems almost certain, was consecrated not by another bishop but by the council of his presbyters in Lugdunum.[23] This practice of presbyteral consecration continued

[22] *The Apostolic Ministry*, p. 40.
[23] See E. Molland: *Journal of Ecclesiastical History* (1950), i, pp. 12–28.

until the fourth century in Alexandria.[24] The doctrine of the manual transmission of grace for episcopacy in succession from the apostles is first found in third-century Latin Christians. It is interesting, as T. M. Lindsay points out, to note that many of its inventors were lawyers, men like Cyprian, Tertullian and Augustine. 'Apostolic succession in the dogmatic sense', he says, 'is the legal fiction required by the legal mind to connect the growing conceptions of the authority of the clergy with the earlier days of Christianity. It served the Christian lawyer in much the same way that another curious legal fiction assisted the pagan civilian. The latter insisted that the government of the Emperors from Augustus to Diocletian was the prolongation of the old Republican constitution; the former imagined that the rule of bishops was the prolongation through the generations of the inspired guidance of the original apostles who were the planters of the Church.'[25] So much for a Presbyterian summary of the situation, written fifty years ago. The Anglican church historian, Dr. Telfer, who has contributed the most recent review of the evidence, agrees. 'These Latin churchmen created a historical myth, the unhistorical nature of which they were secure from discovering. This was to the effect that the apostles had provided for the future of the Church by creating an order of monarchical bishops. The first of these they ordained, according to this myth, with their own hands, and set them to govern the several churches with which they were concerned.'[26]

4. Is it Anglican doctrine?

In the first place, it is important to remember that the Church of England requires no one to believe as necessary any doctrine which cannot be proved from Scripture (Art. VI). This doctrine of apostolic succession in the third sense defined above (p. 63) cannot be so proved, and therefore we would expect to find nothing in the formularies of the Church of England to require its acceptance. That is precisely what we do find. Succession is not included in the marks of the Church (Art. XIX); it is not mentioned in Art. XXIII which deals with the subject of ministering in the congregation; and the Preface to the Ordinal carefully refrains from unchurching non-episcopal

[24] See E. W. Kemp: *Journal of Ecclesiastical History* (1955), vi, pp. 125–142; see also W. Telfer: *J.E.H.* (1952), iii, pp. 1–13.
[25] *The Church and the Ministry in the Early Centuries*, p. 279.
[26] *The Office of a Bishop*, p. 119.

bodies, while giving good grounds for the retention of the threefold ministry in our own church. A sentence from the Preface to the Prayer Book is relevant here: 'In these our doings we condemn no other nations, nor prescribe anything but to our own people only.' Furthermore, the Church of England explicitly claims to uphold the doctrine of justification by faith only (Art. XI); in other words she unashamedly takes her stand with the churches of the Reformation on this issue which divided Christendom in the sixteenth century. This does not mean for one moment, as Dix rather loosely asserts, that 'where the doctrine of "Justification by faith alone" is held, no question of church order can be anything but entirely secondary, even meaningless' (op. cit., p. 301), but it assuredly does mean that where this doctrine is held, no one form of the ministry should be or can be regarded as essential for the existence of the Church. Presbyterians, for instance, have the highest regard for the importance of regular and public succession to the ministry, and yet hold jealously to the doctrine of justification. They ground the validity of their succession not so much in historical continuity (to do so would be to have 'confidence in the flesh', Phil. 3: 3), but in the promise of Christ to be with the Church down the ages. 'Ministerial succession in no way secures the possession of the Holy Spirit, nor does it guarantee a lawful ministry. But because it is the apostolically appointed ordinance, it cannot be condemned or neglected without disobedience and loss.'[27]

This seems to me to be not only the spiritually healthy attitude to succession, but the one that has been most characteristic of the Church of England since the Reformation. The Reformers themselves freely intercommunicated with their brethren in the Reformed and Lutheran Churches on the Continent; this practice continued for over 200 years. Bishop Joseph Hall, who in 1618 attended the Synod of Dort as a representative of the Church of England, could write in his book *Peacemaker* on his return: 'There is no difference in any essential matter betwixt the Church of England and her sisters of the Reformation. We accord in every point of Christian doctrine, without the least variation.'[28]

[27] *Manual of Church Doctrine according to the Church of Scotland*, ed. Torrance and Selby Wright, p. 98.
[28] Quoted by N. Sykes: *The Church of England and Non-Episcopal Churches*, p. 23.

Richard Hooker, that most representative of Anglicans, prized episcopacy very highly, and yet refused to conclude that it is absolutely necessary. He gives as one exception, 'when God Himself doth of Himself raise up any, whose labour He useth without requiring that men should authorize them'; as another, 'when necessity doth constrain to leave the usual ways of the Church which otherwise we would willingly keep' (*Eccl. Pol.* VII, xiv, 11). This was the situation which forced Luther to break with Rome. The papacy of his day would allow no appeal from itself to Scripture. Luther had to choose between sound doctrine and episcopal consecration. As R. F. Hettlinger justly observes: 'The Lutherans were ready to preserve unity even if the bishops personally rejected their doctrines, so long as they would ordain men who believed in justification by faith, but "they admit none except they will swear not to teach the pure doctrine of the Gospel" (Augsburg Confession of 1530)'.[29] Hooker himself concluded that 'the Church hath power by universal consent to take it [episcopacy] away, if thereunto she be constrained through the proud, tyrannical, and unreformable dealings of her bishops' (*op. cit.* VII, v, 8). Episcopacy, though valuable, is not indispensable.

The late Professor Norman Sykes has shown in two influential books, *Old Priest and New Presbyter* and *The Church of England and Non-Episcopal Churches in the Sixteenth and Seventeenth Centuries* that this was the characteristic Anglican position, including most of the high church Caroline divines, until the Oxford Movement, when in the first of the celebrated *Tracts for the Times* Newman wrote of the bishop in ordination that 'he but *transmits*; and thus the Christian Ministry is a *succession*. And if we trace back the power of ordination from hand to hand, of course, we shall come to the Apostles at last. We know we do, as a plain historical fact (!) . . . We must necessarily consider none to be *really* ordained unless they have been *thus* ordained'. The Anglo-Catholic doctrine of the *exclusive* validity of those orders which come within the apostolic succession was something quite novel in the Church of England.[30] It is not doctrinally sound, scripturally based, historically reputable, or part of the teaching of our Church. Indeed, the Anglo-Catholic historian Darwell Stone admits

[29] *Episcopacy and Reunion*, Mowbray (1953), p. 81.
[30] See the evidence set out in J. W. Hunkins, *Episcopal Ordination and Confirmation in relation to Inter-Communion and Reunion.*

that it is impossible to argue 'that the present formularies and the post-Reformation English divines are committed to the necessity of episcopal ordination as distinct from the practical requirement in the Church of England'.[31]

In view of this, it seems astonishing that this dogma of apostolic succession should be allowed to bedevil the promising conversations at present in progress with a view to reuniting the Protestant churches in these islands. Anything done here would give a great impetus to such reunions elsewhere in the world. The Church of England may quite properly ask that those with whom she enters into union shall accept the fact, without any 'particular theory or interpretation',[32] of episcopacy from then onwards. It would, however, be a gross impropriety to stipulate that those ministers entering the united church shall be episcopally ordained. Time and time again Anglicans have been thought muddled or, what is worse, insincere, because despite repeated protestations such as the Lambeth Appeal of 1920 (which spoke of the 'spiritual reality of Free Church ministries'[33]), and the Memorandum of the Joint Conference which followed it (and which so far from finding Free Church ministries 'invalid, that is null and void', declared, 'we regard them as being within their several spheres real ministries in the Universal Church'[34]), there has, nevertheless, been a marked unwillingness to admit the churches concerned to communion without the explicit or implicit reordination of their ministers.

'The challenge of the single successful experiment in reunion from the Church of South India,' wrote Sykes,[35] 'and the contrast between its unequivocal taking of episcopacy into its system, and the equivocal response of Lambeth 1948, have

[31] Quoted in N. Sykes: *Old Priest and New Presbyter*, p. 212.
[32] *Lambeth Conference Report* (1930).
[33] 'We do not call in question for a moment the spiritual reality of the ministries of those communions which do not possess the Episcopate. On the contrary, we thankfully acknowledge that these ministries have been manifestly blessed and owned by the Holy Spirit as effective means of grace' (*Lambeth Report* (1920), 9.7).
[34] See G. K. A. Bell: *Documents on Christian Unity* (1924), p. 158. As R. F. Hettlinger comments (*op. cit.*, p. 95), Bishop Kirk recognizes the unpalatable fact that this Memorandum gives away the Anglo-Catholic case, and therefore devoted two pages to showing that it is patient of another legitimate interpretation (see Kirk: *op. cit.*, pp. 42–45).
[35] *Old Priest and New Presbyter*, pp. 237 f.

raised . . . the query whether from the Anglican side episcopacy has not assumed the elusive characteristic of the ghost of Hamlet's father "*Hic et ubique*: then we'll shift our ground". The differences between Lambeth in 1930 and in 1948 have evoked the suspicion that in fact a particular interpretation of the historic episcopate (and not the adoption of that institution alone) is being asked of non-episcopal churches as a condition of full union or intercommunion; and, further, that this interpretation is not the traditional Anglican doctrine of episcopacy but the exclusive theory of Tractarian *provenance* and championship.'

It is very much to be hoped that the next Lambeth Conference will reassert the truth that the Church of England has never held episcopacy to be of the *esse* of the Church, and that the widespread assumption among our nonconformist brethren that this is the official Anglican doctrine, is a misconception, unsupported by Scripture, our formularies, or our historical practice. In fact, more than once in our history (notably between 1610 and 1638 in our relations with Scots when episcopalians did not reordain those whom presbyterians had already ordained, and later for many years in India[36]) there have coexisted for a period after union two types of ministry, those episcopally and those not episcopally ordained. It is tragic that these precedents were not, apparently, known to the Lambeth Bishops in 1948 who said, in defence of their equivocal attitude to the Church of South India: 'We have never yet entered into full communion with any church which does not possess a fully unified ministry, episcopally ordained.' It would be more tragic still if the prospect of reunion with the Methodists and Presbyterians were marred by similar intransigence upon this point.

While it is right to respect the views of minorities as far as possible, *is* it right that a view which was introduced into Anglicanism with the Tractarians, a view which led their most consistent thinkers to join the Church of Rome, should be allowed to prejudice the reunion of the Anglican Church with some of her sister churches of the Reformation? And if it be argued that reunion with these churches on these terms would

[36] See Bishop Stephen Neill in *The Ministry of the Church*, p. 21, and Sykes: *op. cit.*, p. 236, also G. E. Duffield's article 'Intercommunion and the Ministry', in *The Churchman*, December 1963, pp. 235 ff.

prejudice our eventual reunion with Rome and the Orthodox Church,[37] this must be resisted; for these churches do not believe that our orders are valid in any case! They do not accept that we have the precious gift which we are so anxious to pass on to others. So reunion with other Reformation churches is unlikely to alter our future relations with Rome. There is great value in a bridge, provided it reaches both sides of the gulf. But there is not much value in a 'bridge church', as the Church of England delights to be, if it fails to reach either side. And that is precisely the danger that the Church of England has been running since the Tractarian Movement alienated us from the Reformed churches without gaining for us recognition from the 'Catholic' side.

[37] For the rather complex evidence on Orthodox views of Anglican orders, see T. Ware: *The Orthodox Church*, pp. 324 ff.

CHAPTER SEVEN

BARRIERS TO REUNION—SACRIFICIAL PRIESTHOOD

As we saw in an earlier chapter, the word 'priest' is derived in terms both of etymology and function from the 'elder' (Greek *presbyteros*) of the New Testament. There is, however, another meaning commonly associated with the word—one who offers sacrifice. The Greek word for such a person is quite distinct, *hiereus*, a sacrificing priest. This is not a mere matter of playing with words. The meaning is important for the whole conception of the Christian ministry. Calvin complained of the Roman Catholic bishops that 'by their ordination they create not presbyters to rule and feed the people, but priests to offer sacrifice'. Does the Church of England do this? The answer which appears increasingly to underlie modern Anglican pronouncements is 'Yes'. The idea is that the priest, duly ordained in the apostolic succession, has entrusted to him the authority and power to offer the sacrifice of the eucharist. It is of this that the Minority Report in the Anglican-Methodist Conversations complains (p. 60): 'Whatever the etymology of the English word *priest*, in this report it means more than *presbyter*. It is expressly connected with sacrificial views of the Eucharist.' Because this conception of the priesthood in the Church of England is undoubtedly a grave barrier to any hopes of reunion, we must examine both the New Testament evidence and the historic position of the Church of England.

A. PRIESTHOOD AND SACRIFICE IN THE NEW TESTAMENT

1. *The Priesthood of Christ and His Sacrifice*

I do not think that it is necessary these days to go over much of the old ground again. It is recognized on all sides now that Christ sums up in Himself all that was symbolized by the sacrificing priesthood of the Old Testament. He has Himself so discharged the office of a *hiereus* that no other priest is needed, and no needs of the human soul remain unmet. His sacrifice is admitted by Anglo-Catholic and Evangelical alike to be unique and unrepeatable. All this is solid gain. I suppose, there is hardly a priest of any learning within the Anglican Communion who would argue the old medieval dogma of Catholicism that in the eucharist the priest offers Christ for the sins of the living and the dead. It is now, thank God, universally recognized that Christ's priesthood is final and complete, and that His sacrifice of Himself upon the cross for man's forgiveness can neither be added to nor repeated. Thus Father Hebert asserts, 'the sacrificial action is not any sort of re-immolation of Christ, not a sacrifice additional to His one sacrifice, but a participation of it', and he strongly repudiates 'any idea that in the eucharist we offer a sacrifice to propitiate God'.[1] So far so good. It is difficult to see how any other view could ever have gained acceptance amongst any familiar with the argument of the Epistle to the Hebrews, with its reiteration of the finality of Christ's sacrifice and the sufficiency of His sacrifice (for example 7: 23–28; 9: 24–28; 10: 1–22, especially 10–14, 16–21). 'Christ thus abolishes all further human priesthood,' writes Prof. A. Richardson.[2]

One might go further and point out that any such priest would suffer from the same three defects which marred the efficacy of the old Jewish priesthood. In the first place, he would be a sinner, himself needing forgiveness, and therefore unable to procure it for others (Heb. 7: 26, 27). Secondly, he could not offer a sacrifice which is acceptable to God, for whom nothing is good enough but the total obedience of a life of utter love to Him (10: 4–10), and from whom sin makes a complete separation (Is. 59: 1, 2; Rom. 6: 23). That is why the sacrifice of Calvary, when Christ offered up His perfect, sinless life of love and obedience for us, and so broke down for ever the barrier caused by sin (Heb. 9: 12; 10: 12), needs and admits of no addition or repetition. And thirdly, of course, no other priest can create for man a permanent and satisfactory relationship with God, because he dies, whereas Jesus can always save those who come to God by Him, because the very

[1] In *Ways of Worship*, cited with approval in the *Lambeth Report* (1958), 2.85.
[2] *An Introduction to the Theology of the New Testament*, S.C.M. (1958), p. 201.

presence in heaven of the crucified and risen Saviour is the guarantee of their acceptance (7: 25; cf. 10: 12–14). No wonder, in view of all this, that the author of the Epistle to the Hebrews cries out in triumph, 'We have such an high priest' (8: 1).

2. *The Priesthood of all Christians and their Sacrifice*

The New Testament sees in the person, life, death and resurrection of Jesus the perfect way to God for all to take; He is the great high priest through whom we can approach God with every confidence (Heb. 10: 21 f.). It is hardly surprising, therefore, that we do not hear of any priestly caste or group within the Christian Church. And yet, of course, it *is* surprising; it is simply staggering in view of the background of these New Testament writers, steeped as they were in the priestly system of the Old Testament, that never once do they use the word *hiereus* of the Christian minister. The Aaronic analogy for their ministry lay obviously to hand. But they refused to use it. It is hard to overrate the significance of this point when we notice that they *did* use it *of the whole Christian community*! Just as the ideal of the Servant originally applied to the whole of Israel, but shrank and shrank until it was embodied in Jesus alone, and thenceforward belonged distinctively to His Body, the Church; so it was with priesthood. Originally the whole nation of Israel was called to be a nation of priests (Ex. 19: 6) to bring the Gentile world to God and represent God to the Gentile world. But Israel did not fulfil her function; neither did the Aaronic priesthood; neither did the high priest himself; it was only Jesus who brought God to men and brought men back to God. He is *the* priest *par excellence*. But now His people share His office. They cannot, to be sure, make sacrifice for sins; that expiatory part in the function of the Priest, as in that of the Servant, Christ has fulfilled alone, and once for all. But the other elements in the priestly role have devolved upon the whole Christian community without distinction. The Christian Church, in fact, realizes the ideal which the Jewish Church recognized but never achieved. For the Church *is* a nation of priests (Rev. 1: 6; I Pet. 2: 9; cf. Ex. 19: 6). What that means is expressed in three ways in the New Testament, in terms of access, mediation and offering.

In the first place, the priesthood common to all believers

carries with it unrestricted access to God. In the Old Testament this had been the prerogative of the priests, and supremely of the high priest. Only he could venture, and that but once a year and with sacrificial blood, into the Holy of Holies. Now the way into the holy presence of God has been made open once and for all, through the sacrifice of Christ. And now every believer has the priestly privilege of immediate access to God through Jesus (Rom. 5: 2; Eph. 2: 18; Heb. 4: 16; 10:19; I Pet. 3: 18). No other intermediary is either possible or necessary.

Secondly, priesthood in the Old Testament was mediatorial. The priest represented God to the people, when he declared to them God's will, and the people to God, when he interceded with Him on their behalf. Now the Christian Church is to bear this double responsibility. 'You are a chosen race, a royal priesthood, a holy nation, God's own people, that you may declare the wonderful deeds of Him who called you out of darkness into His marvellous light' (I Pet. 2: 9). It is the job of every member of the Church both to *go* into all the world and preach the Gospel to every creature, and to *pray* for that world to God (I Tim. 2: 1). This two-way mediation of evangelism and prayer is the solemn, lifelong calling of every Christian, and it is significant that these two activities are both spoken of as priestly ministries in the New Testament (Rom. 15: 16; Rev. 8: 3 ff.).

In the third place, the Church, and every Christian in it, inherits the priestly task of offering gifts and sacrifices to God (I Pet. 2: 5). Of course, for this had always been the task of the priest under the Old Testament (Heb. 8: 3). The sacrifices which are mentioned in the New Testament are the sacrifices of praise and thanksgiving (Heb. 13: 15), of faith (Phil. 2: 17), almsgiving (Acts 24: 17; Phil. 4: 18), a godly generous life (Heb. 13: 16), and supremely the sacrifice of ourselves, the yielding of our bodies as a thank-offering to God (Rom. 12: 1, 2).

Two things are noteworthy about this priestly work. In the first place, it belongs to every Christian, not to any ministerial group. In the second place, 'our offerings are not propitiations, for nothing that we could do could have turned away God's wrath. It is solely because of what God has done that we are able to approach Him and bring offerings in which He will take pleasure. It is because of Christ's one, true, effective sacrifice, offered once for all, that our unworthy oblation is possible.'[3]

3. The Priesthood of Ministers, and their Sacrifice

Priesthood is never associated with *presbyters* in the New Testament. Christian ministers are no more priests, and no less so, than any other members of Christ's priestly Body. The idea of a priestly ministerial caste came originally into Christianity from pagan sources,[4] and was furthered by analogies from Jewish practice. Even so, it was not until Cyprian in the middle of the third century that we find the word *hiereus* being regularly used of the Christian minister. Cyprian himself did much to transform the New Testament presbyter into the 'Catholic' priest.

Furthermore, the eucharist is never, in the New Testament, called a sacrifice, though, of course, Christ's death, which it displays, was *the* sacrifice for sins. But the holy communion is not seen as one of the many things we offer to God. It is something He offers to us; that is why it is called a sacrament of the *Gospel*. The primary movement in both the Gospel and its sacrament is from God to man, and not from man to God — a form of Pelagianism which has considerable currency today. It is significant that the Lambeth Report of 1958 quoted with approval these words of Dr. Hebert: 'The true celebrant is Christ the High Priest, and the Christian people are assembled as members of His Body to present before God His Sacrifice, and to be themselves offered up in sacrifice through their union with Him'; and the bishops themselves go on to say: 'We are partakers of the sacrifice of Christ (I Cor. 10: 16) . . . Christ with us offers us in Himself to God.' There is a great deal of truth in this eirenic statement, as there is in the following citations from a Roman Catholic writer, but there are unbiblical emphases in each. In speaking of the mass as a sacrifice, a characteristic exponent of the modern liturgical movement in the Roman Church writes:[5] 'At the mass Jesus does not die. The Risen Christ never dies again . . . but we are saved through His death. The Cross is the very source of our life.

[3] Richardson: *op. cit.*, p. 303.
[4] See Lightfoot: *op. cit.*, pp. 123 ff., Lindsay: *op. cit.*, p. 308, cf. Tertullian: *de Baptismo* 5.
[5] *Les Albums Liturgiques — La Messe*, Fleuret-Louvel, Paris, p. 9 (my translation from the French).

And it is the mass that presents it to us. For there are not two sacrifices, that of the Cross and that of the mass. There is the once-for-all sacrifice of Christ. . . . It is Jesus who does the offering; same Priest, same Victim, same Sacrifice.'

So far so good, as in the earlier part of Dr. Hebert's statement, which is, of course, influenced by current Roman thinking. But then we read on: 'It is not only Jesus who offers for us His Sacrifice to the Father, the whole Church joins with Him in making the offering. . . . It is the assured conviction of the Church when she celebrates mass that she offers the Sacrifice of Jesus. The Sacrifice is ours because it was offered for us. It is ours because at the mass we unite our sorrows, small though they be, with the great sufferings of Jesus. It is ours, because we present it in our turn.' I cannot find any great difference between this Roman Catholic statement and the position recommended by the Lambeth Conference. Both contain much that is helpful, but both, it seems, depart from Scripture at one or two significant points.

When it is suggested that the Church offers to God Christ's unique offering, this is something quite alien to the New Testament, which sees Christ as the One who made that sacrifice not *with* us but *for* us when He took the world's sin upon Himself once for all upon the cross, and then sat down in the place of honour and victory at God's right hand. It cannot be the case that He is now offering His sacrifice in the heavenly sanctuary, while the Church offers it on the earthly altar, as Moberly, Bicknell, Hicks and others suggest. For, according to the imagery of Hebrews, there is no altar in heaven any more than there was an altar in the Holy of Holies in the Jewish Tabernacle (Heb. 9: 24). As a Roman Catholic writer himself put it, 'the idea that Christ officiates before the throne of God by any sort of liturgical action or by any active pleading of His passion is nowhere to be found' (in Hebrews or in the rest of the New Testament for that matter). 'There is no heavenly sacrifice of Christ, but the living Priest holds all the power of His sacrifice in His living humanity.'[6] That is just the point. Jesus is not constantly offering to the Father His sacrifice once made. Chrysostom rightly says: 'Do not think, because you have heard that Jesus is a priest, that He is always offering sacrifice. He offered sacrifice once and for all,

* W. Leonard: *The Authorship of the Epistle to the Hebrews* (1939), pp. 73, 75.

and thenceforward He sat down' (*Hom. in Heb.* 13: 8). He is now, in Richardson's phrase (*op. cit.*, p. 202), 'seated in the seat of the Vizier, not standing in the posture of the suppliant'.

But does the New Testament not say that Jesus is praying for His people (Rom. 8: 34; Heb. 7: 25)? It does, but a rare and significant word is used. It does not mean that He is asking for our acceptance, as though from a Father who is reluctant to grant it. For the Father has already accepted the sacrifice which Jesus made for sins, and the resurrection is the abiding proof of it (Rom. 4: 25). Indeed, the Father *shared in* the sacrifice of Calvary (II Cor. 5: 19). How should He need a reminder of it?[7] How should He need to have it pleaded? This doctrine of the heavenly sacrifice of Christ, invented to find room for a priestly offering by men in the eucharist, in fact drives a wedge between the attitude of the Father and the Son in our redemption. It gives us a flattering doctrine of eucharistic sacrifice at the expense of a Christian doctrine of God! Westcott saw long ago what the heavenly intercession of Christ did and did not mean: 'The modern conception of Christ pleading in heaven His passion, offering His blood on behalf of men, has no foundation in Hebrews. His glorified humanity is the eternal pledge of the absolute efficacy of His accomplished work. He pleads by His very presence on the Father's throne.'[8]

Our difficulties here are at least partly due to the ambiguities of language. Thus Christ does not *plead* His sacrifice, in the normal sense of the word, because it is already accepted; but He can properly be said to 'plead His sacrifice' if by that is meant that His presence as the Lamb once slain in the midst of the throne (Rev. 5: 6) is the silent plea for our acceptance. He does not *present* His sacrifice, if by that is meant constantly to offer to the Father the sacrifice of Calvary; but He may rightly be said to 'present' it (and so, indeed may we) if by that is meant to draw attention to the sacrifice once offered. It will be disastrous for ecumenical advance if some churchmen take fright at the language others are using, without

[7] This doctrine evoked John Knox's protest long ago: 'Is there any oblivion or forgetfulness fallen on God the Father? Hath He forgotten the death and passion of Jesus Christ, so that He needs to be brought in memory thereof by any mortal man?'

[8] *Hebrews*, Macmillan (1892), p. 230.

pausing to analyse whether such terms are necessarily to be construed in the most sinister way!

A further ambiguous phrase which causes great heart-burning is any talk of our 'uniting our sufferings' or 'joining our offerings' to those of Christ. This can so easily detract from the uniqueness of Christ's work. His sufferings were atoning; ours are not. His sacrifice removed the sin of the world; ours does not. The New Testament does not speak of our 'offering Christ' or 'presenting His sacrifice'; we do not associate ourselves and our offering of fitful obedience and thanksgiving with His offering which bore away the sin of the world. We are indeed 'partakers of the sacrifice of Christ', but partakers in the *benefits* that flow from that sacrifice, not in the *making* of it. Our offering of ourselves is not part of the offering of Christ, but a grateful response to His prior act.

All this is a most important emphasis which tends to be neglected today in a good deal of eucharistic discussion which verges on obscuring the distinction between the Saviour and the saved. Nevertheless there is a sense in which we share in sacrifice with Christ as well as responding to His initiative. It is most important both to recognize and to isolate this sense of sharing in the sacrifice of Christ.

If we talk about Christ's death as a sacrifice, we use Old Testament language. The Old Testament knew two different kinds of sacrifice; the sin offering, which came under divine displeasure, and the burnt offering, etc. which was a sweet-smelling savour and pleasing to God. The sacrifice of Christ fulfilled both these Old Testament types of offering. Viewed as a sin-offering, His sacrifice was utterly unique; we can only accept its benefit and respond to it in gratitude. Viewed as a burnt-offering it is unique indeed, in its perfection, but not in its character, for it is the pattern and ideal of our own self-offering (Eph. 5:2). In this sense we do share with Christ in His self-oblation. It is because Christ's sacrifice was at the same time both expiatory and dedicatory, whereas ours is only the latter, that the confusion arises. His atoning sacrifice is the *root* of our salvation; our responsive sacrifice of praise, thanksgiving and surrender is the *fruit* of it. The two must never be confused.

It is true that the Christians in the second and third centuries often spoke of the holy communion, as well as prayer, evangelism and so on, in sacrificial terms. But never did they suggest that our sacrifice is incorporated in Christ's. Instead they saw the eucharist as the fulfilment of the prophecy of Mal. 1: 11 and of the Old Testament meal-offering. It was a 'sacrifice of thanksgiving' which the Church 'offers to God for having made the world and all that is in it for man's sake, and also for having set us free from evil'.[9] The eucharist was 'a sacrifice in the sense of a real offering to God of money, goods, devotion and prayer; it was not designed in any way to ensure the forgiveness of sins; and it was offered by the entire priestly body, that is the whole Church'.[10] As a Roman Catholic liturgiologist puts it: 'The Church is a priestly body to offer up spiritual sacrifices through Jesus Christ. I am sure that it is no accident that the primitive Church did not apply the term *hiereus* to either bishop or presbyter. It was applied in the first place to Christ. He is the priest, the high priest eternal. Secondly, they applied it to the assembly of Christians. ... It was only in the third instance that *hiereus* and *sacerdos* were used of Christian ministers ... they occupied an altogether different position from that of pagan priests or even the Old Testament priest.'[11] The 'altogether different position' that they occupied is defined in F. D. Maurice's distinction, taken over by Lightfoot, that the Christian priesthood is '*representative* without being *vicarial*'. That is to say, when a presbyter of the Church celebrates the communion, he is exercising the double representative function which we have seen to characterize the priesthood of all believers. He acts on behalf of God when in God's name he proclaims the Gospel of grace, and declares God's willingness to forgive the truly penitent. Again, he acts as Christ's representative when he utters the words and performs the actions with which Christ instituted the sacrament. He acts on behalf of men in leading the prayers and praises and presenting the offerings of the congregations. He is acting as a *representative*. He does not thereby take away the Christian layman's right of direct access to God, nor of assuring a penitent friend whom he has led to faith of God's certain pardon, nor his responsibility to offer his all to God and to proclaim to the unbelieving God's way of salvation. When the minister acts as God's mouthpiece, 'he

[9] Justin: *Dialogue* 41.
[10] E. M. B. Green in *Eucharistic Sacrifice*, ed. J. I. Packer (London, 1962), p. 77. The early patristic evidence is there surveyed.
[11] J. A. Jungmann: *The Early Liturgy*, D.L.T. (1960), pp. 17 f.

does not interpose between God and man in such a way that direct communion with God is superseded on the one hand, or that his own mediation becomes indispensable on the other'.[12] And when he acts as the mouthpiece of the congregation, as 'the delegate of a priestly race . . . here too his function cannot be absolute and indispensable. It may be a general rule . . . that the highest acts of congregational worship shall be performed through the principal officers of the congregation. But an emergency may arise when . . . the layman will assume functions which are otherwise restricted to the ordained minister.'[13] Such is Lightfoot's conclusion of the whole matter. I do not believe that any other can be derived from Holy Scripture.

B. PRIESTHOOD AND SACRIFICE IN ANGLICAN TEACHING

Cranmer, the architect of the Prayer Book, has this to say of the Christian priesthood: 'The difference between the priest and the layman in this matter is only in ministration; that the priest, as a common minister of the Church, doth minister and distribute the Lord's Supper unto other, and other receive it at his hand.'[14] Logically, therefore, he used 'priest' and 'minister' interchangeably in the Prayer Book. Of sacrifice, he has this to say: 'One kind of sacrifice there is which is called a propitiatory or merciful sacrifice, that is to say, such a sacrifice as pacifieth God's wrath and indignation, and obtaineth mercy and forgiveness for all our sins. . . . And although in the Old Testament there were certain sacrifices called by that name, yet in very deed there is but one such sacrifice whereby our sins be pardoned . . . which is the death of God's Son, our Lord Jesus Christ; nor never was any other sacrifice propitiatory at any time, nor never shall be. This is the honour and glory of this our high priest, wherein he admitteth neither partner not successor. . . . Another kind of sacrifice there is, which doth not reconcile us to God, but is made of them which be reconciled by Christ . . . to show ourselves thankful to Him; and therefore they be called sacrifices of laud, praise and thanksgiving. The first kind of sacrifice Christ offered to

---

[12] Lightfoot: *op. cit.*, p. 134.
[13] *Ibid.*
[14] *The Lord's Supper*, V.11.

God for us; the second kind we ourselves offer to God by Christ.'[15] Logically, therefore, he constructed the Communion Service in such a way that it would make this distinction perfectly plain. No mention of our sacrifice of 'ourselves, our souls and bodies' is made until after our reception of the elements which make real to us 'His one full, perfect and sufficient sacrifice for the sins of the whole world'. It is in order to maintain this vital distinction between Christ's sacrifice and ours, and not because of any innate conservatism, that evangelicals are anxious that the Prayer of Oblation should remain in the position in which Cranmer put it.

If this was the view of Cranmer, what of Hooker? 'I rather term the one sort [of clergy] *presbyters* than *priests*, because in a matter of so small moment I would not offend their ears to whom the name of priesthood is odious, though without cause.' (Hooker then explains the derivation of priest from *presbyteros*, but admits that it is commonly associated with sacrifice.) 'Seeing then', he continued, 'that sacrifice is now no part of the church ministry, how should the name of priesthood be thereunto applied? . . . Wherefore whether we call it a priesthood, a presbytership, or a ministry it skilleth not: although in truth the word *presbyter* doth seem more fit, and in propriety of speech more agreeable than *priest* with the drift of the whole Gospel of Jesus Christ.'[16]

It would be tedious to show how this view remained characteristic of the Church of England until the Oxford Movement. This has been superbly done by Professor Sykes.[17] It simply cannot be denied that at the Reformation the notion of a sacrificial priesthood was firmly repudiated. Indeed, at the ordination of a priest, the medieval habit of giving the man a patten and chalice as the emblem of his priestly office was significantly altered. From now on, he was given a Bible. It is hardly surprising, therefore, that Anglican orders are condemned by Rome because they lack the intention to make a man a priest in the sacrificial sense. The old priest has become the new presbyter. That is the position of the Church of England. Whatever the views of some of her members, a church's doctrine must be judged by her formularies. There is no doubt that the formularies of the Church of England, the

[15] *Op. cit.*, v.3.
[16] *Eccl. Pol.*, v.78.
[17] *Old Priest and New Presbyter*, C.U.P., 1956.

Bible, the Book of Common Prayer, and the Articles of Religion, do not favour the interpretation of priesthood and sacrifice advocated by 'Catholic' Christendom. Newman began the Oxford Movement convinced that he could, by subtle casuistry, reconcile the Articles with the Council of Trent. He later realized the dishonesty of such an attempt, and left the Anglican for the Roman fold.

The Church of England is comprehensive, and it is good that those with divergent theologies should live together in one Church (within the limits imposed by its formularies) and thereby show that Christian love and fellowship go deeper than theological differences. But those Anglicans who do not adopt Tractarian views of the ministry and sacraments have a right to ask that these comparatively recent intrusions into the historic ethos of Anglicanism should not be regarded as the quasi-official view of the Church. In particular, let there be an unequivocal recognition of those ministries of orthodox Christian communions which do not claim to stand within the apostolic succession.[18] To commend episcopacy, wrote the Bishop of Woolwich, 'not as the source and symbol of unity but as a gimmick for validating sacraments — this is what neither Presbyterians nor Methodists, nor any other non-

[18] There is one way in which we could, perhaps, help our friends in the reformed tradition to understand us at the present time. We could revert to the name *presbyter* for *priest*. The two reasons advanced by Hooker are more than ever relevant today; it would remove the offence from those to whom the name *priest* is odious, and it would bring us more into line with primitive church practice and the Gospel of Christ. It is difficult to see that the change would be offensive to any section within the Anglican Communion. The historically minded would be glad to see the undoubted linguistic and historical meaning of the word *priest* demonstrated in this way; it is astonishing how many people seem unaware that 'priest' is an English contraction of the word 'presbyter'. The High Churchman would remember that the Scottish Episcopalian Prayer Book of 1637 has *presbyter* for *priest* throughout; and undoubtedly that Book, influenced as it was by Laud, has a more 'Catholic' flavour than the Book of Common Prayer of 1662. Even the Roman Catholic Church retains vestiges of the primitive usage which for centuries they employed, when they call the priest's house the presbytery. And the ecumenically minded would note that *presbyter* is the title used in the Church of South India. The restoration of this, the most primitive name for the Christian ministry, might go a long way towards removing barriers to reunion. A golden opportunity to restore it was missed in the Report of the Anglican-Methodist Conversations, and the failure to do so very properly called forth the protest of the Dissentients (*Report*, p. 60).

episcopalian church will stand *or ought to stand*.[19] If our Church does adopt this intransigent attitude to other communions she will be denying her past history since the Reformation, and will be repudiating whatever claim she still retains to be the Church *of England*. It was not without reason that Dr. Alec Vidler in *The Times* (7 December 1961) asked if the Church of England were to remain the Catholic Church of the land, or to become an episcopalian sect? If sacerdotalism and an exclusive doctrine of apostolic succession ever become the doctrine of our church, that is precisely what it will become.

[19] Bishop J. A. T. Robinson's *On Being the Church in the World*, S.C.M. (1960), p. 105. The whole essay on Episcopacy and Intercommunion is an important and penetrating piece of work.

CHAPTER EIGHT

EPILOGUE

THERE have inevitably been many omissions in a short book of this nature.

There has not been room to say much about the making of a minister of the Gospel. It is usual to recognize three elements; the call of God, of which the candidate is assured (cf. Acts 26: 16–18), the approval of the congregation of Christian people recognizing the divine call (cf. Acts 6: 3, and I Tim. 3: 7), and the solemn commissioning and authorizing to this ministry by the imposition of hands with prayer (Acts 6: 6; I Tim. 4: 14; II Tim. 1: 6). To this one might add explicitly what is implicit in the first of these conditions, namely that the candidate must have a personal knowledge of God's mercy to himself, a sinner (I Tim. 1: 12–14). Without that he cannot proclaim the Gospel of God's mercy to others with any conviction; and he will not himself survive the pressing temptations and deep discouragements that make fruitless the ministry of many sincere men who, like the young Wesley, are well equipped for their ministry—except that they lack the prime essential, a personal relationship to their Lord.

There has not been room to say anything about training for the ministry. One who is at present engaged in this work cannot help being concerned at the present overemphasis on intellectual compared with practical preparation for the ministry. In particular, many men are ordained with little experience of youth work, less of preaching, and some with no experience at all of evangelism. The intellectual equipment of men who will have to hold down a regular ministry in a parish is clearly of great importance; so is the spiritual experience of living together as a Christian community in a theological college. But this is no substitute for practical experience of the work of the ministry such as would be gained by having a year of one's training as an assistant to an active vicar in a vital congregation. I was impressed in South Africa recently to learn that candidates for the Methodist ministry there normally have three years of experience as lay ministers before their academic training. There was, not unnaturally, a far greater maturity and understanding of the real needs of people among them than could be seen in the Anglican ordinands in that country, or in our own, for that matter.

Despite these and other omissions and shortcomings in this treatment of the Christian ministry, the factors here considered do seem to be of cardinal importance. We *must* take seriously the ministry of Jesus as a pattern for service rather than rule, for the function rather than the office of Ministry. We *must* talk less about what a layman can or cannot do, and more about what he is *called* to do within the Christian Body. We *must* think less in terms of hierarchy and more about the mutual relationships of different members of the Body of Christ.

As regards the threefold ministry, we must beware both of giving up a division of ministry which has eminent justification in Scripture, history and reason, and at the same time of compelling others to accept it on pain of excommunication; there was, we must recall, a variety of polity even within the New Testament Church, and yet this was not allowed to hinder their table-fellowship. It befits us rather to take seriously the threefold ministry whose excellencies we so loudly proclaim.

1. Let us, then, not attempt to commend episcopacy on the wrong grounds, but take the first steps towards a more biblical and primitive pattern of episcopacy by increasing the number of dioceses and decreasing the number of administrative tasks which a bishop is expected to fulfil, and thus restore to the bishop his proper function of being the chief pastor, overseer and teacher of his people.

2. Let us not attempt to commend the priesthood to non-conformists on grounds which are neither to be found in Scripture nor in the historic position of Anglicanism, but rather seek to recover the New Testament meaning of presbyter as a man who is the teacher[1] (II Tim. 4: 5; 2: 2; 1:13; I Tim. 3: 2; 4: 6, etc.), pastor (I Tim. 4: 12–5: 3; Tit. 1: 9, 10;

[1] In the Pastoral Epistles teaching, preaching, wrestling with the Word of God, commending it, defending it—all this is seen as the permanent duty of the presbyter. It is worth considering what sort of priority it is given today—and what fruit we reap in ignorance, false doctrine and apathy among Christian people.

2: 1–10) and leader (I Tim. 1: 18; 5: 21; I Thess. 5: 12) of his people; a man who can teach without dogmatizing and lead without domineering, a man who is prepared to suffer with them and for them, following the example of the Suffering Servant of the Lord (II Tim. 2: 3, 9, 12, 24; cf. I Cor. 4: 8–10).

3. Let us seek to recover the primitive diaconate in some relevant form instead of retaining it as a fossilized relic of bygone usefulness, a one-year probationary period for the priesthood. We bemoan the shortage of clergy, and hanker after an auxiliary ministry, while all the time the remedy is within our own hands, the weapon lies rusting in our own armoury. Let us ordain men to the diaconate for life, a diaconate which embraces and swallows up the post of lay-reader and catechist, yes, and that of lady worker as well. Let them be the chief assistants to the presbyter in every parish. Of course, they will continue with their secular job — St. Paul and Aquila and others did in the New Testament period (Acts 18:3; 20: 34), as did perhaps the majority of Christian ministers for the next three hundred years. In this way the presbyter will be relieved of much of the administrative and secretarial work which so largely hinders him doing the work for which he was ordained; he will be set free so that he can give himself to the task of building up the saints for the work of service. Furthermore, the yawning gulf between the clergyman and the man in the street will be to some extent bridged by these deacons who manifestly serve God both in the Church and in the world.

Above all this little book has sought to emphasize the pattern of the Servant for the ministry of the Church. It will require a tremendous reversal of our current attitudes, both on the part of the laity and of the clergy. The layman will need to get a new idea of the ministry. No longer will he be satisfied with responding from time to time to appeals to 'help the Church', by which, of course, we clergy mean the institution of which we are the hub. He will have to realize that the very reason the ordained ministry exists is to equip the ordinary Christian for his ministry in the world. The pattern of the Servant thus holds good for both laity and clergy. 'We must not be satisfied,' writes Professor A. T. Hanson, 'until it is quite natural for the ordinary Christian to approach his minister for advice or action with the request, "Won't you help the Church . . .?"'[2]

² *The Church of the Servant*, p. 106.

It will require no less of a revolution in the attitude of the clergy if the pattern of the Servant ministry is to be realized among us. It is we clergy, with our prejudices, our dogmas, our talk of the validity and regularity of orders, that so often hinder the oneness of Christ's people. Of course, we must not sacrifice truth in the quest of unity, but so often it is not truth by prejudice that holds us up, doctrines and practices which we refuse to examine dispassionately in the light of Scripture. If we really took seriously the example of Jesus our Servant, and the Servant-status and function that He has bequeathed us, we would repent of proud and hierarchical attitudes adopted in the past, recognize each other's ministers as brethren in Christ, and co-operate forthwith in the work of the Kingdom of God. What an impetus for their own sacrificial service it would give to the people of God throughout the world, if they saw their leaders following in the path of the Servant! What progress it would mean for the Gospel of God if Christian leaders really behaved in this revolutionary way of their Founder, a way so contrary to the natural man that it could not fail to impress men with the power of this message which at last the Christians both preach *and live*! And what joy it would bring to the heart of the Saviour who on the last most solemn evening of His life gave this charge to His disciples: 'If I then, your Lord and Teacher, have washed your feet, you also ought to wash one another's feet. For I have given you an example, that you also should do as I have done to you. Truly, truly, I say to you, a servant is not greater than his master; nor is he who is sent greater than he who sent him. *If you know these things, blessed are you if you do them*'!

SELECT BIBLIOGRAPHY

H. S. Box, ed., *Priesthood*, S.P.C.K., 1937.
E. Brunner, *The Misunderstanding of the Church*, Lutterworth, 1952.
K. Carey, ed., *The Historic Episcopate*, Dacre Press, 1954.
G. Dix, *The Question of Anglican Orders*, Dacre Press, 1943.
Mgr. L. Duchesne, *Christian Worship*, S.P.C.K., 1903.
A. Ehrhardt, *The Apostolic Succession*, Lutterworth, 1953.
E. R. Fairweather, *Episcopacy Reasserted*, Mowbray, 1955.
E. R. Fairweather and R. F. Hettlinger, *Episcopacy and Reunion*, Mowbray, 1953.
P. T. Forsyth, *The Church and the Sacraments*, Longmans, 1917.
A. T. Hanson, *The Church of the Servant*, S.C.M. Press, 1961.
A. T. Hanson, *The Pioneer Ministry*, S.C.M. Press, 1961.
A. G. Hebert, *The Form of the Church*, Faber, 1944.
J. W. Hunkin, *Episcopal Ordination and Confirmation*, Heffer, 1929.
D. T. Jenkins, *The Nature of Catholicity*, Faber, 1942.
J. A. Jungmann, S. J., *The Early Liturgy*, D.L.T., 1960.
K. E. Kirk, ed., *The Apostolic Ministry*, Hodder and Stoughton, 1946.
T. M. Lindsay, *The Church and the Ministry in the Early Centuries*, Hodder and Stoughton, 1902.
J. B. Lightfoot, *The Christian Ministry*, Thynne & Jarvis, 1927.
T. W. Manson, *The Church's Ministry*, Hodder and Stoughton, 1948.
B. Minchin, *Every Man and his Ministry*, D.L.T., 1960.
R. C. Moberly, *Ministerial Priesthood*, John Murray, 1899.
L. Morris, *Ministers of God*, I.V.F., 1964.
C. F. D. Moule, *Worship in the New Testament*, Lutterworth, 1961.
Stephen Neill, *Anglicanism*, Pelican, 1958.
Stephen Neill, ed., *The Ministry of the Church*, The Canterbury Press, 1947.
L. Newbigin, *The Household of God*, S.C.M. Press, 1957.
J. I. Packer, ed., *Eucharistic Sacrifice*, Church Bookroom Press, 1962.
O. C. Quick, *The Christian Sacraments*, Nisbet, 1927.
A. Richardson, *An Introduction to the Theology of the New Testament*, S.C.M. Press, 1958.
C. Robinson, *The Ministry of Deaconesses*, Methuen, 1898.

W. Sanday, *The Conception of Priesthood*, Longmans, 1898.

E. Schweizer, *Church Order in the New Testament*, S.C.M. Press, 1961.

W. J. Sparrow Simpson, *The Ministry and the Eucharist*, S.P.C.K., 1942.

B. H. Streeter, *The Primitive Church*, Macmillan, 1929.

H. B. Swete, ed., *The Early History of the Church and Ministry*, Macmillan, 1918.

N. Sykes, *Old Priest and New Presbyter*, Cambridge University Press, 1956.

N. Sykes, *The Church of England and Non-Episcopal Churches in the Sixteenth and Seventeenth Centuries*, S.P.C.K., 1948.

T. F. Torrance, *Royal Priesthood*, S.J.T. Occasional Papers, 1955.

W. Tulfer, *The Office of a Bishop*, D.L.T., 1962.

Timothy Ware, *The Orthodox Church*, Penguin, 1963.

R. Whateley, *Apostolic Succession Considered*, Longmans, 1912.

H. J. Wotherspoon and J. M. Kirkpatrick, *A Manual of Church Doctrine according to the Church of Scotland*, revised and enlarged by T. F. Torrance and R. Selby Wright, Oxford University Press, 1960.

Catholicity, Dacre Press, 1947.

The Catholicity of Protestantism, Lutterworth, 1950.

Conversations between the Church of England and the Methodist Church: a Report, Church Information Office and Epworth Press, 1963.

The Fulness of Christ, S.P.C.K., 1950.

BUT FOR THE GRACE OF GOD...

DIVINE INITIATIVE AND HUMAN NEED

by

PHILIP EDGCUMBE HUGHES

CONTENTS

FOREWORD

CHRISTIAN FOUNDATIONS is a series of books written
by evangelical churchmen and designed to reaffirm the
doctrine of the New Testament in the light of
the past history, the present needs, and the future
development of the Church. The series appears under
the auspices of the Evangelical Fellowship in the
Anglican Communion, and the authors are all members
of that Communion. But their concern is for the whole
Church, and not for just one portion of it. They have
no desire to promote any kind of narrow denominationalism or to avoid involvement in the contemporary
ecumenical debate. As the Archbishop of Sydney said
in his Foreword to the British edition, 'These books have
a truly catholic scope, and accordingly they can speak
with clarity and also charity to those on either side of
Anglicanism, and indeed, to many who at present are
outside the fellowship of Christian believers.' The unity
that the authors covet for the Church is unity in the
truth—not unity at any price, least of all at the price of
dispensing with the foundations of the faith which has
been once delivered to the Church. They are convinced
that, as evangelicals, they have a full and essential
contribution to make, especially in advocating the
recovery of the dynamic witness, the apostolic teaching,
the fellowship in worship, and the victorious living of
the New Testament; for these, they believe, are the
vital principles of Christian unity in faith and action.

In view of the fact that some of the books deal with
controversial issues it is not expected that there will

always be agreement with each particular position that may be propounded; but it is hoped that the books will be received in the spirit in which they are offered, which is not one of contention but of goodwill and reasonableness. The authors only ask for an unprejudiced hearing. Naturally they seek to persuade; yet where they fail to do that, they will be content if any discussion that arises is conducted before the bar of the scriptural revelation. They wish that all together, however different their viewpoints, might follow the example of the Christians in Beroea who searched the Scriptures to see whether the things they had been told were true (Acts 17:10 f.). To do just this could in itself hardly fail to have the effect of bringing us all closer together.

This book deals with a theme that is basic to the whole range of Christian faith. There is no single word or concept that is more radical to the Christian message than that of grace. Yet, regrettably, the deepest divisions within the Church are related to differences in the understanding of the scope and means of divine grace, with the unhappy result that, instead of being joyfully united in the grace of God, the denominations are separated from each other by diverse and sometimes contradictory expressions of this central doctrine. This constitutes a crucial issue for the Church more than ever today as the healing of divisions is being sought. Indeed, it may be affirmed that in this connection nothing is more important than that those who profess the name of Christ should grasp and be united in the biblical doctrine of grace. One of the main aims of this book is to examine the more important of these diverse and dividing views of grace and to emphasize the essentials of the New Testament presentation of the doctrine, which must be authoritative, or canonical, for all Christians. In doing this, controversial questions have had to be faced and analyzed, but always with the hope that the New Testament may be allowed once again to speak to and control our situation today.

P. E. H.

Note: In this book and in others of the CHRISTIAN FOUNDATIONS series, mention of the 'Articles' in general, or of certain 'Articles' in particular (for example, 'Article XI' or 'Article XXXVII'), should be understood to refer to the Thirty-Nine Articles of Religion of the Church of England (1563). Parallels to many of the statements in these doctrinal formulae could have been cited, of course, from sixteenth-century Reformation confessions such as the Augsburg Confession (1530), the Second Helvetic Confession (1566), and the Scottish Confession (1560), and from later statements such as the Westminster Confession (1647).

CHAPTER ONE

WHAT GRACE IS

THE doctrine of grace lies at the very heart not merely
of all Christian theology but also of all Christian experience. If we have an incorrect or inadequate understanding of the biblical teaching on grace, our whole
grasp of the meaning and purpose of Christianity will
be deficient in consequence. There is, accordingly, no
subject which is more vital for our study and com-
prehension than this subject of the grace of God.

The term 'grace', of course, has a variety of connota-
tions in the English language, and also in Holy Scripture. As used in this book, grace has the meaning of
undeserved blessing freely bestowed on man by God,
and, still more particularly, the blessing of salvation, in
all the rich significance of that term, freely given to sinful man in and through Jesus Christ. The saving and
transforming effect of this grace is graphically illustrated in the dynamic experience of every regenerate
life, as it was in a very wonderful manner in the experience of the apostle Paul. 'By the grace of God I am
what I am,' he testifies to the Corinthians; 'and His
grace toward me was not in vain. On the contrary, I
worked harder than any of them, though it was not I
but the grace of God which was with me' (I Cor.
15: 10). This verse indicates that Paul attributed not

9

only his conversion to God's grace, but also all that he was able to do and achieve throughout the course of his life and ministry as an apostle. In other words, the grace of God is determinative of the whole pilgrimage of the Christian, from conversion to glorification.

Grace speaks of God's initiative, of the priority of God's action on behalf of us poor sinners. 'You know the grace of our Lord Jesus Christ,' Paul says to the Corinthians again, 'that though He was rich, yet for your sake He became poor, so that by His poverty you might become rich' (II Cor. 8: 9). Grace enriches, and the enrichment it brings is owed entirely to God's prior action of mercy in Christ Jesus. Divine grace precedes all. That is the whole point of grace. Thus to the Christians in Rome Paul writes: 'God shows His love to us in that while we were yet sinners Christ died for us' (Rom. 5: 8); and John declares: 'In this is love, not that we loved God but that He loved us and sent His Son to be the expiation for our sins.' Consequently: 'We love, because He first loved us' (I Jn. 4: 10, 19).

Verses like these show the manner in which the apostles stressed the priority of God's grace. The coming of Christ into the world is the evidence of God's love and mercy in initiating our salvation; for apart from this divine initiative there would be no salvation for the sinner and no Good News for the preacher. Man is indebted for his salvation entirely to the prior goodness of God. God has acted freely and finally in Christ Jesus, and graciously offers sinful man redemption that is full and complete in Him. The work of atonement has been done, once for all: to the perfection of that work man can add nothing – indeed, to attempt to add anything would be to mistrust and to call into uncertainty the completeness of what God has done for us in His Son. That is why Paul reminds the Ephesian believers that salvation came to them when they were 'dead in sins' (and therefore incapable of doing anything at all to save themselves), from which there follows only one conclusion, namely, that it is *by grace* that they have been saved. Both now and for all eternity the Christian will be indebted to 'the immeasurable riches of His grace in kindness toward us in Christ Jesus' – for, Paul insists, 'by grace you have been saved through faith; and this is not your own doing, it is the gift of God: not because of works, lest any man should boast' (Eph. 2: 5ff.).

CHAPTER TWO

GRACE AND FAITH

BUT, someone may object, if salvation is *by grace alone*, why is it also said that salvation is *by faith alone*? What does it mean that we have to exercise faith ('by grace you have been saved *through faith*')? Does this not conflict with the concept of salvation by grace alone? These are questions which are very rightly asked. The answer is that 'by grace alone' and 'by faith alone' are two sides of the same coin. They are in no way contradictory concepts. If grace is God's initiative, faith is man's response to that initiative. And yet faith is not a 'work' of man; indeed, it implies the very opposite of work. Moreover, man's faith is not in any sense something that earns or deserves or qualifies him for salvation: his faith is part of his salvation; it cannot be isolated from the grace of God. That is why Paul, having declared, 'by grace you have been saved through faith,' insists: '*and this is not your own doing, it is the gift of God.*' It is to God, then, that man owes the whole of his salvation: even his faith belongs to the gift of God's grace.

Faith, then, must not be considered in isolation from grace. Nor, further, can it be understood in isolation from the object to which it is directed. There is no such thing as faith in a vacuum, without origin and without object. The object of Christian faith is God – the Trinitarian God – God the Father who so loved us that He sent His only Son into the world – God the Son, our only Saviour and Mediator, who died for our sins on the Cross and rose again for our justification – and God the Holy Spirit, who rouses us from the death of sin and applies the saving work of God-in-Christ in every believing heart. Christian faith, accordingly, is God-centred, not man-centred or self-centred. 'That we say, faith only justifies, ought to offend no man,' writes William Tyndale in his *Prologue to the Epistle to the Romans*. 'For if this be true, that Christ only redeemed us, Christ only bore our sins, made satisfaction for them, and purchased us the favour of God, then must it needs be true that the trust only in Christ's deserving and in the promises of God the Father, made to us for Christ's sake, doth alone quiet the conscience and certify it that sins are forgiven.'[1]

Archbishop Cranmer explains Paul's teaching in the Epistle to the Romans by pointing out that there are 'three things which must concur and go together in our justification: upon God's part, His great mercy and grace; upon Christ's part, justice, that is the satisfaction of God's justice, or price of our redemption, by the offering of His body and shedding of His blood, with fulfilling of the law perfectly and thoroughly; and upon our part, true and lively faith in the merits of Jesu Christ, which is yet not ours, but by God's working

[1] William Tyndale: *Doctrinal Treatises* (Parker Society edition, Cambridge, 1848), p. 509. *The Prologue to the Epistle to the Romans* was originally published as a separate pamphlet in 1526.

in us ... And therefore,' he says, 'St. Paul declares here nothing upon the behalf of man concerning his justification, but only a true and lively faith; which nevertheless is the gift of God, and not man's only work without God.'[2]

It may perhaps be objected that to ascribe everything in this way to the grace of God would seem to leave no place for the exercise of good works, whereas the New Testament has a great deal to say about the importance of Christian conduct. But this objection is based on a misunderstanding. It is not at all a question of repudiating good works, as though these have no proper place in the Christian life. What is denied is that by good works we can in any way contribute to our salvation. That is why Article XI declares that 'we are accounted righteous before God only for the merit of our Lord and Saviour Jesus Christ by faith, and not for our own works or deservings.'

There is no denial, however, that good works are an essential part of the Christian life. But, it must be stressed, they are not the cause but the consequence of a man's salvation. They are, in fact, a necessary outward evidence of his salvation. They are not the root but the fruit of faith. Accordingly Article XII describes good works as 'the fruits of faith' which 'follow after justification . . . and do spring out necessarily of a true and lively faith, insomuch that by them a lively faith may be as evidently known as a tree discerned by the fruit.' This

[2] Thomas Cranmer: *Works*, Vol. II (Parker Society edition, Cambridge, 1846), p. 129. The quotation is from the *Homily of Salvation*, originally published in 1547.

14

teaching is in complete harmony with the teaching of the New Testament, which emphasizes throughout that the Christian, who owes his salvation to divine grace alone, is under obligation to do everything to the glory of God and to conduct himself in a manner that does not contradict his profession of faith (cf. I Cor. 6: 20, 10: 31; Rom. 15: 6; Jn. 15: 8). To the same effect is the solemn admonition that 'we must all appear before the judgment seat of Christ' to render an account of what we have done during this life (II Cor. 5: 10). Good works, then, so far from being neglected or despised, play a vital role in the Christian scheme. The situation is best summed up for us by Paul in the very place where he insists that salvation is by grace through faith and not of works; for he immediately adds: 'For we are His workmanship, created in Christ Jesus for good works, which God prepared beforehand, that we should walk in them' (Eph. 2: 10). If verses 8 and 9 of Ephesians 2 are kept, as Paul placed them, in the closest conjunction with verse 10, misunderstanding of this kind we have been discussing will be avoided.

Paul is not theorizing in propounding this doctrine of the grace of God: he is speaking of what he knows by experience. Indeed, the history of the apostle Paul provides us with an outstanding illustration of the practical significance of this teaching. No man could have been more fiercely opposed to the Gospel of God's grace in Christ Jesus than was Paul. He was driven by a murderous determination to make havoc of the Christian Church (Acts 8: 3, 9: 1) – until in one crucial moment of destiny he was brought face to face with the risen Jesus on the road to Damascus (Acts 9: 3ff.). This was the turning-point of his whole life. But it was not something he had sought. It was not even that he had some inclination towards the Christian faith; for he was violently hostile to it. If one thing stood out with unmistakable clearness, it was that his conversion was due entirely to the sovereign mercy of God, and not at all to his own strivings. It never ceased to be a cause of wonder and thanksgiving to him that God had called him by His grace (Gal. 1: 15) – him, Saul the persecutor – and transformed him into Paul the apostle. So he wrote to Timothy, many years after this dramatic experience: 'I thank Him who has given me strength for this, Christ Jesus our Lord, because He judged me faithful by appointing me to His service, though I formerly blasphemed and persecuted and insulted Him; but I received mercy because I had acted ignorantly in unbelief, and the grace of our Lord overflowed for me . . .' (I Tim. 1: 12ff.). How could Paul say anything else than: 'by the grace of God I am what I am' (I Cor. 15: 10)?

But this redeeming grace whereby the believer is created anew in Christ Jesus is not something empty or vain or fruitless. It does not absolve us from the obligation to keep the law of God and to perform the good works that it enjoins. Indeed, it is precisely God's grace that enables us to keep His law. The fruit that the Holy Spirit produces in the believer is a cluster of nine graces: love, joy, peace, patience, kindness, goodness, faithfulness, gentleness, self-control. 'Against such there is no law,' says Paul (Gal. 5: 22) – why? because

the manifestation of these graces is precisely the fulfilment of the law, and there is no law against the keeping
of the law! (The relationship between grace and law is
discussed more fully on pp. 29 ff. below.)

It is by grace that sin is overcome and man is set free
from its tyranny. For this purpose God's grace is more
than just adequate: it is superabundant! 'Where sin
increased, grace abounded all the more,' Paul asserts
(Rom. 5: 20). But, Paul imagines someone objecting,
if sinning provides the opportunity for grace to prevail,
why should we not go on sinning, so that grace may
abound more and more? This form of argument, however, shows a complete miscomprehension of the nature
and purpose of grace. Hence Paul's explosive rejoinder: 'God forbid! How can we who died to sin still
live in it?' To go on living in sin is in fact a contradiction of grace. Remember that you have been baptized,
Paul says in effect to such an objector, and that baptism
signifies identification with Christ with dramatic
clarity: going down under the water symbolizes dying
and being buried with Christ, and coming up out of the
water symbolizes being raised with Christ from death,
so that 'we too might walk in newness of life.' The logic
is compelling: 'For if we have been united with Him in a
death like His, we shall certainly be united with Him in
a resurrection like His. We know that our old self was
crucified with Him so that the sinful body might be
destroyed, and we might no longer be enslaved to sin.
For he who died is freed from sin.' Accordingly, we
must reckon ourselves to be 'dead to sin and alive to
God in Christ Jesus.' Whereas prior to our experience

of God's grace we yielded our bodily members 'to sin as instruments of wickedness,' now we are to yield ourselves 'to God as men who have been brought from death to life,' and our members 'to God as instruments of righteousness.' The Christian life is intended to be and by God's grace is enabled to be fruitful unto holiness. The Christian calling is precisely to a new life of sanctification. *That* is how grace abounds and prevails. (See the whole of the 6th chapter of Romans.)

To sum up, the salvation of the sinner is achieved *by God's grace alone.* God's grace is not bought or merited or induced by anything that man may do. It is *freely* bestowed on those who do not deserve it. God's grace is *God's initiative.* Hence it is important always to emphasize the *priority* of divine grace, which is in no way dependent or consequent on the religious activity of man. Moreover, the truth that salvation is all of grace should be a source of great comfort to the believer, for as it is *God's* work, so also it is a *sure* work: it cannot fail or be frustrated. If it were man's work, even partially, it would be marked by imperfection and insecurity. But God's work is indefectible, and the Christian believer may rejoice in the assurance that what God has begun He will also bring to completion. This is the explanation of Paul's confidence that God who had begun a good work in the Philippian believers would also carry it through until its consummation in the day of Jesus Christ (Phil. 1: 6; cf. Rom. 8: 30). The grace of God is the very ground, and the only ground, both of the believer's assurance of eternal salvation and of the preacher's confidence that God's Word will not

18

return to Him void (Is. 55: 11). And faith is the proper response of man to the grace of God, for faith is the closing with and the appropriation of all that is offered us in Christ by God's grace. Hence the assertion of Article XI: 'That we are justified by faith only is a most wholesome doctrine, and very full of comfort.'

CHAPTER THREE

GRACE AND WORKS

BUT, it will be asked, are we to conclude from this doctrine of grace that prior to the experience of God's redeeming grace everything that a man does is bad and sinful – that, in fact, he is incapable of performing any good works at all? And is not this what Article XIII states when it says: 'Works done before the grace of Christ and the inspiration of His Spirit are not pleasant to God, forasmuch as they spring not of faith in Jesus Christ, neither do they make men meet to receive grace . . . yea, rather, for that they are not done as God hath willed and commanded them to be done, we doubt not but they have the nature of sin?'

This question is fair enough. In answering it, it must be pointed out, in the first place, that Articles X to XIII are primarily concerned with the all-important subject of man's justification before God. While, further, the truths that these articles affirm are truths which are valid for all times and all circumstances, yet it should not be forgotten that the Articles were formulated within the framework of the Reformation conflict with Roman Catholicism. According to Roman Catholic teaching, unregenerate man possesses the natural ability to turn to God and to contribute by his deeds and dispositions to his own justification. This is the background of Article X, which declares: 'The condition of man after the fall of Adam is such that he cannot turn and prepare himself, by his own natural strength and good works, to faith and calling upon God. Wherefore we have no power to do good works pleasant and acceptable to God, without the grace of God by Christ preventing [preceding] us, that we may have a good will, and working with us, when we have that good will.'

This, like Article XIII, is not merely a positive affirmation of a truth about man and justification, but also a clear rejection of the erroneous teaching of Roman Catholicism. What was this erroneous teaching? It was, briefly, this: that the consequence of the fall of man was his loss of 'original righteousness', which is explained as an extra gift that was added to man after his creation; that the fall, accordingly, left man in a purely natural state, regarded not as a state of depravity, but as a neutral state in which man's will is free to choose between good and evil; that man must co-operate to obtain the grace of justification, preparing and disposing himself by the motion of his own will; that justification, once received, may be increased before God by good works; that, therefore, the good works of a justified man are meritorious, deserving of an increase of grace and also of eternal life; that a man may even accumulate merits in excess of what is required for justification, and that these surplus merits are preserved, so to speak in a spiritual treasury, and may be made available by the Church to those who are running short of merit. It is taught, further, that grace, or the state of justification, may be lost. The justification of the sinner is effected, according to Roman Catholicism, by baptism, whereby he is restored to the state which he enjoyed before the fall. Sins committed after his baptism, however, find their expiation in this system (at least as regards their so-called 'temporal' punishment), not in the work of Christ, but by way of penitential exercises, indulgences, good works, and, after this life, the cleansing flames of purgatory.

The uncertainty in which the Roman Catholic doctrine of grace and justification leaves a man is increased yet further by the teaching that for baptism to effect what is claimed for it there must be the intention of the priest administering it to perform a valid sacrament. If the priest does not intend to do what the sacrament is intended to do, then the grace of the sacrament is not transmitted – its recipient does not enter into a state of justification. But the intention of a priest, or of anyone else, is invisible. Consequently, in the Roman Catholic Church, no baptized person can be absolutely sure that he is justified and in a state of grace. Yet, even if he were assured of the right intention of the priest who baptized him, he could have no assurance that he would not lose his justification. In a system which depends so much on the collaboration of man – whether it be on the intention of the priest, or on the dispositions which prepare a man for the reward of justification, or on the works which have to be performed to atone for sins committed after baptism – it would be unreasonable to expect to find assurance of salvation.

It is against this background that the whole group of

Articles from X to XVII must be understood. Their primary purpose is to assert the uniqueness of God's grace, the sole sufficiency of Christ's sacrifice for the forgiveness of all sin, and consequently, the truth that a man is justified through grace alone by faith alone in the perfect atoning work of the incarnate Son of God. To teach that man must co-operate in his own salvation and that his works contribute meritoriously to his acceptance with God is not only irrelevant: it is blasphemous in that it detracts from the uniqueness, the perfection, and the sole merit of the saving work of Christ.

The grace of God in Christ avails for sins committed both before and after baptism, or, in the case of those baptized as infants, for 'actual' sins as well as for 'original' sin. It is the blood of Christ, and nothing else, that cleanses from *all* sin, without reservation (I Jn. 1: 7). Hence the assertion of Article XVI (Of Sin after Baptism): 'After we have received the Holy Ghost we may depart from grace given and fall into sin, and by the grace of God we may arise again and amend our lives. And therefore they are to be condemned which say they can no more sin so long as they live here, or deny the place of forgiveness to such as truly repent.' And in Article XVII the indefectibility of the grace which God bestows is expressed with reference to the biblical doctrine of predestination to life, in the declaration that 'they which be endued with so excellent a benefit of God be called according to God's purpose by His Spirit working in due season: they through grace obey the calling: they be justified freely:

they be made sons of God by adoption: they be made like the image of His only-begotten Son Jesus Christ: they walk religiously in good works, and at length, by God's mercy, they attain to everlasting felicity.'

The importance of the Thirty-Nine Articles is seen especially in their affirmation of these cardinal truths of the New Covenant. These great facts of the Christian faith – that man owes his salvation entirely and solely to the grace of God; that man's part is by faith to appropriate the benefits of Christ's finished work of atonement, disclaiming any merit of his own; that the only purgatory for all sin is the blood of Christ; and that salvation in Christ, as it is *God's* work from beginning to end, cannot fail to reach its heavenly consummation – do not change. Theological fashions may change; but these truths remain constant. They are as true today as they have ever been throughout the history of the Church. And they are the very heart of the Christian Gospel.

Moreover, the teaching of Roman Catholicism on grace and justification is radically the same today as it was in the sixteenth century. Hence, *vis-à-vis* the theology of Rome, the Articles have lost none of their appositeness. There is just as much need for these evangelical truths to be proclaimed, in love, today as there was in the day of the Reformers – in fact, more need, since the background is now enlarged to include the various brands of Protestant liberalism which, to a greater or lesser degree, assert the adequacy of man in the work of salvation, and to that degree discredit the Christian doctrine of the grace of God.

But let us return to the question proposed at the beginning of this section. While it is important to realize that the articles to which reference has been made relate primarily to the theme of man's justification before God, yet the questioner may still urge his inquiry. Granted, he may say, that no work can be described as good in the sense that through it man may merit justification, and, further, that dependence on one's own good works for salvation, in whole or in part, is a mark of sinful self-sufficiency; yet is there really no distinction between good and bad prior to regeneration? No one will dispute the fact that it is bad for a man to be cruel and unjust and dishonourable; but can it seriously be denied that it is good, even for the unregenerate man, to be kind and just and honourable? Is not this a distinction between good and bad which is made every day, without first having to ask whether a person is regenerate or not?

There are two things which must be said by way of response. Firstly, the goodness of the unregenerate man is at best humanistic: his 'good works' are not performed to the glory of God. The deep spring or motive of his action is a will and a heart estranged from God by the rebellion of sin; and for this reason the 'good works' of the unregenerate man may be described as 'sinful'. Their aim or end is not the only proper one for the creature in all that he does, namely, the glorification of His beneficent Creator.

Yet, secondly, this does not mean that all the works of the unregenerate man are equally bad, or that there are no degrees of goodness and badness in what he does.

It is obvious that there are such degrees. A man, albeit unregenerate, who is honourable and law-abiding is a good citizen, and a man who loves his wife and family is a good husband and father. Standards of goodness are part of the fabric of civil government and social co-existence. What is more, they point beyond themselves to the moral structure of the universe in which man has been placed: the very concept of goodness implies an absolute standard, the standard of the perfection of God's goodness. In comparison with this absolute standard – 'You, therefore, must be perfect, as your heavenly Father is perfect' – the sinfulness of all men, even at their best is apparent.

If it is asked why, since sin is the rejection of God's standard and disobedience to His law, the fallen state of man does not manifest itself in universal wickedness and lawlessness and in the total corruption of humanity – why, since to reject Light is to choose darkness and to reject Life is to choose death, unregenerate society is not the scene of complete darkness and death – the answer is to be sought in what is sometimes described as *common grace*. As distinct from the *special grace* of of God manifested in the coming of Christ into this world to save sinners, there is a grace of God which is enjoyed by all in general, whether they are regenerate or not. This grace is extended indiscriminately to the whole of humanity; for God has not abandoned His rebellious creatures, as He might have done, to the full outworking of the consequences of their sin. Sin left to itself and unrestrained by God's providential hand would soon have turned the world into a vile cesspool of iniquity, in which good government and community life would have been an impossibility. That domestic, economic, and political order are enjoyed by the generality of mankind is due to the undeserved goodness and grace of God.

For this reason, then, the beneficial organization of human society is a general reality, with the result that man, though no longer God-centred, can be humanitarian in his behaviour and the community of men can enjoy the cultural and scientific advantages of civilization. Common grace, however, involves the restraint not the suppression of sin; and so at the same time the sinfulness of man is ever defiantly endeavouring to burst these bounds, displaying itself in the setting up of tyrannical governments, in international and inter-racial hostilities, in personal selfishness and animosity, and in the terrible misuse of the remarkable inventions of scientific progress for the dissemination of falsehoods and the destruction of human beings. This is the awful nemesis of sin, and a constant reminder to the thoughtful of how intolerable a place the world would be but for the common grace of God whereby the sinfulness of man is curbed.

For an example of common grace in operation we may turn to Romans 13: 1 ff., where Paul speaks of the office of the civil government. Every person, he says, should be subject to the higher authorities, because these authorities themselves are ordained of God, and thus to resist them is to resist the ordinance of God. A law-abiding citizen has nothing to fear from the civil magistrate, for it is for the punishment of evildoers that he wields the sword. The apostle even calls him a *minister of God* whose concern is the maintenance of a well ordered society. And let us not forget that the state of which Paul was a proud citizen was not a Christian state but the notoriously *pagan* state of imperial Rome.

It would be difficult to find a better illustration of the doctrine of God's common grace than this: the pagan rule of Rome operating in general for the benefit and security of the multi-racial society over which it held sway, and doing so by God's ordinance. From this it is evident, as Paul explains, not only that the Christian, as well as any other citizen, owes obedience to the authority of the state, but also that the state derives its authority from God, the sovereign Ruler of the whole universe. The state, therefore, is not the supreme authority: *it is under God*. To God accordingly it in turn owes obedience; and if it decrees anything which is clearly contrary to God's Word, the Christian can only reply: 'We must obey God rather than men' (Acts 5: 29 – though, significantly, these words were spoken to the *ecclesiastical* authority; they apply, however, to the Christian's relationship to any kind of authority).

To God's grace, then, we must thankfully attribute the fact that human society is tolerable and governable, that it is possible for fallen human beings to live together in a generally orderly and co-operative manner in national, civic, and domestic spheres, to show mutual forbearance, and to cultivate together the artistic, scientific, and humanitarian pursuits of civilization.

CHAPTER FOUR

GRACE AND LAW[1]

FROM what has been said about common grace it follows that law and grace are not of themselves contrary to each other, for the rule of equitable law is one important aspect of the operation of common grace in the process of human history.

But, it may be asked, does not the New Testament speak very plainly of law and grace as being antagonistic to each other? Why does Paul admonish his fellow-Christians that they are not under law but under grace (Rom. 6: 14), or that if they are led by the Spirit they are not under the law (Gal. 5: 18)? And why does he call the law 'the dispensation of death' if it is not opposed to the life-giving Gospel (II Cor. 3: 7 ff.)?

These are important questions, and a proper understanding of the biblical doctrine of grace will depend very largely on the answer that is given to them. In particular, we must avoid the mistake, which has often

[1] The term 'law' is used in this section with reference to the moral law, particularly as it is summed up in the ten commandments. The distinction between the moral law and the ceremonial and civil prescriptions of the Old Testament is explained in Article VII: 'Although the law given from God by Moses, as touching ceremonies and rites, do not bind Christian men, nor the civil precepts thereof ought of necessity to be received by any commonwealth; yet notwithstanding, no Christian man whatsoever is free from the obedience to the commandments which are called moral.'

been made, of jumping to conclusions on the basis merely of texts in which law and grace are contrasted with each other. To begin with, let us see what the New Testament really teaches about the nature of the law. Christ's attitude to the abiding importance of the law is emphatically stated: 'Think not that I have come to abolish the law and the prophets; I have come not to abolish them but to fulfil them. For truly, I say to you, till heaven and earth pass away, not an iota, nor a dot, will pass from the law until all is accomplished' (Mt. 5: 17f.). This is clear enough. But why, then, it may further be asked, does Christ go on to utter a sequence of statements each introduced by the formula: 'You have heard that it was said. . . . But I say to you. . . .'? Does not this show that the old law is superseded by His teaching? Not at all; for a careful reading of these utterances will disclose that, so far from wishing to depreciate the law, Christ's intention was to display the deep inner significance of the old commandments, and thereby also to expose unworthy interpretations of the law which were commonly taught in His day.

Thus to the commandment 'You shall not kill' the admonition had been added that 'whoever kills shall be liable to judgment.' But Christ declares that there is more to this commandment than the external act of manslaughter: 'But I say to you that every one who is angry with his brother shall be liable to judgment' (Mt. 5: 21 f.). In other words, the outward action springs from an inward emotion: hatred, the wish to see another man dead, even if the external action does not follow, is a breaking of the sixth commandment.

Similarly, with reference to the commandment 'You shall not commit adultery,' Christ explains, in condemnation of the merely external, and therefore superficial, interpretation of the law then current, 'But I say to you that every one who looks at a woman lustfully has already committed adultery with her in his heart' (Mt. 5: 27 f.). Indeed, these and the following utterances are a denunciation of the elaborate system of moral casuistry which had been developed over the years and which completely failed to penetrate to the true spirit and purpose of the law. Hence the solemn warning: 'I tell you, unless your righteousness [that is, morality or keeping of the law] exceeds that of the scribes and Pharisees, you will never enter the kingdom of heaven' (Mt. 5: 20).

The situation is pointedly summed up in the last of this series of utterances: 'You have heard that it was said, "You shall love your neighbour and hate your enemy." But I say to you, 'Love your enemies and pray for those who persecute you' (Mt. 5: 43 f.). His meaning is simply this, that the foundation of the law of God is a foundation of love, and the true keeping of the law is the manifestation of love. To teach that it is lawful to love some people and to hate others is a serious perversion of the law.

Christ, in point of fact, was propounding nothing new. His summary of the law in two great commandments – 'You shall love the Lord your God with all your heart, and with all your soul, and with all your mind. This is the great and first commandment. And a second is like it, You shall love your neighbour as yourself' (Mt. 22: 37 ff.) – was but a repetition of what Moses, the mediator of the law, had taught centuries earlier (cf. Deut. 6: 5, Lev. 19: 18). On these two commandments of love, Christ affirmed, all the law and the prophets depend (Mt. 22: 40).

So, too, Paul explains the law explicitly in terms of love. 'He who loves his neighbour has fulfilled the law,' he says, with reference to the second table of the law. Since, in the sphere of human relationships, it is the essence of love, that it 'does no wrong to a neighbour,' therefore, he concludes, 'love is the fulfilling of the law' (Rom. 13: 8 ff.). Consistently with this, he has already written earlier in the same epistle that 'the law is holy and the commandment is holy and just and good' (Rom. 7: 12).

None the less – and this is where the contrast between law and grace comes in – the law stands over us in condemnation: not, however, because there is anything monstrous or evil in the law itself, but precisely because man, when confronted by the law, sees himself to be a sinner, a law-breaker, since he has failed to keep its precepts. Hence Paul repudiates with horror any suggestion that the law is sin (Rom. 7: 7); for, on the contrary, it is the perfect righteousness enjoined by the law which reveals the abject sinfulness of man.

Indeed, the law may even be spoken of as a way of life: 'You shall therefore keep My statutes and My ordinances, by doing which a man shall live,' said God to Moses (Lev. 18: 5 – an assurance which is repeated in Neh. 9: 29, Ezek. 20: 11, 13, 21, and Gal. 3: 12). To fulfil the whole law is indeed to be righteous before God.

But the ominous aspect of the law consists just in this, that man has failed to keep its precepts, injunctions of love though they are, with the result that, instead of being an instrument of life, it has become an instrument of death to him. The law has become a document which is against us with its legal demands (Col. 2: 14). It has become the dispensation of death and condemnation (II Cor. 3: 7 ff.) because it accuses man of his guilt and condemns him as a law-breaker. Just as the law brings life to him who keeps it, so it brings death to him who breaks it. 'The wages of sin is death' (Rom. 6: 23): and since 'all have sinned and fall short of the glory of God' (Rom. 3: 23) all are under sentence of death.

It is in this perspective that man's desperate need of grace is seen. Man's great need is to be delivered from the condemnation of God's law, which he is bound to keep, but which, because of the corruption of his nature through sin, he is unable to keep. Hence the anguished cry: 'Wretched man that I am! Who will deliver me from this body of death?' (Rom. 7: 24). The answer, gratefully embraced by the apostle, is that deliverance is *through Jesus Christ our Lord* (Rom. 7: 25). The grace of deliverance from the bondage and penalty of sin is indissolubly associated with the person and work of the Lord Jesus Christ (cf. II Cor. 13: 14).

Grace, it is true, is the expression of the pure and undeserved love of God to man. But it is not, as some theologians have wished to maintain, the contradiction of law. Forgiveness in Christ, though undeserved by man, is not something legally unjust. Christian redemption is not a demonstration of divine flexibility and independence of law or of God's elbowing aside of the law in order that grace may prevail, as though it were diametrically opposed to law. Nor is grace the abrogation of law. God was not faced with a choice between the rigours of justice and the supposed injustice of being merciful.

As we have seen, the fulfilment of the law is synonymous not merely with justice but also with love. It is a false, and even a shocking, dilemma that we place God in if we suppose that to be gracious He had to be unjust. What sort of a god could this be who had to choose between being unloving or being unjust? Modern theories which postulate an antithesis between law and grace are but new variations of the old heresy of Marcionism – though Marcion, who lived in the second century, may be thought to have shown more good sense than some theologians of our day when, starting from the presupposition of the incompatibility of law and grace, he postulated an absolute distinction between the god or demiurge of the Old Testament, who created the material universe and imposed the law on mankind (Marcion together with other exponents of Gnosticism affirmed that matter was evil) and the God and Father of Jesus Christ, whose kingdom is the spiritual kingdom of love, and by whom the evil demiurge was destined to be overthrown.

The concept of a *dialectic* of law and grace, as exemplified, for instance, in the writings of the Swiss theologian Emil Brunner, is not entirely free from Marcionist overtones, though it would be unwarranted to charge it with being a recrudescence of Marcionism. According to this dialectic, the law is explained as the polar opposite of the Gospel of grace: the law is negative, grace is positive; the law is impersonal, grace is personal; the law is strictly just in its demands, grace is the 'injustice' of love; the law is rational, grace is irrational. Forgiving grace is praised as the abrogation of the law: God, in other words, dispenses with the norms of the law when He shows grace in Christ Jesus. Yet at the same time law and grace are viewed as inseparable, though disparate; they are held in tension with each other, the former being the necessary preliminary to the latter. The law is regarded as God's 'strange work' (*opus alienum*) which leads man to God's 'proper work' (*opus proprium*) of grace.

Still more radical are the postulates of contemporary personalistic theology which dismisses the law altogether as being legalistic, impersonal, and the opposite of love, and affirms the sole authenticity of interpersonal relationships governed by the spirit of love. In this perspective the human I-thou situation becomes the sphere of the divine; prescriptive laws, whether of the decalogue or of Christ Himself, are discarded on the supposition that in itself nothing may be described as always wrong; and the encounter of man with man must be without any condition at all except that of love. Grace, then, ceases to belong to any sort of supernatural category, but is sought at the human 'depth' of personal being and encounter. Everything, in short, is reduced to the dimensions of this-worldly experience; a sentimental concept of love becomes the determining ethical factor; the absolutes, whether of conduct or

35

faith, are dismissed in favour of a pliable relativism; and the objectivity of God is replaced by the subjectivity of humanistic pseudo-christianity.[2]

As we have seen, however, the biblical teaching, so far from making law a contradiction of love, stresses that it is precisely love which the law enjoins – love of God and love of one's fellow-man. It is a dangerous fallacy, therefore, to imagine that the law must be eliminated before grace can appear. That the demands of the law and the grace of God in Christ Jesus are not incompatible with each other is shown in three main respects.

Firstly, Jesus when He came to save the world did not set aside the law: He fulfilled it – that is to say, He kept the law fully, without fault or lapse. In contrast, to all other men, who are law-breakers, He is the sole lawkeeper. He alone is without sin (Heb. 4: 15, 7: 26, I Pet. 2: 22). He alone is full of grace and truth (Jn. 1: 14, 14: 6). He is Jesus Christ the Righteous (I Jn. 2: 1). This perfect obedience of Christ to the law is an essential element in the salvation which He came to procure for us. In becoming man, the Son of God identified Himself radically with mankind; and the first stage of His work of salvation required that, as man, He should keep fully the law of God which mankind had broken. Only thus would He be qualified to offer Himself, as the spotless Lamb of God (I Pet. 1: 18), in sacrifice for man.

[2] For a popular advocacy of this position see J. A. T. Robinson: *Honest to God* (London, 1963) and the writings to which he refers in his book. Cf. also my monograph *Scripture and Myth* (London, 1956).

Secondly, Christ's suffering and death on the Cross, while indeed a demonstration of pure love, was also closely associated with the demands of God's law. Indeed, apart from the law the Cross would have become no more than a symbol of human tragedy. But Christ's redemptive identification of Himself with mankind involved not only the keeping of the law on man's behalf but also the endurance, in man's place, of God's judgment against sin. He became man in order that *as man* He might take man's place as a condemned sinner and suffer the punishment of the law-breaker. The saving grace of God is seen in the fact that 'for our sake He made Him to be sin who knew no sin, so that in Him we might become the righteousness of God' (II Cor. 5: 21). This grace can be understood only in conjunction with the fulfilment of the law; otherwise it fails to make sense. That is why Peter asserts that 'Christ died for sins once for all, *the Righteous for the unrighteous,* that He might bring us to God' (I Pet. 3: 18). God's redeeming grace is made operative by the exchange of the life of Christ's law-keeping ('Do this, and you will live', Lk. 10: 28) for the death of our law-breaking ('The soul that sins shall die,' Ezek. 18: 4. See Gal. 3:13).

Thus at the Cross law and grace meet together. The law is not abrogated. At Calvary Christ paid to the full the penalty incurred through the disobedience of men, while the perfection of His obedience is, by pure grace, transferred to the account of guilty sinners. The justification of the sinner, therefore, is not a legal fiction. In the atoning life and death of Christ the requirements of the law and the punishment due to man's sin have been fully met, with the result that through this perfect redeeming work of Christ the sinner is able to experience the grace of God, to rejoice in the peace of sins forgiven, to know the vital power of the Holy Spirit, and to be assured that he has passed from death to everlasting life. Believers are 'justified by God's grace as a gift, through the redemption which is in Christ Jesus.' At Calvary God displays His righteousness in that He is both just (in accordance with His law) and also the justifier (in accordance with His grace) of all who have faith in Jesus (Rom. 3: 24, 26).

Thirdly, that there is no antipathy between the law and the Gospel is shown by the fact that the believer who has been freely justified by God's grace is still under obligation to keep the law. The law has not become an irrelevance as far as he is concerned. He has, it is true, been transferred into the realm of grace; but not that he should leave the law behind. Why, then, it may be asked, does Paul say to the Christians in Rome, 'You are not under law but under grace'? Does not this imply that Christians have said goodbye to the law? Not at all; for when the Apostle says that they are not under law he means that, thanks to the grace of God in Christ Jesus, they are no longer subject to the commandments of the law for their justification – which means also, because man in his fallenness is a law-breaker, that they are no longer under the condemnation of the law which they have broken. Paul, in fact, rejects outright the false conclusion that, because we are not under law but under grace, therefore we are at liberty to sin, that is, to break or disregard the law.

The implication of justification is not freedom *to* sin but freedom *from* sin. Thus Paul tells his readers that, as previously they have yielded their members to sin as instruments of wickedness, now, as men who have been brought from death to life, they are to yield their members to God as instruments of righteousness. 'Thanks be to God,' he exclaims, 'that you who were once slaves of sin have become *obedient from the heart* to the standard of teaching to which you were committed, and, *having been set free from sin*, have become slaves of righteousness.' They have left behind them the way of sin and death, and the way before them is one of holiness (that is, loving observance of God's law) and life (Rom. 6: 13 ff., see also Rom. 8:4).

The grace of God in Christ Jesus, then, freely and fully justifies the believer who could not be justified, but only condemned, by the law which he had failed to keep. And, furthermore, the grace of God in Christ Jesus actually enables the man who was once a law-breaker to be a law-keeper. That is why throughout the New Testament the Christian is enjoined to be holy, to be pure, to be loving, to do the will of God, to abound in the work of the Lord – in a word, to be like Christ. It is only by the grace and power of God in which he now rejoices, however, that he is enabled to advance along this road of sanctification, not by any virtue or ability of his own. The discussion of the terms and promises of God's covenant of grace which follows will assist us to a better understanding of this truth.

CHAPTER FIVE

GRACE AND THE COVENANT

THE divine covenant of grace has its roots in the very first promise of grace to fallen man, recorded in Genesis 3: 15, where the coming of a Deliverer, the seed of the woman, who would crush the serpent's head is foretold. In bringing Noah and his family to safety through the waters of judgment, God reaffirmed his covenant (Gen. 6: 18, 9: 8 ff.). The nature of the covenant of grace was declared with much greater explicitness to Abraham, the great type in the Old Testament of all who are justified by faith in God and His promises. 'I will establish My covenant between Me and you and your seed after you throughout their generations for an everlasting covenant to be God to you and to your seed after you,' God said to Abraham (Gen. 17: 7). It was never intended, however, that the scope of the blessing of the covenant should be narrowly limited to those who could count themselves among Abraham's physical descendants; on the contrary, it extended to all mankind. Hence the further declaration: 'In your seed all the nations of the earth shall be blessed' (Gen. 22: 18). God's purposes of grace have ever been worldwide in their amplitude.

What is no less important, Christ was and is ever the focus or nucleus of the covenant of grace. God's grace is centred in Christ and flows from Christ, always. This is implicit in the *protevangelium* of Genesis 3 : 15, where the promise of the conquest of evil by the seed of the woman looks ahead to the victory of Calvary and Easter (cf. Gal. 4: 4 f.). And Paul specifically explains the covenant promise made to Abraham – 'in your seed all the nations of the earth shall be blessed' – as being a preaching of the Gospel beforehand to Abraham which had its fulfilment in the single person, or seed, of Christ (Gal. 3: 8, 16), and continues to have its fulfilment in all who, not by mere physical descent but by faith, are one with Christ and therefore the seed of faithful Abraham: 'If you are Christ's,' he says, 'then you are Abraham's seed, heirs according to the promise' (Gal. 3: 9, 26 ff.).

This demonstrates the continuity of the covenant of grace throughout Scripture, in both Old and New Testaments. But the promises of God's covenant are also closely bound up with the keeping of God's law. Obedience is an essential element and condition of the covenant. This is made plain, for example, in a passage like Deuteronomy 7: 9 ff.: 'Know therefore that the Lord your God is God, the faithful God who keeps covenant and steadfast love with those who love Him and keep His commandments, to a thousand generations ... You shall therefore be careful to do the commandment, and the statute, and the ordinances, which I command you this day. And because you hearken to these ordinances, and keep and do them, the Lord your God will keep with you the covenant and the steadfast love which He swore to your fathers to keep.'

While, however, the condition of the covenant is the keeping of the law, the principle of the covenant is the internal principle of grace, whereby man, in his weakness, is encouraged to look to God for strength to be faithful to the covenant. Grace on God's part calls forth faith on Man's part. And this response of faith, even in the Old Testament dispensation, is faith centred in Christ – a faith symbolized for the saints of the Old Testament period sacramentally in the Passover lamb, and in other ways (cf. I Cor. 5: 7, 10: 1 ff.). Their faith was by way of anticipation of the fulfilment of the covenant promises. Thus Christ said to the Pharisees: 'Your father Abraham rejoiced that he was to see My day; and he saw it and was glad' (Jn. 8: 56). And the coming of Christ into the world is the proof that God has remembered 'His holy covenant, the oath which He swore to our father Abraham' (Lk. 1: 72 f.); 'for all the promises of God find their Yes in Him' (II Cor. 1: 20).

Accordingly, Augustine[1] affirms that prior to Christ's advent 'righteous men believed in the same way in Him who was to come as we believe in Him who has come. Times change, but not faith . . . At different times, indeed, but by the one doorway of faith, that is by Christ, we see that both have entered.' And, referring specifically to I Corinthians 10: 1 ff., he asks: 'Was not the same faith theirs by whom these signs were employed, and by whom were foretold in prophecy the very things which we believe?'; and answers: 'Certainly it was: but they believed that they were yet to

[1] Augustine (354–430): Tractate XLV on the Gospel of John.

come and we, that they have come'. So, too Article VII declares that 'the Old Testament is not contrary to the New; for both in the Old and the New Testament everlasting life is offered to mankind by Christ, who is the only Mediator between God and man.'

But, it may be objected, if there is but one covenant of grace, why does Scripture speak as though there are two covenants, one old and one new (cf. especially Heb. 8: 6 ff.)? The answer to this is that the distinction between old and new covenants is precisely the distinction between law and grace. When mention is made of the old covenants the allusion is not to the covenant established with Abraham and his seed, but to the giving of the law through Moses – 'the covenant which I made with their fathers when I took them by the hand to bring them out of the land of Egypt, My covenant which they broke' (Jer. 31: 32). The reference here, then, is to the law viewed as an *external* principle, 'the document which stood against us with its legal demands' (Col. 2: 14), accusing us of our failure to keep its prescriptions. The 'old covenant', with its condition: 'Do this, and you will live' (Lk. 10:28), exposed the sinfulness and power-lessness of fallen man, and hence his need of justification.

The 'new covenant' is both one with and at the same time the fulfilment of the *original* covenant of grace established by God with Abraham, and even before that with Adam. It is also, in its effect, the enablement of man to perform the demands of the 'old covenant'. It does not cancel the law, except as an instrument of condemnation, but transposes the law so that it now

43

becomes an *internal* principle – no longer as it were written outwardly on accusing tablets of stone, but written inwardly on the vital tablet of the heart, and thus not the despair but the delight of the believer, because now, by the grace of God, it is part of his own being and will. The terms of the new covenant are defined in Jeremiah 31: 31 ff.: 'Behold, the days are coming, says the Lord, when I will make a new covenant with the house of Israel and the house of Judah . . .

I will put My law within them, and I will write it upon their hearts; and I will be their God, and they shall be My people'; and again in Ezekiel 11: 19 f.: 'I will give them one heart, and put a new spirit within them; I will take the stony heart out of their flesh and give them a heart of flesh, that they may walk in My statutes and keep My ordinances and obey them; and they shall be My people, and I will be their God.' These terms could hardly be more explicit. They show that the purpose of the new covenant is to empower man to keep that same law which before he had been unable to keep, and to do so in a relationship of the most intimate fellowship with God.

The Mediator of the new covenant is Christ (Heb. 12: 24). His blood shed on the Cross for the remission of our sins is the blood of the new covenant (Mt. 26:28, I Cor. 11: 25, Heb. 13: 20). When Paul describes the Corinthian believers as 'a letter from Christ . . . written not with ink but with the Spirit of the living God, not on tablets of stone but on tablets of human hearts,' and of himself as a minister of the new covenant

44

(II Cor. 3: 3, 6), he is referring to the promises, fulfilled through Christ's atoning work, contained in the passages in Jeremiah and Ezekiel which we have cited. He explains that the old covenant, which by reason of man's disobedience became a dispensation of condemnation and death, was none the less glorious, as was indicated by the glory which shone from the face of Moses, the mediator of the old covenant; but that the Gospel dispensation of righteousness is superlatively glorious with a glory that never fades (II Cor. 3: 7 ff.; cf. Heb. 8: 6 ff.).

Apart from grace, therefore, the law, which in itself is good and glorious, becomes an instrument of death, exposing and condemning the sinfulness of man; whereas the grace of God in Christ Jesus as it were transplants the law, placing it at the vital centre of man's being; with the result that the heart, which previously, when unregenerate, found it natural to rebel against the law, now, when regenerate, finds it natural to obey the law, and delights to do so. Thus in the new-man-in-Christ law and grace meet together and are wedded in perfect harmony.

While it is true that all the blessings of the covenant of grace are available to us here and now, yet there is a final and crowning consummation of the covenant for which we still wait. The reference of the covenant of grace, in other words, is not merely to this present pilgrimage, but it looks beyond and ahead to the eternal glory of heavenly perfection. The central blessing of the covenant of grace, which comprehends within itself all other blessings, is defined in the often repeated declaration: 'I will be their God, and they shall be My people,' coupled with the assurance that God will dwell with his people in perfect communion with them (cf. Lev. 26: 11f.; Jer. 31: 33; Ezek. 11: 20; 37: 26 f.). The realization of this blessing of God's presence takes place in two stages. Firstly, God came down in the person of the incarnate Son and dwelt among us, full of grace and truth (Jn. 1: 14), reconciling us to Himself through the obedience and death of Christ, and thus restoring the fellowship between Creator and creature which had been interrupted by sin. Through the regenerating and sanctifying work of the Holy Spirit, every believer knows the indwelling presence of God within him as the supreme reality of existence (cf. Jn. 14: 16f., 23; 17: 23; Gal. 2: 20. Eph. 3: 17; Col. 1: 27; I Cor. 6: 19; II Cor. 6: 16;) Christians have been made the temple of the living God. Where two or three are gathered together in Christ's name He is present in their midst (Mt. 18: 20).

All this is unspeakably wonderful: it is the irruption of the eternal into the temporal, of the heavenly into the mundane. But there is much more to come! What we now experience, though it is essentially the ultimate reality, is but the foretaste of the fullness of the glory yet to be revealed (Rom. 8: 18). It is only the earnest, the first instalment, the surety of the 'inheritance which is imperishable, undefiled, and unfading, kept in heaven for us' (I Pet. 1: 4). And all who are sealed by the Holy Spirit have the assurance of this supreme expectation (Eph. 1: 13 f.; II Cor. 1: 22; 5: 5). This consummating glory will be attained when at the end of this age Christ comes again in majesty, bringing in 'new heavens and a new earth in which righteousness dwells,' and from which all sin and imperfection will be for ever absent (II Pet. 3: 13, Rev. 7: 9 ff.). In this new, or renewed, creation all God's purposes in creation will be fulfilled. It is then, when we see the Saviour face to face, that our sanctification will at last be complete, for *we shall be like Him* (I Jn. 3: 2). And this will be our everlasting glorification!

It should be noticed that God's purposes of grace are *cosmic* in their scope, involving the renewal of the whole creation, and, further, that the terms in which the ultimate state of glory is described are precisely the terms of God's covenant of grace: 'Behold, the dwelling of God is with men. He will dwell with them, and they shall be His people, and God Himself will be with them; He will wipe away every tear from their eyes, and death shall be no more, neither shall there be mourning nor crying nor pain any more, for the former things have passed away' (Rev. 21: 3 f.). This is the consummation to which the grace of God, in faithfulness to the promises of His covenant, will bring us.

CHAPTER SIX

GRACE AND THE SACRAMENTS

In the Catechism of the Church of England a sacrament is defined as 'an outward and visible sign of an inward and spiritual grace given unto us, ordained by Christ Himself, as a means whereby we receive the same, and a pledge to assure us thereof.' In this section we propose to examine this threefold definition of a sacrament as a sign of grace, a means of grace, and a pledge of grace, and in doing so to determine the nature of the connection between grace and the sacraments.

Firstly, then, a sacrament is a *sign of grace*. The function of a sign is to point to a reality other and greater than itself. The sacramental sign is 'outward and visible', and the reality to which it points is 'inward and spiritual'. If the sign is effectively to point us to this reality, it must speak clearly to us: it must be an *eloquent* sign. There can be no such thing as a dumb sign. By itself, water or bread or wine is not a sign: a word or words must be added to the element for it to become significant as a pointer to the reality of divine grace. That is why, with reference to baptism, Augustine says: 'Take away the word, and the water is neither more nor less than water. The word is added to the element, and there results the sacrament, as if itself also a kind of *visible word*.'[1]

[1] Augustine: Tractate LXXX on the Gospel of John.

This concept of a sacrament as a visible word is most important if we are to understand the proper relationship of the sacrament to the experience of grace. It is seriously misleading to speak of the ministry of the word and the ministry of the sacraments as though they were two distinct ministeries. There is but one ministry of grace, and that is the ministry of the word and sacraments. Indeed, it would be still more accurate to say that there is but one ministry of grace, and that is the ministry of the word; for the administration of the sacraments is but an aspect of or an adjunct to the ministry of the word. Paul declares that 'faith comes from hearing, and hearing comes by the word of Christ' (Rom. 10: 17). The clear proclamation of the word or Gospel of Christ is the central function of the Christian ministry. The sacraments, as well as the sermon, must proclaim the word of Christ. The word of grace which is audible from the pulpit should be visible in the sacraments. If the sacraments do not vividly point us to the glorious promises of the covenant of grace, it is because they have become divorced from the word; and if they are divorced from the word, they cease to be signs and degenerate instead into harmful superstitions. Hence, alluding to what Paul says about cleansing 'by the washing of water with the word' (Eph. 5: 26), Augustine states that the cleansing 'would on no account be attributed to the fleeting and perishable element, were it not for what is added, 'with the word'' '.[2] The sacraments of the Gospel, then, are signs of grace because they point to and thereby

[2] Augustine: *loc cit*.

49

declare the message of grace to those who receive them.

Secondly, a sacrament is a *means of grace*. The sacraments ordained of Christ are not merely signs but also, in the words of Article XXV, '*effectual signs of grace and God's good will towards us, by the which He doth work invisibly in us, and doth not only quicken but also strengthen and confirm our faith in Him.*' But their efficacy as means of grace is not automatic (*ex opere operato*), as though the outward ceremony and participation were all that was necessary for the reception of grace through the sacraments; for the external sign by itself is powerless to produce any spiritual effect. Water cannot cleanse, nor bread and wine nourish, the soul. The efficacy of a sacrament is indissolubly linked to the word of promise of which it is a sign – not, however, to the word as a mere pronouncement of a formula of consecration, but to the word as a proclamation of the Gospel to those who receive the sacrament. As such, as a visible word, the sacrament not only proclaims the covenant promises; it also demands a response, the response of faith, from those it confronts. And where there is this response the sacrament is a veritable means of grace.

That is to say, the sacraments, to be effective, must be addressed, word-wise, to men and women as to intelligent, responsible, and needy persons of whom it is required that they should inwardly believe the word thus outwardly proclaimed to them. This principle is admirably displayed in the words of administration of the sacrament of Holy Communion, which exhort the recipient to feed on Christ '*in thy heart by faith with thanksgiving*. 'Whence,' inquires Augustine regarding baptism, 'has water so great an efficacy, as touching the body to cleanse the soul, save by the operation of the word; and that *not because it is uttered, but because it is believed*?'[3] When Christ admonished the multitude: 'Do not labour for the food which perishes, but for the food which endures to eternal life, which the Son of man will give to you.' He was asked the question: 'What must we do to be doing the works of God?' And to this He replied: 'This is the work of God, that you believe on Him whom He has sent' (Jn. 6: 27 ff.). Commenting on this passage, Augustine explains that to believe on Christ is to eat the food which endures to eternal life. 'To what purpose do you make ready teeth and stomach?' he asks. 'Believe, and you have eaten already.'[4] Again, he declares that to eat of the bread which comes down from heaven (Jn. 6: 50 f.) 'belongs to the virtue of the sacrament, not to the visible sacrament'; it is the eating of the man 'who eats inwardly, not outwardly, who eats in his heart, not who presses with his teeth.'[5]

Bishop John Jewel emphasizes the same truth in his famous *Apology of the Church of England*: 'We affirm,' he says, 'that Christ doth truly and presently give His own self in His sacraments: in baptism, that we may put Him on; and in His supper, that we may eat Him by faith and spirit, and may have everlasting life by His cross and blood . . . For, although we do not touch the

[3] Augustine: *loc cit*.
[4] Augustine: Tractate XXV on the Gospel of John.
[5] Augustine: Tractate XXVI on the Gospel of John.

body of Christ with teeth and mouth, yet we hold Him fast, and eat Him by faith, by understanding, and by the spirit.'[6]

The effect of the sacraments, therefore, cannot be dissociated from the manner in which they are received. They are means of divine grace only to the heart which gratefully believes the promises of which they are signs. To quote again from Article XXV: 'In such only as worthily receive the same they have a wholesome effect or operation'; and the words of invitation in the communion service remind us that it is those who draw near *with faith* who take these holy symbols to their comfort. Richard Hooker is also quite emphatic concerning the manner of the efficacy of the sacraments as a means of grace. The benefit received through them, he says, is received 'from God Himself the Author of the sacraments, and not from any other natural or supernatural quality in them,' and 'they contain *in themselves* no vital force or efficacy, they are not physical but *moral instruments* of salvation, duties of service and worship, which unless we perform as the Author of grace requireth, they are unprofitable. For,' Hooker adds, 'all receive not the grace of God who receive the sacraments of His grace.'[7]

It is necessary to affirm, moreover, that the Christian sacraments are not without effect even when received

[6] John Jewel: *Works*, Vol. III (Parker Society edition, Cambridge, 1848), p. 64. The original Latin edition of Jewel's *Apology of the Church of England* was published in 1562. Lady Bacon's English translation appeared two years later.

[7] Richard Hooker: *Laws of Ecclesiastical Polity*, V, lvii, 4; originally published in 1597.

unworthily; but when so received it is the opposite effect which they mediate: they then become, not means of grace, but means of judgment. Hence the further assertion of Article XXV that 'they that receive them unworthily purchase to themselves damnation, as St. Paul saith' (the reference is to I Cor. 11: 29); and similarly Article XXIX says of the eucharist that 'the wicked and such as be void of a lively faith, although they do carnally and visibly press with their teeth (as Saint Augustine saith) the sacrament of the body and blood of Christ, yet in no wise are they partakers of Christ; but rather, to their condemnation, do eat and drink the sign or sacrament of so great a thing.' Hypocritically to associate oneself with those who partake of these eloquent symbols of the Gospel is to show a contempt for the Gospel and its promises far worse than that displayed by those who hold themselves aloof from the worship of the Church.

Thirdly, a sacrament is a *pledge of grace*. While the necessity of faith for a right reception of the sacraments is very properly stressed in the Book of Common Prayer, it would be quite mistaken to conclude that the grace of God is in any way created or induced by the faith of man. As we have previously said, God's grace is God's initiative on behalf of man who is helpless because of sin. Divine grace precedes all. Faith, as response to the initiative of grace, embraces with humility and wonder the saving promises of the Gospel. Absence of faith cannot nullify the fact or the reality of the work of Christ. Nor can it invalidate the word of God, which, visible in the sacraments, is prior both to those sacraments and also to that faith of which their participation is an expression. God's word remains true, however much men may spurn it.

Accordingly it is customary to speak of a sacrament not only as a sign and a means of grace but also as a pledge of the faithfulness of God's word. It does not add anything to the promises of the covenant of grace, but it confirms them to the believing heart, or, it may be, to the doubting heart – just as an engagement ring is a visible pledge which confirms, but does not add to, the promise of marriage that has been spoken and heard between a betrothed couple. Thus a sacrament, like a seal attached to a royal proclamation, is a visible assurance of the authenticity of God's proclamation of the Gospel, which apart from the sacramental pledge is none the less authentic. And as a seal by itself, attached to a wordless sheet of paper, is void of all value and significance (since nothing can fulfil the function of a pledge unless it is associated with a promise), so, too, the sacraments, if divorced from the word of God, degenerate into empty ceremonies.

These considerations show plainly enough the great importance of the sacraments within the sphere of grace. They may indeed be described as instruments of grace, but not in some special sense distinct from that in which the preaching of the Word is an instrument of grace. It is, in fact, plain throughout the New Testament that preaching is the *primary* means of grace – the sacraments being properly, as we have said, a part of the ministry of the Word and as such visible manifestations of the message of grace (cf. I Cor. 1: 17 f.; 21,

23 f., 9: 16; Rom. 1: 15, 10: 14 f.; Acts 1: 8, 20: 14 ff.; Gal. 1: 8; II Tim. 4: 2). That is why Bishop Hugh Latimer described preaching as 'God's instrument of salvation.'[8] 'This office of preaching,' he declared, 'is the office of salvation'[9] and, again, when himself preaching before King Edward VI in 1549: 'We cannot be saved without hearing of the word: it is a necessary way to salvation. . . . There must be preachers if we look to be saved.'[10] To this essential ministry of the Word sacraments are annexed.

It is the attribution to the sacraments of a status as a means of grace *on their own*, independently of the word, that in the history of the Church has led to the atrophy of preaching and the misuse of the sacraments. The effect, when this has taken place, has been to elevate the sacraments to a position over against preaching – as though the ministry of the word and the ministry of the sacraments were two virtually unrelated functions – with the consequence that the celebration of the sacraments, rather than preaching, has come to be regarded as essential to salvation. The *ex opere operato* doctrine, whereby it was taught that grace was as it were automatically conveyed through the sacraments, encouraged people to put their faith in sacraments instead of in the word (to which the proper function of

[8] Hugh Latimer: *Works*, Vol. I (Parker Society edition, Cambridge, 1844), p. 155. The quotation is from a sermon preached before King Edward VI on 29 March 1549.

[9] Hugh Latimer: *op. cit.*, p. 349. The quotation is from the second of the sermons on the Lord's Prayer which were preached in 1552.

[10] Hugh Latimer: *op cit.*, p. 200. The sermon was preached on 12 April 1549.

the sacraments is to testify). With the ascendancy of this false dichotomy, the proclaiming and hearing of the word entered so far into eclipse that the liturgy came to be conducted in a language (Latin) which the people could not understand. The priority of preaching was abandoned for the priority of priesthood. The dispensation of grace was placed to all intents and purposes exclusively in the hands of the priest, regarded, in particular, as the offerer of the so-called eucharistic sacrifice. The Christian table of fellowship was replaced by the altar of the mass. The teaching of transubstantiation focused attention on the 'consecrated' elements and induced the practice of 'reservation' and adoration of an inanimate object the substance of which, it was taught, had been changed into the very substance of the physical body of Christ. Baptism, priestly absolution, and the sacerdotal offering of masses, for both the living and the dead, became the prime necessities in the scheme of salvation.

Thus we find that the Council of Trent in the middle of the sixteenth century pronounced anathemas against any who maintain that 'the sacraments of the New Law do not contain the grace which they signify,' or that 'grace, on God's part, is not given through these sacraments, always, and to all men', or that 'by these sacraments of the New Law grace is not conferred through the act performed (*ex opere operato*), but that faith alone in the divine promise suffices for obtaining grace.'[11] The same Council affirmed, when defining transubstantiation, that 'by the consecration of the

[11] Session VII, canons 6, 7, and 8.

bread and the wine a conversion takes place of the whole substance of the bread into the substance of the body of Christ our Lord, and of the whole substance of the wine into the substance of His blood; which conversion is conveniently and properly called transubstantiation by the holy catholic Church'; and the faithful are enjoined to 'exhibit in veneration the worship of latria, which is due to the true God, to this most holy sacrament.'[12] Accordingly, further anathemas are pronounced against any who deny 'that in the sacrament of the most holy eucharist the body and blood, together with the soul and divinity, of our Lord Jesus Christ, and consequently the whole Christ, are verily, really, and substantially contained,' or who assert that 'in the holy sacrament of the eucharist Christ, the only-begotten Son of God, is not to be adored with even the external worship of latria . . . or is not to be exposed publicly to the people to be worshipped, and that those who worship it are idolaters.'[13]

These and the many other declarations and anathemas of Trent are still binding in the Roman Catholic Church today. They reflect a doctrine of grace which is far removed from that propounded in the New Testament. Anglicanism has no cause for complacency, however, for the indications that it is moving away from the scriptural understanding of the communication of grace, recovered at the Reformation, and in the direction of the teaching of Romanism are too plain to be ignored. It is true that the doctrine of

[12] Session XIII, chapters 4 and 5.
[13] Session XIII, canons 1 and 6.

transubstantiation is generally repudiated; but the normal accompaniments of this doctrine, such as a sacerdotal priesthood, reservation and adoration of the sacrament, fasting communion, and the erection of altars and candles, show (even if these comparatively recent introductions are not invariably associated with Romish teaching) that Anglicanism is in danger of departing from its scriptural heritage. The fact that the 'altar', placed within the 'sanctuary', is commonly treated as the most holy part of a church – much 'holier' than the pulpit – speaks volumes in itself, as also does the fact that the pulpit may be occupied by a layman, but not the 'sanctuary'.

The most incisive contemporary challenge to this whole system of 'churchianity' has come from the pen of Emil Brunner, who said that the reception of his book *The Misunderstanding of the Church*, published in 1952, 'showed how hard it is to make a critical examination of the customary conception of the Church,' and that in the writing of this book it became clear to him 'how the situation of the Church as time goes on makes such an examination a more and more urgent necessity.'[14] Brunner's contention is that the development of 'the Ekklesia' of the first century into 'the Church' has in fact been a 'disastrous misdevelopment', and that 'the end product of this development – the Roman Catholic Church – is certainly not identical with what we know as the Ekklesia of the New Testament, but something fundamentally different.'[15] He

[14] Emil Brunner: *Dogmatics*, Vol. III (London, 1962), p. xi.
[15] Emil Brunner: *op. cit.*, p. 58.

draws attention to 'the emphatically non-cultic, one might almost say everyday, character of the celebration of the Supper' in the New Testament, insisting that the primitive Christian Lord's Supper is 'fundamentally different from what was later called the Sacrament of the Altar or the Mystery of the Eucharist.' 'If it were a Sacrament, that is, the bestowal of salvation,' says Brunner,[16] 'then it would necessarily be clearly taught as the decisive thing, and would be made the central theme of the preaching . . . An unprejudiced reader of the New Testament would never think that this meal was the decisive thing, and yet it would have to be, if it were a Sacrament.' But in the system of the Church the eucharist 'gains a dominating significance and becomes incomparably more important than any spoken word.' In the New Testament, moreover, 'not a word is said of a differentiation between the one who administers and the one who receives. But if what is distributed is itself the means of salvation, it is inevitable that differentiation should enter in . . . The Ekklesia becomes the Church of the priests who, as mediators of the means of salvation, stands over against the laymen.' With the conception of the eucharist as a sacrifice, 'the Old Testament sacrificial cultus penetrated the Church, a cultus which according to the Epistle to the Hebrews had once for all been

[16] Brunner is using the term 'sacrament' here in a somewhat idiosyncratic sense that serves to draw attention to the sacramental uses of Roman Catholicism. In itself, however, the term 'sacrament' is not objectionable, and is common currency in the churches of the Reformation, including the Church of England, in a sense which is not at variance with New Testament truth, as we have sought to show in the opening part of this section.

blished by Christ. . . . Thus the structure of the ἐκκλησία has suffered a total change through this new understanding of the Lord's Supper as the Sacrament of the altar. The brotherhood of Christ has turned into the sacramental priestly Church.'[17]

This no doubt is, and is liable to be dismissed as, a *radical* criticism; but it is a criticism which is radical in the right sense, namely, that it returns to the *roots* of Christianity in the New Testament. In doing this Brunner is serving the cause of genuine Christianity, for the New Testament is the standard with which the Church, whether 'Protestant' or 'Catholic', must always be compared and by which it must always seek to re-form itself. While Brunner's criticism must itself be open to criticism in terms of the same standard, it is certain that the Church is in urgent need, not least at this present ecumenical juncture, of a radical reconsideration of itself and its institutions in the light of the New Testament revelation.

[17] Emil Brunner: *op. cit.*, pp. 63 ff.

CHAPTER SEVEN

GRACE AND BISHOPS

CLOSELY connected with what we have been saying about grace and the sacraments is the notion that a 'valid' ministry of grace is in some way bound up with the possession by a church of bishops in the 'historic succession'. In the New Testament, as has often been pointed out, the terms 'presbyter' (elder) and 'bishop' are synonymous and interchangeable. The elevation of the office of bishop above that of presbyter belongs to the sub-apostolic period. The bishop, however, was not regarded as belonging to a different ministerial order, but as being the first among equals. As Jerome wrote in the fourth century, 'the word bishops includes presbyters also.'[1] The evolution of the distinction between bishop and presbyter was at first in the interests of the government and superintendence of the spreading Church. The bishop's function was that of pastoral oversight. He was regarded as the centre of unity and (through his faithful transmission of apostolic teaching) the guarantor of orthodoxy. But it was not long before a sacerdotal concept of the ministry, alien to the teaching of the New Testament, began to gain ground in the Church, and indeed to dominate the ecclesiastical scene. Bishops were exalted above all

---

[1] Jerome (c. 342–420): Letter CXLVI, to Evangelus.

others to an eminence of dignity as 'successors of the apostles', presidents of the 'altars' under their jurisdiction, and the channels of Christian grace. Ordination at the hands of a bishop became an essential prerequisite for the exercise of a priestly ministry purveying grace through the sacraments of the Church. The final refinement was the elevation of the bishop of Rome to the highest eminence of all as successor of Peter and vicar of Christ. The Church had become a hierarchical institution, which through its pope, bishops, priests, and sacraments dispensed grace to the community. 'There is,' observes Brunner, 'a fundamental difference between the saying, "Where two or three are gathered together in My name, there am I in the midst of them", and the legally constituted Church, which exists only where the bishop is present.'[2]

Again, is not Brunner right when he explains that, 'as late as the first letter of Peter, it is only because there are as yet no special persons who hold the rank of priest and exercise the priestly right of administering the Sacrament that the Ekklesia can be called the priestly people?'[3] The same conclusion was, of course, set forth a century ago by Bishop J. B. Lightfoot in his famous dissertation on the Christian ministry, in which he affirms of the kingdom of Christ that 'above all it has no sacerdotal system. It interposes no sacrificial tribe or class between God and man. . . . Each individual member holds personal communion with the Divine Head. To Him immediately he is responsible,

[2] Emil Brunner: *op. cit.*, p. 68.
[3] Emil Brunner: *op. cit.*, p. 64.

62

and from Him directly he obtains pardon and draws strength.'[4] It is true that in the early Church it became necessary to appoint particular officers. 'But,' says Lightfoot, 'the priestly functions and privileges of the Christian people are never regarded as transferred or even delegated to these officers. They are called stewards or messengers of God, servants or ministers of the Church, and the like: but the sacerdotal title is never once conferred upon them. The only priests under the Gospel, designated as such in the New Testament, are the saints, the members of the Christian brotherhood.'[5]

The classical Anglican position is defined by Bishop Jewel in his *Apology of the Church of England*: 'For, whereas some use to make so great a vaunt, that the pope only is Peter's successor, as though thereby he carried the Holy Ghost in his bosom, this is but a matter of nothing, and a very trifling tale. *God's grace is promised to a good mind, and to one that feareth God, not unto sees and successors.*'[6] Significantly, and consistently with this, Article XIX makes no mention of bishops when describing the nature of the Church: 'The visible Church of Christ,' it states, 'is a congregation of faithful men [that is, believers], in the which the pure Word of God is preached, and the sacraments be duly administered according to Christ's ordinance . . .' And this tallies with the definitions of the other Reformed churches which, for one reason or another, had adopted a presbyterian form of church

[4] J. B. Lightfoot: *St. Paul's Epistle to the Philippians* (2nd edition, London, 1869), p. 179.
[5] J. B. Lightfoot: *op. cit.*, pp. 182 ff.
[6] John Jewel: *Works*, Vol. III (*ut supra*), p. 103.

government. They were not in principle opposed to episcopacy, and their lack of bishops was no barrier to the enjoyment of full and reciprocal intercommunion with the Church of England. Neither the adequacy of their sacraments nor the validity of their orders was called in question. On the contrary, freedom of intercommunion was normal and interchange of ministries was not abnormal. What mattered was not the particular form of church order – though Anglicans valued episcopacy as being ancient and estimable – but unity in the Gospel and the teaching of the apostles.

The essential apostolic succession was succession in apostolic doctrine. Thus Jewel replied to his critic Thomas Harding: 'Succession, you say, is the chief way for any Christian man to avoid antichrist. I grant you, if you mean the succession of doctrine.'[7] Other things, though not unimportant, were optional and should not be forced on other churches. This principle is clearly stated in the treatise 'Of Ceremonies' which was prefaced to the Book of Common Prayer in 1549 (and which has been retained in all subsequent revisions): 'In these our doings,' it is declared, 'we condemn no other nations, nor prescribe anything but to our own people only: for we think it convenient that every country should use such ceremonies as they shall think best to the setting forth of God's honour and glory, and to the reducing of the people to a most perfect and godly living, without error or superstition.'

[7] John Jewel: *Defence of the Apology*, in *Works*, Vol. III (*ut supra*), p. 348.

The unity of the Church of England as a national church was shattered by the rigid enforcement of the Act of Uniformity of 1662. The consequent development of nonconformity certainly created a new situation; but, drastic though the change was that then took place, it was not radical in respect of liberty of worship: the Lord's Table remained open to dissenters, as the practice of 'occasional conformity' showed. Changes that really were radical in this respect were introduced by the adherents of the Oxford Movement in the nineteenth century, whose aim was, among other things, to revive the concept of episcopacy as the essential apostolic ministry, belonging to the very *esse* of the Church and therefore constitutive of its existence, and as the only authentic channel of grace – grace being understood primarily in terms of sacrament and priesthood. The advance of this type of basically unreformed churchmanship has been such that it has now become a dominant factor in the Anglican scene. Its modern restatement will be found in the large volume *The Apostolic Ministry*, which was published under the editorship of the late Bishop K. E. Kirk in 1946.

Those who hold that episcopacy is of the absolute essence (the *esse*) of the Church are no more than a minority, but an influential minority, in the Church of England. Perhaps more numerous are those who maintain that bishops in the historic succession belong to the fullness of being (the *plene esse*) of the Church. Their case has been put forward in *The Historic Episcopate*, edited by Bishop (as he now is) K. M. Carey, which appeared in 1954. Although the position propounded in this book does not regard episcopacy as essential to the Church's being, yet it places non-episcopal ministries in an unfavourable light, since, while refusing to dismiss such ministries as invalid, it does regard them as deficient because of their lack of episcopacy. Its advocates see the historic episcopate as a necessary element for the realization of the fullness of the Church in any scheme of reunion.

There are others, again, in the Church of England who, while valuing episcopacy as, at its best, an excellent form of church government, make no special claims for it and would not insist on its acceptance as a prerequisite to reunion or intercommunion. They cannot sympathize with any prelatical concept of episcopacy and would welcome the introduction of a 'modified' form of episcopal government, such as was advocated by Archbishop Ussher and others in the seventeenth century,[8] which would place more emphasis on and allow more scope for genuine pastoral oversight than the present demands of bureaucratc administration allow. This, in the main, is the position defended in the symposium entitled *The Ministry of the Church*, edited by Bishop Stephen Neill, which was published in 1947 as a rejoinder to *The Apostolic Ministry*.

But there is yet another view of episcopacy which

[8] Cf. James Ussher: *Reduction of Episcopacy unto the Form of Synodical Government received in the Ancient Church*, first published in 1641; and for a modern discussion of the proposals put forward in the seventeenth century see A. Harold Wood: *Church Unity without Uniformity* (London, 1963) and the symposium entitled *From Uniformity to Unity* (London, 1962) edited by G. F. Nuttall and Owen Chadwick.

should not fail to be taken into account. Theologians of the Church of Scotland, for example, maintain that, 'while the word "bishop" has, for historical reasons, fallen into desuetude in the Church of Scotland, the idea of episcopacy, as oversight, is not new or alien to the Presbyterian doctrine of the Church'; indeed that 'there is and always has been a Presbyterian episcopacy, whose origin lies in the New Testament, where the "Elders" were at first identical with the "Bishops" and are referred to sometimes as presbyteroi and sometimes as episcopoi.'[9] This same publication, *Glasgow Speaks*, criticized insistence 'on the "historic episcopate" and on episcopal ordination as a *sine qua non* for any valid and regular ministry of Word and Sacrament,' as 'a lower doctrine of the Church' than the doctrine of 'the fundamental unity and catholicity of the Church' held by the Church of Scotland.[10] Instead, it was suggested that 'mutual recognition' would open the door to full sacramental communion and to interchange of ministries, and should form the chief topic of further conversations[11] – a proposal that would have the ready sympathy of a large section, both clergy and laity, of the Church of England.

As is well known, the proposals of the Joint Anglican-Presbyterian Report were rejected by an overwhelming majority – and the chief reason for their defeat was

[9] *Glasgow Speaks* (Glasgow, 1959), p. 20, edited by G. M. Dryburgh. This booklet was a rejoinder to the Joint Report on Anglican–Presbyterian Relations, published in 1957, which proposed that Presbyterianism should take episcopacy into its system under the guise of 'bishops-in-presbytery'.

[10] *op. cit.*, p. 15.

[11] *op. cit.*, p. 30.

precisely the insistence on the acceptance of episcopacy as an essential preliminary to reunion or intercommunion. This, in fact, is the great stumbling-block which may be expected, if it continues to be insisted on, to overthrow all schemes for unification. It has occurred again in the Report of the Conversations between the Church of England and the Methodist Church, in which it is clearly implied that in the proposed service of reconciliation, during which the bishop's hands are laid on the Methodist ministers, the latter are endued with 'grace for the office of priest'.[12] The four authors of the vigorous 'Dissentient View' which is appended to the Report declare that 'historic episcopacy is entirely without support in the New Testament,' and that therefore 'no ecclesiastical body has the right to demand participation in historic episcopacy as a qualification for communion or union with itself.' They hold, further, that 'the belief that the full and true being of the Church is dependent upon its possession of historic episcopacy is inconsistent with the New Testament doctrine that the existence of the People of God depends wholly upon God's gracious election, grasped by faith only.'[13]

In recent years, probably the most notorious expression of the rigorist doctrine of episcopacy as being in some way essential for the valid transmission of sacramental grace was the categorical declaration, contained in the Report of the last Lambeth Conference (1958), that 'Anglicans conscientiously hold that the celebrant of the Eucharist should have been ordained by a bishop

[12] Anglican–Methodist Report (London, 1963), p. 43.
[13] op. cit., p. 59.

standing in the historic succession, and generally believe it to be their duty to bear witness to this principle by receiving Holy Communion only from those who have thus been ordained,' with the consequence that it is 'in practice impossible to envisage the establishment of fully reciprocal intercommunion at any stage short of the adoption of episcopacy by the churches of Presbyterian order, and the satisfactory unification of the Presbyterian and Anglican ministries.'[14] The fact is that there are large numbers of Anglicans who entirely repudiate any such view, regarding it as a deplorable departure from the outlook and policy of classical Anglicanism and an unwarranted impediment to the realization of unity.

Not surprisingly, it is a view that fails to commend itself to non-episcopal churches which cannot conscientiously assent to a procedure whereby a serious question-mark is placed over the character of the grace and blessing they have enjoyed for centuries. Thus, speaking for the Baptists, Dr. E. A. Payne has said that 'they could not agree to any scheme which appeared to question the validity of their ministries or to involve them in theories of episcopal succession and authority which would seem to deny their whole history and experience.' Principal John Huxtable, speaking for the Congregationalists, has questioned 'whether the facts bear out the theory, whether it is true that churches with such an episcopal succession are more certain of sacramental grace than those without . . . We cannot doubt,' he adds, 'that God has honoured our ministries,

[14] *The Lambeth Conference 1958* (London, 1958), 2.44.

that through the ministry of Word and Sacraments in our gathered churches God's grace has been conveyed and received, and that our corporate life is in its measure a fellowship in the Holy Spirit.' Dr. A. Marcus Ward, speaking for the Methodists, has written: 'What they object to is the conclusion that episcopacy is . . . the constitutive element of the Church. This seems to involve a conception of the working of grace which is historically unreliable and contrary to the nature of the Gospel.' And, speaking for the Presbyterians, J. M. Ross has complained that this insistence on episcopacy seems 'to imply that the existing ministry of the Presbyterian Churches is not a true ministry in the Church of Christ and needs to be validated in this way before intercommunion can take place.'[15]

In promulgating what is commonly known as the 'Lambeth Quadrilateral' (according to which Holy Scripture, the Nicene creed, the sacraments of baptism and holy communion, and the historic episcopate are stipulated as essentials for unity) the Lambeth Conference of 1920 at the same time gave the following assurance: 'It is not that we call in question for a moment the spiritual reality of the ministry of those Communions which do not possess the Episcopate. On the contrary we thankfully acknowledge that these ministries have been manifestly blessed and owned by the Holy Spirit as an effective means of grace.' If this is indeed so, it is legitimate to ask why the Lambeth divines should have insisted on a

[15] *The Churches and Christian Unity* (London, 1963), pp. 143, 161, 187, 207, edited by R. J. W. Bevan.

procedure that conveys exactly the opposite impression.

This whole concept of episcopacy was strongly attacked by Professor G. W. H. Lampe in an article on Episcopacy and Reunion published in the March 1961 issue of *The Churchman*. Holding that 'neither the efficacy nor the validity of the sacraments depends upon the maintenance of a particular type of Church Order,' Dr. Lampe complained that the many Anglicans who repudiate the view propounded in the 1958 Lambeth Report (quoted above) 'yet find themselves committed against their own conscience to a position which they conceive to be illogical and indefensible. It is illogical,' says Dr. Lampe, 'because it is constantly asserted, on the one hand, that the ministries of the English Free Churches and the Church of Scotland are real ministries within the Catholic Church of Christ, and that Anglicans do not for a moment wish to question their spiritual efficacy; yet at the same time Anglicans are told that they should not receive Holy Communion at the hands of those ministers, but should wait until the Church of England is reunited organically with the bodies to which they belong and they have been given episcopal ordination. Thus what is asserted in word is denied in practice . . . The words and actions of Anglicans in these circumstances are contradictory. Anglicans are thus committed to the belief in the historic episcopate as the "essential ministry", which many of them repudiate as warmly as do their non-episcopal brethren.' A true doctrine of priesthood, Dr. Lampe concludes, will enable us to recognize 'that the doctrine of the ministry need not be a barrier to intercommunion; and we shall be increasingly reluctant to be committed, as Anglicans, to a position in which our church too often seems to the rest of the world to be concerned with a gospel which is no gospel, a gospel of the grace of God in bishops.'[16]

To the same effect the celebrated Open Letter on Intercommunion addressed to the Archbishops of Canterbury and York in November 1961 by thirty-two theologians of the Church of England stated: 'We recognize that it is our Lord who calls and commissions His ministers, and that He is not tied to any one form of ministry. The raising up of non-episcopal ministries was the almost inevitable consequence of the Reformation and post-Reformation divisions of the Church, following from the necessary duty of maintaining the truth of the Gospel as this was conscientiously understood. We believe that our Lord conveys through these ministries the same grace of the Word and the Sacraments as He bestows through the historic ministry of bishops, priests, and deacons, and that He does this, not as an act of uncovenanted mercy, but because they are real and efficacious minis'ries within the Body of His Church.'

Distinguished theologians of other lands have also spoken critically of the ecumenical demands which are now associated with the official (though not the general) voice of Anglicanism. Thus the German scholar Professor Wilhelm Niesel asks: 'By making apostolic succes-

[16] G. W. H. Lampe: 'Episcopacy and Reunion' in *The Churchman*, Vol. LXXV, No. 1 (London, March, 1961), pp. 7 ff.

sion in the episcopal office an indispensable condition for any union of churches, is not Anglicanism laying upon others a law which these others cannot rightly accept ?'[17] And he offers the pointed comment: 'It is plainly dangerous to extol the episcopal office of apostolic succession as a symbol of church unity, in the way the Anglican Church does, for surely Rome can offer a much more impressive symbol of such unity ?'[18] Wise words have also been written by Bishop Gustaf Aulén of Sweden: 'The episcopal office, with or without "unbroken" succession, may be treasured for various reasons,' he says, 'but not because it guarantees the effectiveness of the means of grace. The Word and the Sacrament do not lose their power if this is omitted. They have their validity in themselves . . . It is not the office of the ministry that makes the means of grace a means of grace, but rather it is the means of grace which enables the ministry to function according to the commission and authority of Christ. Everything is dependent on the fact that the means of grace have their validity and power in themselves, or rather through Christ, because through them the living Lord carries on His redemptive work in His Church.'[19]

That there is a way forward that involves the retention of episcopacy in a manner which is acceptable at least to the great majority of both episcopalians and non-episcopalians has been demonstrated by the Church of South India. This united church was inaugurated in

[17] Wilhelm Niesel: *Reformed Symbolics* (London, 1962), p. 317.
[18] Wilhelm Niesel: *op. cit.*, p. 314.
[19] Gustaf Aulén: *Reformation and Catholicity* (Edinburgh 1962), pp. 163 f.

1947 by the coming together of Anglicans, Presbyterians, Methodists, and Congregationalists to form a single ecclesiastical body with more than a million members. It is expected that before long the Lutherans too will join the Church of South India. In the planning of this union, it was agreed that the form of its ministry and government should be that of historic episcopacy, but at the same time the doctrine of apostolic succession through bishops was rejected. The recognition of the genuine authenticity of the orders of ministers belonging to the non-episcopal denominations was demonstrated without ambiguity by the fact that they were welcomed into the united church and accorded the full rights of ministerial office without having to submit to any ceremony that might in any way be interpreted as reordination – though naturally, in an episcopally constituted church, all ordinations of new candidates coming forward for ordination are performed by bishops. Professor Rajaiah D. Paul has explained the stand which the Church of South India takes in this respect as follows: 'It does not accept that episcopally ordained priests are superior, in any sense, to non-episcopally ordained ministers. We consider all our ministers to be on an equal footing and on a complete parity of status . . . Our aim is not to replace the ministers of the non-episcopal churches with an episcopal ministry, but to preserve for the whole Church of South India all the grace and authority which Christ has given to our ministries in their separation.'[20]

It is not enough for the 1958 Lambeth Report to say

[20] *The Churches and Christian Unity* (*ut supra*), pp. 245 f.

74

that 'we can indeed thank God for the grace which He has bestowed upon the bishops, presbyters, and people of the Church of South India in these past ten years, and for the response to that grace shown in the growth of inner coherence and missionary zeal.'[21] For Anglican officialdom to thank God for grace bestowed, and yet to refuse the tangible recognition of full communion to the body on which that grace has been bestowed, strikes the onlooker as ludicrous and lacking in seriousness. Indeed, the Lambeth fathers must not be surprised if some interpret this as an example of cant and hypocrisy. The Bishop of Derby, Dr. G. F. Allen, has pertinently observed: 'If the Church of England says that the position in South India is anomalous, they may fairly reply, that it is in England that the anomaly exists, since we are still divided and they are not. . . . At least it must be said that the Church of South India, by its unity and its subsequent life, has given a challenge to the rest of Christendom.'[22] Must we expect the response to this challenge to be blocked indefinitely by a minority theory of grace through episcopal succession which (as described by Professor Lampe) is both illogical and indefensible? That is the question which confronts the Church, and not least Anglicanism, today.

[21] *The Lambeth Conference 1958*, 2.28.
[22] *The Churches and Christian Unity (ut supra)*, p. 122.

CHAPTER EIGHT

GRACE AND MARY

IN the worship of Roman Catholicism the Virgin Mary is given a prominence which rivals that of Christ Himself. The Ave Maria enjoys a prestige to all intents and purposes on a level with that of the Lord's Prayer. Legitimate respect for Mary, the 'calling her blessed' (Lk. 1: 28, 42, 48), has been replaced by excessive veneration and devotion to her as in a special sense the dispenser of grace. In the course of this chapter we shall hope to show that the mariology of the Roman Catholic Church is a logical outworking of that church's doctrine of grace and salvation.

Support for the veneration of Mary as the dispenser of grace is claimed in the angelic greeting of the annunciation (Lk. 1: 28), which the Latin version known as the Vulgate (the official Roman Catholic Bible) renders: '*Ave, gratia plena,*' that is, 'Hail, thou that art full of grace.' Hence the terms of the Ave Maria: 'Hail, Mary, full of grace, the Lord is with thee. Blessed art thou amongst women, and blessed is the fruit of thy womb, Jesus. Holy Mary, mother of God, pray for us sinners now and at the hour of our death. Amen.' The original Greek of Luke 1: 28,[1] however, does not mean

---

[1] Κεχαριτωμένη

76

'thou that art full of grace,' but simply 'thou favoured one' or 'thou recipient of grace'. The most that can be said for the Vulgate rendering has been said by the commentator Alfred Plummer (and even he stretches a point in saying it): 'The *gratia plena* of the Vulgate is too indefinite. It is right, if it means "full of grace, *which thou hast received*; wrong, if it means "full of grace, which thou hast to bestow".'[2] But it is precisely the latter impermissible meaning that Rome daily assigns to the expression. And this conception of Mary as one who mercifully mediates grace to those who call upon her is the basis of the unrestrained worship that is offered to her in the Roman Catholic Church.

The rationalization of the supreme position to which Romanism has exalted Mary has been expressed in the following terms: 'As the mother of God, Mary transcends in dignity all created persons, angels, and men, because the dignity of a creature is the greater the nearer it is to God. And of all created things after the human nature of Christ . . . Mary is nearest to the Triune God. As a true mother she is related by blood to the Son of God according to His human nature. Through the Son she is associated intimately also with the Father and the Holy Ghost. The Church honours her on account of her position as Mother of God, and on account of her high endowment with grace deriving from her position as daughter of the Heavenly Father and spouse of the Holy Ghost.' It is even argued that in

[2] Alfred Plummer: *Commentary on the Gospel according to St. Luke* (ICC, 4th edition, Edinburgh, 1910), p. 22.

a sense Mary's dignity is infinite, 'since she is the Mother of an Infinite Divine Person.'[3] To describe Mary in this way as both the daughter of God (the Father) and the mother of God (the Son), and also the spouse of God (the Holy Ghost), is more than thoroughly confused: it takes us back into the sphere of the theogonies of the ancient paganisms, in which female deities figured prominently.

Mary is described, further, as the new Eve, parallel with Christ who is the new Adam. Just as the sinful disobedience of the first Eve led to the fall of mankind, so also, it is maintained, the sinless obedience of the new Eve resulted in the salvation of mankind. The Roman Catholic Church teaches not only that Mary was conceived without taint of original sin (a dogma binding, since 1854, on all its members) but also that during the whole of her life she was free from all concupiscence and all personal sin and, after the completion of her earthly life, was assumed body and soul into the glory of heaven (another dogma binding, in this case since 1950, on all its members). Now, as Queen of Heaven, she is said to be in a position to bestow saving grace on all who call upon her. 'Mary is our Lady and Queen,' Ludwig Ott writes, 'because she, the new Eve, has shared intimately in the redemptive work of Christ, the new Adam, by suffering with Him and offering Him up to the eternal Father. Mary's sublime dignity as the Queen of Heaven and Earth makes her supremely

[3] Ludwig Ott: *Fundamentals of Catholic Dogma* (5th edition, Cork, 1962), p. 197; cf. Thomas Aquinas: *Summa Theologica*, I, xxv, 6.

powerful in her maternal intercession for her children on earth.'[4]

It is by virtue of her co-operation in the work of redemption that Mary is stated to be qualified to mediate all graces to men. Her co-operation is seen in her response of acquiescence to the message of the annunciation: 'Behold, I am the handmaid of the Lord; let it be to me according to your word' (Lk. 1:38). Thus viewed, the incarnation of Christ and the salvation of mankind were dependent on her assent. It was to show that there was 'a certain spiritual wedlock' between the Son of God and human nature, says Thomas Aquinas, that the Virgin's consent was awaited as the representative of all human nature.[5] Moreover, Mary is viewed as now co-operating in heaven in the application of the grace of redemption to men, especially through her maternal intercession. Thus it is commonly taught, firstly, that Mary is the channel of all graces in that she gave the Redeemer, who is the source of all graces, to the world, and, secondly, that since her assumption into heaven no grace is conferred on man without her actual intercessory co-operation.

Mary, then, is regarded as performing a work which is mediatorial and redemptive, in co-operation with that performed by our Mediator and Redeemer Jesus Christ. Roman Catholicism, it is true, affirms the sole mediatorship of Christ, in theory at least, for this is clearly asserted in the New Testament (I Tim. 2:5); but then inconsistently assigns to Mary a 'secondary

[4] Ludwig Ott: *op. cit.*, p. 211.
[5] Thomas Aquinas (c. 1225–1274): *Summa Theologica*, III, XXX, 1.

mediatorship' (which amounts to a contradiction of the *sole* mediatorship of Christ), and in the realm of popular devotion encourages the supplication of Mary in such a way as to suggest that she is the real mediator between God and men. 'Who can ever deny,' wrote Alphonsus Liguori, the eighteenth century founder of the Redemptorist order, 'that it is most reasonable and proper to assert that God, in order to exalt this great creature, who more than all others honoured and loved Him during her life, and whom moreover He had chosen to be the mother of His Son, our common Redeemer, wills that all graces that are granted to those whom He has redeemed should pass through and be dispensed by the hands of Mary? We most readily admit that Jesus Christ is the only Mediator of justice . . . and that by His merits He obtains us all graces and salvation; but we say that Mary is the mediatrix of grace, and that . . . whatever graces we receive they come to us through her intercession.'[6]

An astonishing refinement of this doctrine of the mediation of grace through Mary is the description of her as the mediator between us and the Mediator. This has the effect of making Christ seem, by comparison, remote and even hostile to us. In Christ, it is said (as the quotation in the preceding paragraph suggested), there is the mediation of justice by way of merit, whereas in Mary there is the mediation of grace by way of her intercessions on our behalf – a distinction which places

[6] Alphonsus Liguori (1696–1787): *The Glories of Mary* (London, 1852), p. 124. The original Italian edition was published in 1750.

Christ's work in an unfavourable 'legalistic' light and fails culpably to take into account the *love* of God in Christ. Mary, furthermore, is depicted as especially close to us because she is motherly, compassionate, and benign. The saving emphasis is shifted from Christ to her. Accordingly, the Roman Catholic is assured that if Mary undertakes his defence he is certain of gaining the kingdom of heaven; that under her mantle 'all sinners, without exception, find refuge for every sin that they have committed,' and that, while we dare not invoke the Lord whom we have offended, Mary will speak on our behalf and ask all that we need. 'If I have thy favour,' Mary's clients are taught to pray, 'I do not even fear an angry God; for a single prayer of thine will appease Him.' Bernard of Clairvaux, in the twelfth century, rationalized this attitude in the following way: 'There is no doubt that Jesus Christ is the only mediator of justice between men and God, that, in virtue of His own merits and promises, He will and can obtain pardon and the divine favours for us; but because men acknowledge and fear the Divine Majesty which is in Him as God, for this reason it was necessary to assign us another advocate, to whom we might have recourse with far less fear and more confidence, and this advocate is Mary, than whom we cannot find one more powerful with His Divine Majesty, or one more merciful towards ourselves. . . . A mediator then was needed with the Mediator Himself, nor could a more fitting one be found than Mary.'[7]

Any student of the New Testament will recognize

[7] Alphonsus Liguori: *op. cit.*, pp. 66, 89, 90, 143, 159 f.

how repugnant all this elaborate teaching about Mary is to the doctrine of grace in the New Testament – indeed, how blasphemous it is to instruct the sinner that in approaching Mary he may have less fear and more confidence than in approaching Christ. This is a religion entirely foreign to that of the New Testament. It should be realized that one of the hidden pillars by which mariology is supported is the supposition that after baptism the blood of Christ no longer avails for the washing away of sin. This carries the implication that from baptism on another mediator must be sought. Mary thus invades and disrupts the uniqueness of the grace and mediation of Christ and is exalted to a position of dignity which is assigned in Scripture to no creature.

But, as already indicated at the beginning of this chapter, mariology, even in its most excessive elaboration, is no more than the logical outworking of the Roman Catholic doctrine of grace. If, as Roman Catholicism teaches, it is the part of man to co-operate in the achievement of his own justification, then his salvation is not altogether dependent on the grace of God – though, as we have seen, the New Testament teaches that it is. Salvation has become jointly the work of both God and man. This being so, it is not unreasonable to suppose that this partial self-saving propensity in man should be representatively concentrated in the person of a single human being (Mary) in whom this potentiality is exhibited and ideally fulfilled. It is reasonable, too, that this human co-operator in the saving work of Christ should be exalted to glory with

Him and become with Him a dispenser of grace to mankind. All this is implied in any system, whether papal or protestant, which assigns to man the ability, in whatever degree, to contribute to his own salvation.

To conceive of salvation in these terms inevitably detracts from the fullness of the grace of God in Christ Jesus. It renders that grace inadequate and demands its supplementation. And it detracts from the glory that is due solely to God, dividing that glory between God and a creature. Professor G. C. Berkouwer has rightly discerned that 'in its mariology the Roman doctrine of grace is most unmistakably manifested,' and that 'this mariology is nothing but a crystallization of the Roman conception of grace and freedom.' He observes that 'we need not be surprised to discover that after the rejection of the *sola gratia* and of the Reformed doctrine of justification by Trent the picture of Mary was more and more elaborated in the centuries that followed.' Beyond doubt, it is true that 'we are here in the centre of Roman Catholic doctrine and not at the periphery.'[8]

The official encouragement and intensification of the cult of Mary is a factor which, in this ecumenical age, is not diminishing but increasing the gulf between Romanism and the churches of the Reformation. Although mariology has undoubtedly had a long history, throughout the centuries it has been a battleground even of papal theologians. In more recent times, however, despite the prior protests of many

[8] G. C. Berkouwer: *The Conflict with Rome* (Philadelphia, 1958), p. 174.

scholars and churchmen, it has become irrevocably entrenched as an integral part of the papal cultus as the result of the promulgation, in 1854, of the dogma of Mary's immaculate conception and, in 1950, of the dogma of her bodily assumption into heaven. The *ex cathedra* proclamation of these dogmas by the pope as absolutely binding on all the faithful has stifled for ever any further disputation on these issues in the Roman Catholic Church. It only remains now for Mary's co-redeemership with Christ to be dogmatically defined by an infallible utterance of the pope; and it is widely expected that this will not be long delayed. Meanwhile the worship of Mary proceeds apace, fostered and promoted by the highest authorities. Especially significant in this respect is the tremendous and constantly swelling popularity of the Marian shrines at Lourdes in France and Fatima in Portugal, which year after year are visited by multitudes of pilgrims.

Pope Pius XII in particular proved himself an ardent promoter of the cult of Mary: in 1942 he dedicated the world to her immaculate heart; in 1950 he proclaimed *ex cathedra* the dogma of her assumption; 1954 he announced as a Marian year, to celebrate the centenary of the definition of the dogma of her immaculate conception; and that same year he instituted the Feast of Mary Queen of Heaven, allocating 31 May as its day. But he was doing no more than following the lead given by his predecessors on the papal throne. Thus, in 1891, Pope Leo XIII had proclaimed that 'as no one can come to the Most High Father except through the Son, so, generally, no one can come to Christ except through Mary';[9] and, five years later, in another encyclical he described Mary as 'mediatrix of the Mediator'.[10] In 1904 Pope Pius X spoke of Mary as the restorer of a fallen world and the dispenser of all the gifts of grace won for us by the death of Christ.[11] In 1918 Pope Benedict XV affirmed that Mary had redeemed the human race in co-operation with Christ. And his successor, Pope Pius XI, expressed his approval of the custom of calling Mary Co-Redeemer. But the peak of the officially encouraged adulation of Mary was surely reached when Pope Pius XII, at the crowning of the Fatima statue of the Virgin in 1946, affirmed: 'Mary is indeed worthy to receive honour and might and glory. She is exalted to hypostatic union with the Blessed Trinity . . . Her kingdom is as great as her Son's and God's.'[12]

The seriousness of such statements cannot be exaggerated. They demonstrate that the cult of Mary has indeed introduced another saviour and another gospel. It is a cult which makes nonsense of the apostolic affirmation that there is salvation in none other than Christ: 'for there is no other name under heaven given among men by which we must be saved' (Acts 4: 12). It overthrows the whole doctrine of grace so plainly delineated in the New Testament, which tells us that grace and truth came alone by Jesus Christ, who Himself alone is full of grace and truth (Jn. 1: 17, 14). It is,

[9] Encyclical *Octobri Mense*, 22 September 1891.
[10] Encyclical *Fidentem*, 20 September 1896.
[11] Encyclical *Ad diem*, 2 February 1904.
[12] I am indebted to W. von Loewenich: *Modern Catholicism* (London, 1959), pp. 188 ff. for many of the facts given above.

quite frankly, to fall into the sin of heathenism, by worshipping and serving the creature rather than the Creator (Rom. 1: 25).

These criticisms are not offered in any spirit of harsh self-righteousness. Prayerfully and charitably, however, we would plead with our Roman Catholic friends to turn to the pages of the New Testament so that they may judge for themselves whether or not what we have said is justified. Above all, we wish that together we might embrace the pure Gospel of Jesus Christ so faithfully proclaimed by His apostles – that we might hear St. John saying to our churches: 'Grace to you and peace from Him who is and who was and who is to come,' even Jesus Christ our Saviour and Advocate, who alone is worthy 'to receive power and wealth and wisdom and might and honour and glory and blessing' (Rev. 1: 4, 5: 12).

CHAPTER NINE

GRACE AND ELECTION

MORE than any other doctrine of Scripture, the doctrine of election throws into relief the absolute priority of divine grace. Election itself is God's sovereignty in terms of grace. Hence in the New Testament it is described as *the election of grace* (Rom. 11: 5). It is important to realize, moreover, that the focus of election is Christ Jesus, and no one else, because all grace is concentrated in Him. All God's purposes of grace revolve round Christ and find their fulfilment in Him. Christ it is who is God's elect, God's Chosen One (Lk. 23: 35), 'foreordained before the foundation of the world' (I Pet. 1: 20), the living, chief corner-stone, elect and precious (I Pet. 2: 4, 6).

Accordingly, God's election of grace operates entirely *in Christ*. Believers, says Paul, have been chosen in Christ before the foundation of the world. In Him they have redemption through His blood. In Him they have been 'destined and appointed to live for the praise of His glory.' In Him they have been sealed with the promised Holy Spirit (Eph. 1: 4, 7, 11–13). Furthermore, election in Christ is election *to be like Christ*: 'God has not called us for uncleanness, but in holiness' (I Thess. 4: 7). Election means to be 'destined by God the Father and sanctified by the Spirit for obedience to

87

Jesus Christ (I Pet. 1: 2; cf. II Thess. 2: 13). The purpose of God's election in Christ is that we should be 'conformed to the image of His Son' (Rom. 8: 29).

Indeed, the whole majestic sweep of God's sovereignty in grace is summarized in the passage from which we have just quoted (Rom. 8: 28–30). Those who are 'called according to God's purpose' are involved in the sequence of grace which Paul explains in the following terms: 'Those whom He foreknew He also predestined to be conformed to the image of His Son . . . And those whom He predestined He also called; and those whom He called He also justifies; and those whom He justified He also glorified.' The whole salvation of man, therefore, from beginning to end, from eternity to eternity, is the gracious sovereign work of God. For that reason it is a work which cannot fail or be frustrated. And it will be consummated in the crowning blessing of glorification, when at last and for ever all who are elect in Christ will be fully conformed to His perfect image (I Jn. 3: 2, Phil. 3: 21). Meanwhile the process of sanctification, which culminates in glorification at Christ's appearing, is the process of being 'changed into His likeness, from one degree of glory to another,' through the operation of the Lord who is the Spirit (II Cor. 3: 18).

Election rules out salvation as being the work of man or the choice of man: 'All this is from God, who through Christ reconciled us to Himself' (II Cor. 5: 18). If all is not of grace, then it is not grace. This holds good for all, including the apostles, to whom Christ said: 'You did not choose Me, but I chose you and appointed you that you should go and bear fruit and that your fruit should abide' (Jn. 15: 16). Likewise the conversion of Saul of Tarsus, though sudden to him, was not sudden in the purposes of God, but according to election; hence the words of Ananias to Saul: 'The God of our fathers appointed you to know His will, to see the Just One, and to hear a voice from His mouth; for you will be a witness for Him to all men of what you have seen and heard' (Acts. 22: 14 f.).

The election of grace is the true key to history – but always operating in a way that is surprising because it is never bound by human conventions or expectations: 'For My thoughts are not your thoughts, neither are your ways My ways, says the Lord. For as the heavens are higher than the earth, so are My ways higher than your ways and My thoughts than your thoughts' (Is. 55: 8 f.). Thus from the beginning of history election is active in this humanly remarkable manner: Abel is chosen, not Cain the firstborn; Isaac, not Ishmael; Jacob, not Esau; David, the youngest and least considered, not any of his older brothers; and, pre-eminently, Christ Himself, Lord of glory and Saviour of mankind, born in abject humility in a stable situated in a town of no distinction. Why is this? Paul answers by explaining that 'God chose what is foolish in the world to shame the wise, God chose what is weak in the world to shame the strong, God chose what is low and despised in the world, even things that are not, to bring to nothing things that are, so that no human being might boast in the presence of God.' It is God, not man, says Paul, who is 'the source of your life in Christ Jesus, whom God made our wisdom, our righteousness and sanctification and redemption.' Therefore if there is any boasting to be done, it must be of the Lord (I Cor. 1: 27–31).

And the calling of election is always purposeful. It is never capricious or haphazard, but leads forward towards the fulfilment of God's grand purposes of grace for the redemption of the world. All these purposes reach their climax and their achievement in Christ, who, in a unique sense, as we have said before, is God's Elect One. There is no election of grace apart from Him. In isolation from Him it is impossible to speak of anyone being elect. But God's purposes in Christ, His Elect One, are purposes of *cosmic* blessing, no less. The covenant promises extend to all the nations of the earth; but, even more, they embrace the whole created order, *the cosmos*. The creation which was cursed through man's fall will also participate in man's restoration. That is why Paul speaks of the creation as being at present 'subjected to futility' and 'groaning in travail', but also as sharing in the assured hope that, together with redeemed mankind, it 'will be set free from its bondage to decay and obtain the glorious liberty of the children of God' (Rom. 8: 19 ff.). That is why we are taught to look for the consummation of a new heaven and a new earth (II Pet. 3: 13, Rev. 21: 1).

As Christ alone is God's Elect One, all election is in Christ. The many who are elected are elected solely in the One, who is Christ. This means identification with Christ, incorporation into Christ, participation in His Sonship of whom alone the voice from heaven has said:

'This is My beloved Son, with whom I am well pleased' (Mt. 3: 17, 17: 5). In union with God's beloved Son we, too, are well pleasing to God (Eph. 1: 6). The elect man is the *man-in-Christ* (II Cor. 5: 17). In Christ we are adopted into the Sonship of the only Son and we are assured of the heritage of Him and with Him who is the only Heir of glory (Rom. 8: 14–18). For this reason Paul is able to declare that believers, whatever their temporal distinctions, are *all one in Christ Jesus* (Gal. 3: 28): the re-begotten are all one in the unity of the Only-Begotten.

It is the cosmic scope of the election of grace which provides the incentive for all Christian evangelistic and missionary enterprise. Contrary to an all too common misconception, the doctrine of election does not stifle evangelism or make it superfluous. The proof of this is seen, for example, in the ministry of the apostle Paul. His insistence on God's sovereignty through election did not inhibit him from proclaiming the Good News of Jesus Christ far and wide. That was the one thing he could not cease doing (I Cor. 9: 16). Paul's labours, indeed, his sufferings, and his journeyings in the missionary cause of evangelization far exceeded those of others (II Cor. 11: 23 ff.; cf. I Cor. 10: 15). It is instructive, too, to find that the ninth chapter of the Epistle to the Romans, in which the doctrine of divine election receives the strongest emphasis – ' "I will have mercy on whom I have mercy, and I will have compassion on whom I have compassion": so it depends not upon man's will or exertion, but upon God's mercy' (Rom. 9: 15 f.; cf. Ex. 33: 19) – is immediately followed by the tenth (though of course in the letter as Paul wrote it there were no chapter divisions) in which the responsibility to evangelize is no less strongly emphasized – 'The same Lord is Lord of all and bestows His riches upon all who call upon Him. For "every one who calls upon the name of the Lord will be saved". But how are men to call upon Him in whom they have not believed? And how are they to believe in Him of whom they have never heard? And how are they to hear without a preacher? And how can men preach unless they are sent?' (Rom. 10: 12 ff.; cf. Joel 2: 32).

That election and evangelism bring us face to face with a mystery cannot be denied. It is a mystery, however, which makes sense in the experience of grace. Faith is ever the response to the proclamation of the Gospel of divine grace: 'Faith comes from hearing, and hearing comes by the preaching of Christ' (Rom. 10: 17). But preaching is precisely the announcement of God's prior grace. The very response of faith, therefore, is an acknowledgment that all is of grace. The believer who has called upon the name of the Lord for salvation knows himself to be elect-in-Christ. He knows that he owes his new life in its entirety to God's sovereign redeeming mercy in Christ. And he knows that he is under obligation to proclaim this same message of grace to others.

Election, finally, is the guarantee of the believer's eternal security in Christ. He who is elect-in-Christ is sealed with the Holy Spirit of God for the day of redemption (Eph. 4: 30, 1: 13; II Cor. 1: 22). He has the inward testimony of the Spirit of adoption that, in Christ, he is a son of God (Rom. 8: 15 f.). He is assured that he has eternal life, and that none can snatch him out of the hand that has saved him (Jn. 10: 27 f.). He has this certainty, that 'God's firm foundation stands, bearing this seal: "The Lord knows those who are His" ' (II Tim. 2: 19), and that He who has begun a good work in him will not fail to bring it to completion at the day of Jesus Christ (Phil. 1: 6). His election, his calling, and his justification in Christ will most assuredly be crowned by his glorification with Christ (Rom. 8: 29 f.). On this ground the confident affirmation of Article XVII is fully justified, that 'they which be endued with so excellent a benefit of God [predestination to life] be called according to God's purpose by His Spirit working in due season: they through grace obey the calling: they be justified freely: they be made sons of God by adoption: they be made like the image of His only-begotten Son Jesus Christ: they walk religiously in good works, and at length, by God's mercy, they attain to everlasting felicity.'

Holding this superb perspective of grace, it is not to be wondered at that the article goes on to affirm that 'the godly consideration of predestination and our election in Christ is full of sweet, pleasant, and unspeakable comfort to godly persons . . . as well because it doth greatly establish and confirm their faith of eternal salvation to be enjoyed through Christ, as because it doth fervently kindle their love towards God.' It should be of unspeakable comfort, also, to every evangelist and missionary, as to the humblest witness for Christ, to know that, while he serves God with all his might, the success of his work does not depend on his own efforts and achievements – for that indeed would be to surround all with human uncertainty and discouragement – but upon God, who already has acted sovereignly in Christ and whose all-sufficient grace he is charged to proclaim. The work is the Lord's, and it is therefore a perfect and infallible work. And for this very reason, that he knows that *in the Lord* his labour is not in vain, the Christian is exhorted always to abound in the work of the Lord (I Cor. 15: 58). The knowledge that it is *the work of the Lord* spurs him to go all out in his labours as a witness to the grace of God in Christ Jesus.

But for the grace of God there would be no Gospel, no Church, no sacraments, no hope. All that a Christian is and has, and all his eternal heritage of glory, he owes to the grace of God, who, faithful to the promises of His covenant, took the initiative in Christ, even while we were yet sinners, without strength to save ourselves, and in revolt against Him (Rom. 5: 6, 8, 10), choosing us, calling us, adopting us, justifying us, sanctifying us, and at last glorifying us. This, the redeeming work of the Triune God, Father, Son, and Holy Spirit, is the amazing content of the election of grace – which is not a theory of dogmaticians but a reality of faith, the truth of which is confirmed not by theological argument but by the experience of God's redeeming grace in Christ and the inner witness of the Spirit of Truth.

94